The Contemporary Circus Handbook

Modern Vaudeville Press
113 E Mayland St
Philadelphia, PA 19144
United States of America
www.ModernVaudevillePress.com
info@modernvaudevillepress.com
ISBN: 978-1-958604-03-8
Library of Congress: 2023907933.

By Eric Bates.

Edited by Kim Campbell with Benjamin Domask-Ruh and Thom Wall.

The Contemporary Circus Handbook:

A Guide to Creating, Funding, Producing, Organizing, and Touring Shows for the 21st Century

Eric Bates

Modern Vaudeville Press

To my family, for always supporting me so that I could dare greatly.

...And to my circus family, ever-growing.

CONTENTS

SECTION TWO: ORGANIZATION

SECTION THREE: FUNDING

SECTION FOUR: PRODUCING

SECTION FIVE: TOURING

SECTION SIX: FINAL THOUGHTS

SECTION SEVEN: APPENDICES

FOREWORD

I've worked with Eric for over 14 years now. He has been my employee, my collaborator, and my friend. As a performer and technician, his talent and excellence are unmatched. I am not surprised by the care and thoroughness with which he has approached *The Contemporary Circus Handbook*. I am not even surprised by his writing chops! But I am a little surprised that, with everything he could be doing with his talent and his time, he chose to put all this down on paper for us, uniting our community in this unprecedented way.

When Eric first told me he was writing a how-to book for circus show and company creating, I didn't love the idea. The thought that my profession—and decades of painful learning—was going to be reduced to a "just add hot water and serve"/ *Circus Directing for the Complete Klutz*-type handbook kind of terrified me. But the more we spoke, and the more I heard the angle of his interview questions, saw the roster of interviewees, noticed the humility and curiosity with which he approached the subject matter—the more I realized it was completely the opposite. He wasn't simplifying a complex process. He was sharing and revealing its complexities. He was attempting to unravel this untouched messy ball of knots that was the "wing it and cross your fingers" circus culture—unravel it and weave it into a cohesive tapestry. The challenges, the lessons, the wisdom and even the stupidities; all generously shared so we can collectively gaze and learn.

Circus is shockingly lawless. We pride ourselves on making our own rules, on functioning off gut and sweat and instinct. We pride ourselves on having our own private methods and rituals, on not following any standardized forms. There is immense beauty in this, but the downside of course is that we are lacking scribes and collective memory; we are often letting the hard-earned lessons disappear with our predecessors. It's hard to evolve at this level—to learn off each other's backs—if we don't have a way of disseminating that knowledge.

Let's face it: circus people don't do circus because it will make them rich and famous, because they randomly chose a major in college, because they want to win a gold medal, because they want their parents' approval, because they want job security or a good pension, because it's the wave of the future—and definitely not because it's the easy way out. It's hard to think of a metier that is more passion-fueled. How crazy-passionate do you have to be, to endure the physical pain, the injuries, the shaky job security, and to literally risk your life daily for so little reward? Except the deeper, more visceral, more soulful kind. Except the bond you forge with your comrades. Except the lives you change, lift and inspire in those seats.

I realized there was something similar with Eric's desire to write this book, something so true to that circus essence. It is passion-fueled, sincere, generous; building bridges between circumscribed companies and philosophies.

This book is meticulously researched and constructed. Founding a company is not the 'easy way', writing this book was not the 'easy way'. Clearly a labor of love, one from which we will all benefit greatly, from what he has generously compiled for us, the readers.

And not only circus readers... A number of this book's lessons go beyond the circus industry. They speak of how to collaborate creatively in a broader sense. From the largest corporations to the tiniest family home, we all struggle with properly collaborating, listening, exchanging. I'd like to say this is the key to "success"—but more importantly—it's the key to humanity. If we better understand the tools of collaboration, we better create a compassionate society.

In the past, circus has had a primarily oral tradition, leading to a lack of writing, research, or simple documentation on the topic. Our legitimacy suffers for this. Quite often circus academics are not those practicing in the field. Although there are serious studies and publications, these documents are rarely coupled with hands-on, real-life proof of concept. This book is an enormous step in the direction of publishing the particulars of our art form and process for posterity.

Is this book going to change the world one circus company at a time? Possibly. But perhaps more importantly, it will help soften all the hard stuff, clarify all the confusing stuff, lighten all the heavy stuff so we can focus on the business of forging bonds and changing lives. Which will in turn absolutely change the world one circus company at a time.

Shana Carroll
Montréal, Canada

PREFACE

If you're anything like me you got into circus because of the community, but also because of the shows. You saw something amazing that made you laugh and marvel and cry, something poetic and human and funny, something that made the world sparkle a little brighter when you left the theater. It wasn't an event, or a cool trick on social media. It was an honest-to-goodness *show*.

Twelve years ago, I was just coming out of circus school and eager to tour the world and make great art. Perhaps you, too, are a recent graduate—or maybe you are doing circus as a passionate hobby and are wondering what the next step could be. I've been in both of those places. Maybe you're a seasoned pro with a dream you want to bring to life and some solid connections in the industry. Maybe you've tried to make a show before and got frustrated with the process. You've probably seen a few shows and know a few companies, but in general, the whole business is still a mystery to you. I don't blame you. I've been there, too.

Accordingly, it's likely you're never heard of me, so let me introduce myself. My name is Eric Bates, I'm a cigar box juggler, Russian bar porter, and co-founder of Cirque Barcode. Our company has made a touring stage show, *Sweat & Ink*; an outdoor environmental show, *Branché*; and a street show out of a live-in camper van, *See You Down the Road*. Maybe you've seen or heard of our productions, but likely you haven't. In the stage show world our company is new on the scene. So who am I to write this book? Why should you listen to me?

My company, Cirque Barcode, consists of four circus artists, most of whom I've worked with for over 10 years. At the Cirque de Demain Circus Festival, I've received an audience's choice award, a bronze medal, and a silver medal for the different acts I've performed—and the rest of my team has some more shiny hardware clinking around from that festival and others. As an artist, I toured in the original creation *Sequence 8* with The 7 Fingers, as well as in their shows Queen of the Night, Vice & Vertu, and on Broadway on *Water for Elephants*—and I've performed at numerous other events with them from fashion shows in the Philippines to La Plus Grande Cabaret du Monde. I've also performed with Cirque Eloize and Cirque du Soleil, including performing for the world's presidents at the G7 summit with snipers on the rooftop, and at a $70 million dollar wedding in India. I've done street shows and won the audience choice award in the Dundas Buskerfest. I've been on six television shows.

And yet...

Despite all these fabulous adventures with other companies, my friends and I had reached a point in our careers where we felt we had done the rounds. We'd put ourselves out there and seen the world. We had performed amazing creations with other companies and done a ton of events, each unique and exciting at the time. Eventually though, the novelty wore off. We had gotten into circus because we loved shows. We loved the lights going down, the personalities you fell in love with onstage, the tension of an entire theater holding its breath and the relief as they released it, the memories that stayed with you long after you went home for the evening. Given our modest success working with the big circus companies and in the events world, we thought ourselves qualified to make a full-length theatrical show.

We were wrong. So wrong.

What followed was an expensive and difficult journey involving years of work, multiple creation periods in multiple countries, re-creation periods, group therapy sessions, several rounds of financing and an infinite supply of unsolicited lessons about making a company and a show. But we managed to get there—in fact, I'm writing this preface at the airport, on my way to play *Sweat & Ink* at Winterfest in Salzburg, then Graz and Prague.

Two years into the journey of making *Sweat & Ink*, while still doing events and creations with other companies on the side, and still learning hard lessons about cargo, lighting and contracts, we started cooking up our second show, *Branché*, in collaboration with the company Acting for Climate. This creation period was different.

We had been through a lot together with Barcode as a team, and had grown a lot. Making a show in collaboration with another company gave us insight into other ways of working, and our expectations were tempered by the lessons we had learned while creating *Sweat & Ink*. At this point a question occurred to me:

Does everyone that wants to make a show have to learn how to do it the hard way?

I began to write down what I had noticed during the creation of *Sweat & Ink*, and the lessons I took from the creation of *Branché*. When we worked for other companies (since we still do events and short runs of shows), I asked questions and took notes on what they did. Still feeling under-qualified to represent myself as any sort of authority on making shows, I then called up over two dozen creators from successful circus and dance companies (both big and small) from around the world and interviewed them about their journeys (if you're curious about who they are, there's a bit more about them in the back). I read and highlighted interviews I found, and poured over books on writing, creation, business, psychology, productivity, and marketing.

This book is a culmination of all of that advice, a book I wish I had had back when we were stumbling through the creation of *Sweat & Ink*. A mashup of my own goof-ups and other people's insights. There are so many amazing artists in the world with amazing ideas, so many beautiful shows still to be created. I hope this book helps them bring those shows to life, helps *you* bring *your* show to life—and you will. You will get there. If you can avoid even a few of the many traps along the way, this book will have done its job.

Happy creating.

Eric Bates
Montréal, Canada

Obligatory disclaimer: While I will talk about companies and fundraising methods, none of this book constitutes legal advice. Talk to a lawyer in your specific country to make sure you understand the laws and best practices in your area.

SECTION 1: CREATION

FIRST STEPS

Vice & Vertu *by The 7 Fingers. Photo by Sebastien Lozé. Artists: Eric Bates, Alexandra Royer, Tristan Nielsen.*

Generating New Work

A spark has been lit in the corner of your mind. For some creators this spark is a book, for others it's an idea, a concept, a place, a group of people. The process of developing the spark into a full-blown show is in large part the process of deciding or discovering what your show is, and what it is *not*.

For our second show *Branché*, it was a question which started us on the path of creating a show: "What would Sustainable Circus look like?"

Audiences and theaters are always looking for something they haven't seen before, so when we made *Branché* we considered it a creative challenge to make something that took our environmental impact into account so we could do our part in the circus world to keep both circus, and the world, healthy.

For Alexandre Fray, co-founder of the French company Un Loup pour L'homme, he says this spark is sometimes "an idea, and to be more precise because I work on acrobatics, it's often a new theory that I want to explore."

For Pia Meuthen, founder of the Netherlands-based Panama Pictures company, "The very first starting point is usually a book. It can be a novel. For *Go north and see what those strangers do* it was multiple books by the Norwegian writer Karl Ove Knausgård. Then I look for what it is about those books that fascinates me."

The Spark Through Exploration

Finding your spark is a process of diving deep, knowing why you have to make this show, and clarifying a reason you can own, as well as a reason you can tell to every person you meet along the way. This reason, this *why*, will serve as your core explanation to grants, festivals, and collaborators as to why you need to bring this show to life. As Twyla Tharp says in her book *The Creative Habit*, this is the 'spine' of your piece. A reason like a candle to light your way when the path gets dark. Any reason can be valid, the important thing is that you know it. Everyone does it differently; here are a few examples.

Gypsy Snider, co-founder of The 7 Fingers in Canada, clarifies her ideas through writing, writing out all sorts of different ideas for shows until they reveal connected themes that reflect the common core of what she wants to talk about.

When making his first show *Filament* for his company Short Round Productions, Joseph Pinzon's process was also to write down his idea, "Write down what you want to see. Maybe it's a discipline, or a random idea. What would I want to see that I haven't seen before? What would I buy a ticket to see? What would I watch over and over again? Get these ideas out, don't shut anything down yet."

Maybe this takes the form of a show with an all-female cast, or a show with a plot you can actually follow, or a show that takes place in the woods. Play with your idea, stretch it in different directions. As Lydia Bouchard, dance choreographer and founder of La Résistance says, "The first time you explain the high level concept, I think you need to give it a wide enough space. The concept needs to be clear and simple, but wide enough that your creators can bring stuff to the table."

When Brent and Maya McCoy (co-founders of Vermont Vaudeville) moved into their home in northeastern Vermont, they sensed a need for good entertainment in the area, both for audiences and as a creative outlet for performers. This spark led to them founding Vermont

Light Check at Dessa, *by Creative Sovereignty. Photo by Eric Bates. Artists: Eve Bigel, Tristan Nielsen.*

29

Vaudeville, a recurring cabaret featuring both local and world-class performers under the slogan, "Laugh Locally."

"For the audience," Maya explains, "this sort of thing wasn't happening in this area... There was a need on the performers' side and on the audience's side. We feel really lucky to have found that, because that seems to be the secret to our success: everyone wants it, needs it."

As this spark begins to glow in your head, start to look around. See what other shows are out there and ask what it took for those shows to get onstage. Start interrogating the choices you see in other shows. As Pinzon says, "You're probably looking at shows and starting to think, 'What do I like? What do I not like? What would I do differently?' And sometimes this manifests as 'This show is onstage? And people are paying to see it? I could make something better than that!' Other times it manifests as, 'This show is amazing, I could never do that.' Both are useful. Keep observing. Keep learning. If you're inspired, see if you can copy processes, not products."

After feeling a spark and its various accompanying inspirations for things he would want to put onstage, Pinzon says his next step is to, "Ask yourself, what do all these different pieces of things that I want to see have in common? Connect the dots. It has to make sense to you, the creator. If it doesn't make sense to you, how are you going to explain that to someone else? How are you going to pitch a concept to a producer if you don't even know what that concept is? A singular idea is not good enough."

Think about both what you want in your show, but also what you don't want. As we'll see throughout the book, limitations can act as helpful creative and logistical forces.

Maya McCoy starts with, "What is the scope of the show you're building? Because that changes [the process] dramatically. For our street show, we had really clear parameters, which was awesome: it had to fit in a suitcase. Building a theatrical performing arts center show, you have to start in a different place."

Mason Ames, who has his own solo street show and who has done numerous creations as an artist with Cirque Eloize, The 7 Fingers and Cirque le Roux, reflected on the motivation when he was creating his solo street show: "It's a combination of 'What the heck can I do?' and 'What is fun to do?' I want to have fun onstage, if I'm not having fun onstage then I don't want to be onstage. So what do I think is fun to be doing? And how do I shape that into something interesting?"

Throughout this book you're going to learn about funding, about building a team, about finding tools that will help you get organized, and tips for planning your creation. When I was talking to Pinzon, he said a lot of people dive in too early and recommended instead to, "think a little more, save yourself some money."

"When then," I asked him, "is it the right time to transition from 'thinking a little more' to 'let's do this'?"

"Everything was there," he said. "I had the money, I had the people. I needed to see it. I thought for four years. Thoughts keep repeating because they are where they need to be. If the thoughts don't change—it's time to start."

KEY TAKEAWAY:

- Inspiration can come from anywhere, and people have different processes to refine and clarify their ideas. Look at other people's methods for finding inspiration and see what works for you.

See You Down the Road *by Cirque Barcode in Graz, Austria. Photo by Eric Bates. Artists: Alexandra Royer, Eric Bates, Mathilde Jimenez, Tristan Nielsen.*

Why Make a Show?

What got you into this career? Was it a show you saw? An event? An act? For me, it was the youth circus Circus Smirkus. When I was a young juggler, the kids in those shows were my idols. Later it was theatrical circus shows—*Traces* from The 7 Fingers, *Rain* from Cirque Eloize. What always inspired me was *shows*. As Charlie Wheeller (co-founder of Barely Methodical Troupe) puts it, "In the circus world the currency you work with is either acts or shows."

As a circus artist, I followed a path that might sound familiar to you: I first developed an act (or acts) that I performed in the context of other companies' shows or cabarets. I then did a longer creation period for another company's show in which I adapted my number to suit that show's theme or story, and participated in other people's acts or transitions, but I was still not in creative control of the show itself.

By the summer of 2017, with my partners at Barcode we had done every sort of gig a small group of freelancers can do, and yet somehow, despite each one being new and exciting, it was getting redundant. We had reached a point where we wanted to make something more substantial than five minute acts. We had reached the point where we wanted to create a cohesive, 70-minute show.

To my surprise at the time, this desire alone wasn't enough. Call me naive, but it turns out that creating a touring show is a much bigger task than I'd understood it to be. Traditional or cabaret style circus shows tend to assemble much quicker, but if you're thinking about making something more in-depth, this will likely be a project that you will work on for years, and then tour for years. So the subject of your show is important. When you're first thinking about creating something, you need to drill down to the core of that idea to make sure it's solid enough to survive the inevitable bumps and detours it will face on the road to making it a reality. You need to interrogate it, make sure it's something you care about enough to fight for and defend for *years* as you work to get it onstage. These interrogations are personal, they are your beliefs about why this show should exist in the world and who it will inspire, as well as why it's important that people see it. It's not the *how*, not the way you make the show—it's the *why*, the subject and the reasons you're embarking on this journey in the first place. This is your well that will keep refilling your spirit when the going gets rough.

Making a show will force you to grow in a lot of different ways you didn't expect as a performer, as with freedom comes the acceptance of responsibility. It will be vastly more work, but these added responsibilities and collaborations will let you do more than was ever possible for you as a solo artist. Lydia Bouchard of La Résistance experienced that opening of possibilities when she transitioned from dancer to director. "At one point, I got to a place where I knew what my talent and limits were. When you start working with other dancers, you can imagine things and ask them to do it, and they have limits you can never even dream of reaching." Suddenly, she had a new color palette to work with. Creatively, she was now able to express herself through other people's abilities, through sets, music, singers, acrobats and more. "It's so much more expansive in a creative way."

James Tanabe, former Senior Director, Business and Creative Strategy/ Senior Innovation Consultant at Cirque du Soleil and 2021 director of Montréal's École Nationale de Cirque, said something similar when he changed from being a hand balancer to a producer. "I'm still trying to connect with an audience. I'm still trying to influence an audience. I'm still trying to make an impact on the world around me, but I was feeling very limited always doing that in a costume, on stage, under spotlights." As artists, he says, we undervalue our toolkits—our abilities to think creatively, to dream and get other people on board with that dream, to make things happen that haven't been seen before—and we forget the impact and power that that toolkit has to make real changes in the world. Finding the team of people who can empower the creative voices, Tanabe says, is a different but equally rewarding way to touch an audience.

You can touch people as an individual artist through your own work or as an artist bringing another director's vision to life. For a long time in my career this was immensely satisfying. But if you're in a place where you want to say something that no one else seems to be saying, or if you want to say something in a way that no one else is saying it, it might be time to start making that idea a reality.

"[Your first show] may not be your end project," Maya McCoy (Vermont Vaudeville) says, "but it's going to advance all of your projects. You're going to learn something from it."

It took Joseph Pinzon (Short Round Productions) four years to bring his idea of an acrobatic high school coming-of-age-story, *Filament,* to life. The first time they ever ran the show was for 200 high-schoolers in the Czech Republic, who Pinzon wasn't even sure would speak English well enough to understand what was going on.

"The next day I got these lovely messages off of Instagram and Facebook from them (turned out they spoke English very well), but there was one in particular, from this girl, that said, 'I'd never seen anything like that before. I didn't know that was possible. I didn't know things like that could exist. The story touched me so much that when I got home I actually came out to my mom. It went really well. I'm going to bring her back to see the show on Friday so she can see why.'"

You don't know what impact your contribution to the world will have. You can't know what ripples it might cause. There's only one way to find out.

KEY TAKEAWAY:

- Making a show of your own is unlike any other experience in the circus world and will lead to a whole new type of growth.

Gaining Gravity

"When you know what your purpose is and it's clear, things fall into place," Pinzon told me when I asked him about making his first show. "The world looks different because you see how it can help you. But it takes time to get to that point. That's what the preparation is." Through good preparation and refining your idea you will make it easy for people to help you. This will in turn grow your project exponentially as you harness the power of other people's skill and enthusiasm.

Sweat & Ink. Photo by JF Savaria. Artists: Tristan Nielsen, Alexandra Royer, Eric Bates.

The first time Barcode did a street show we were super nervous. How do you stop strangers on the street and convince them to watch you, and then convince them to give you money? One of the tricks a professional street performer friend gave to us was this: Don't tell the people walking by that the show is starting in five minutes. Tell them it's starting *now*. Tell them it's *already started.*

Like magic, a few people will stop and watch. Other people will notice them watching and wonder what's interesting enough that those people would have stopped. They stop too. People further off hear your small crowd cheering and they come over to investigate the commotion. It's a snowball effect.

The same thing happens with any project. Do your homework, but instead of saying "I want to make a show one day," say, "I'm making a show. Look, I've already started to lay out the props."

And actually start to make that show.

I call this effect gaining gravity. When you have a cool project you're actively working on (and not just talking about making one day!), it will begin to pull more people and resources into it. The growth adds to the gravity, and suddenly people that you don't even remember telling about your project in the first place are offering to help. This is where things can really start to take off, because it becomes easier to switch your mindset to *who* rather than *how*.

When Barcode started making our first show *Sweat & Ink* we began to develop material and apply for grants, but also asked around to find creation space, a director, a light designer, outside eyes, and all the other things you might want to make a show. Because we had already gotten the ball rolling- writing grants and booking time in creation studios—people took us seriously and offered to help. At the time we didn't know what the show would become—it certainly wasn't called *Sweat & Ink* yet! It was just a vague desire to do a show on the theme of "memory". You might have similar vague ideas and desires, but nothing will bring them to life like taking a proactive step. Maybe this means writing a grant, or committing one day in a studio to try some new ideas, or building the prop you've always wanted to try. Each action step you take will lead to the next thing happening and before you know it your project will start to develop a gravity of its own.

Researching Other Shows

Cirque Barcode's first contract after school was with Circus Flic Flac—located in the rainy town of Dortmund, Germany. We were finishing up and had two weeks before the beloved annual circus competition in Paris, Cirque de Demain, in which our friends Maxim Laurin and Ugo Dario (who later went on to co-found Machine de Cirque) were going to perform. By some stroke of luck, colleagues of ours in Flic Flac were selling their car and because of insurance shenanigans and an imminent return to the US, they were selling it for next to nothing. Alex and I looked at each other. Could we buy a car in Europe and drive to Paris for Cirque de Demain? Alex didn't even have a license!

"If you put your French address on the paperwork, I'll do the driving," I said.

"Sold!"

We took two weeks to drive to Paris, crashing on couches, seeing a show almost every night at every stop along the way. Tigerpalast, Cirque XY, Palazzo, GOP, Wintergarten, Chameleon, Flic Flac, and more. To cap it off, we got to watch Max and Ugo win a gold medal at Cirque de Demain. From having previously only seen shows in Montréal, I had my eyes opened to the variety of what existed out there. That's what I call a successful research trip!

If you haven't started to make your show yet and are still looking at it from afar, congratulations, you're in the research phase. This is a great time! The possibilities feel endless, and you can learn from other people's mistakes before having to make them yourself.

At the time of the above road trip, back in 2011, we hadn't yet thought about making a show and were just interested in meeting people and seeing what was out there. However if you are considering making a show (which I assume you are if you're reading this book), seeing shows is invaluable.

Seeing a lot of shows makes you ask questions—why is this show so good, or so bad? To get more specific, what makes one show click with an audience and another struggle to establish tempo, or relatable characters? What specific elements would you change, and why? And how would you change them? Think bigger than what's onstage: many cabarets in Germany don't pay for the rehearsals, so artists won't come in for long rehearsal periods. The result? Strong acts with transitions that all look like they were made in a weekend... because they were. How could you do this better? Or alternatively, how would you finance a six-month creation if you had to pay the artists the entire time? Is this a venue where you'd see yourself working? Would your show fit? How might you have to change things in order to actually get the gig?

It's easy to be critical of something, it's a lot harder to think of how you could take those same resources and produce something better. If you're genuinely interested in making shows, see every show you can from multiple genres. I recommend taking a critical but humble approach to viewing them. Although seeing many shows will help you clarify your taste, that doesn't mean everything will become clear right away.

The writer Ann Patchett describes the beginning stages of a novel like walking around in a snowstorm.

"In the early stages of thinking up a novel I'm not exactly sure what I would write down anyway. It's like walking through a field in a snowstorm and for a long time I see nothing but the snow, but then in the distance there's something, a tree or a figure or smoke, I just don't know. I always have the sensation that I'm straining to see what's in front of me. The snow lessens for a minute and I catch a glimpse of an idea, but when I get closer the light starts to fade. I squint constantly. It goes on like this for a long time. If I were taking notes they would read: I see something. A shape? I have no idea."

While you're still in the snowstorm, straining for clearer glimpses of your idea, you can complement that work with various forms of research. While you see as many shows as you can, start to ask questions, in your mind or of the creators, of how they got those shows onstage. What do you imagine it took? Were you right?

Backstage at Midnight Circus: Photo by Eric Bates. Artist: Aerial Emery.

Active Spectating

When James Tanabe was doing research for Cirque du Soleil, he saw over 30 shows live and more on video during one season, taking detailed notes on every act, as well as on the overall show. After each show, he and his colleagues would ask each other, "If you had $1k how would you make it better, if you had $100k, if you had $1 million how would you make it better?" This works a muscle in your mind, Tanabe says, of being both a creator and a producer.

You'll find yourself in a similar situation when creating your own show. You'll want to make the show better but only have a certain amount of time and money and it might feel like very little, but if you've practiced this exercise you'll see there's a lot you can accomplish with little money. This builds a habit of thinking about available resources and how they translate to the quality of the show.

For example, if you cut a projector from the show, maybe you could save $5,000 that could be used towards better costumes, or hiring a choreographer to redo the opening, or adding cushions to the chairs for the audience, or all of the above. But cutting a projector might change your lighting or scenography requirements. **Where will you invest your money when you make your own show? Start practicing in your head on other people's shows!**

You can also look at what's been done before on a similar theme as your idea, see who has addressed this topic already. What are the challenges they faced?

What will you do differently? Maybe some ideas you had been thinking about have been done already, and you can see them (or something similar) without having to invest any money or time. Do they look like you thought they would, or are they not as you imagined? Maybe you want to make an ambulatory show where the audience walks around in the space, so you look into *Fuerza Bruta* or *Sleep No More*, *Branché* or *Queen of the Night*, or *Les Minutes* at Montréal Complètement Cirque. Maybe you want to do a show with no props, only group acrobatics, so you look at shows by Gravity & Other Myths or by Cie XY. Want to have live music onstage? What do you think of the piano and guitar scenes from *Traces*? How about Akoreacro's brass band? Or Circa's collaboration with a symphony orchestra? Or Cirque du Soleil's live musicians? Or that show I saw in Belgium with the two guys playing clarinets stuck in a dark corner in the back the whole time? Everything has been done before in one way or another, but we have the chance to keep reinventing it to make it relevant and personal to our times.

You can also do physical, circus research before ever receiving a grant or committing to anything. Get in a room and try to explore your idea today from a physical perspective, without any costumes or lights or extra props beyond what you already have. A rich bank of physical material will serve as fertile ground for the seeds of future ideas to grow from. It will also let you begin to develop the way in which your group likes to create together, especially when developing material that isn't strictly related to your main circus discipline.

KEY TAKEAWAYS:

- What other shows exist that share similarities with my ideas?
- What sort of physical research and creation can I do today, with no budget?
- Where will you invest *your* money when you make your own show? Start practicing in your head on other people's shows!

Getting Started Exercises

- Write, draw or talk through your ideas. Interrogate them. What's exciting to you?
- Write down what you would need in order to start bringing this to life.
- What's your next actionable step?
- What could you start working on today?

Research Exercises

- After seeing a show, think beyond what you liked and didn't like. Use Tanabe's method to analyze what you would have done differently.
- If you had $1k, $100k or $1 million, *what* would you change about the show? What if you had zero dollars?
- *How* would you change those things? Instead of saying "I didn't like the lights," how would you envision them? Would it require a simpler or more complicated setup? Would the artists still be able to see enough to do their disciplines? If you would change the costumes, think of the limitations inherent to circus costumes-resilient yet stretchy materials, when they would have time to change costumes during the show, etc. Think about how all of these changes would impact the budget, creation process, and touring process of a show.
- What did you think the show did well that you *wouldn't* change? What would you try to emphasize? What strengths do you have among your own group that you can celebrate?

The Show Comes First

It can take a long time to take a show from creation to consistent touring. If you want to make a show and play it for long enough that it makes a return on your investment, you have to be prepared to prioritize that show, even if it means making less money initially.

A common challenge of artists creating a show is that it means they will have to turn down better-paying gigs in order to work on their own show. Sometimes you can strike a balance, but if your goal is to make your name as a show or a small company, it will require putting the show first once you've committed to it. It will require turning down gigs in order to perform your show. While it is possible to make a show on the side while working full time on another job, it might require putting in your own money (and certainly your time!) instead of making money elsewhere. Because theaters book far in advance (often 10-18 months ahead of time), it might be a relatively long time before you start to feel the "payoff" of your show- getting to perform it and making enough money to support yourself off of it. This is why you need to know your *why*. You need to know why you're doing this show for reasons other than for money. It's no secret that a performing artist has a limited window for their career based on physical limitations, and this is the time they will likely make the most money while performing. It can feel like a step backwards, at least financially, to work on a show when typically the trajectory of your earnings has only gone up as you gained experience and connections. Still, it is a worthy goal, and will make you a better artist in every aspect as you learn about the other facets of what makes a show work.

In retrospect, I think my personal *why* for making Barcode's first show *Sweat & Ink* was insufficiently clear. Personally, I was interested in making a show for the sake of making a show, for the sake of a new challenge and a reaction to being tired of the type of shallow corporate work we were doing at the time. When we made our second show *Branché* I was much more clear about my artistic reasons- the environmental motivation, the desire to explore a new format, the desire to work closer to home. I knew what it took to make a show, and was able to bring strong enough motivations to get me through the work I knew it would take to bring this show to life.

> **KEY TAKEAWAY:**
>
> • In order to get your own show off the ground you will have to prioritize it over other, possibly better paying opportunities.

OUTSIDE HELP: THE ARTISTIC TEAM

"Collectives are always shitshows."

Shana Carroll says she heard that statement over and over when she was co-founding The 7 Fingers. "Collectives don't work," they said to her. "They can give rise to and spawn other things, but they don't last."

Yet here they are, 20 years later, with award-winning shows around the globe and a massive building with multiple creation studios in Montréal. How did they make it work?

The thing that is hard about collectives is that there is often no clear leader or unified vision that everyone can throw their energy behind. It's important to recognize the power of leaders in different circumstances, even if they're self-assigned, and also to recognize the limits of only directing from within your own group. Even though *Loft* was a collective effort (they even made up a fake director to put on applications because at the time people had so little faith in the collective creation process), they assigned temporary leaders from within their group, and also brought in people to help guide them along the way.

The first thing to recognize when creating collectively without a formal director is that what *feels* good, might not be what *looks* good from the outside. You might not be efficiently communicating what you're trying to communicate to the audience, and not know it since you don't have anyone there to tell you.

In the beginning phases of Barcode's creation for *Sweat & Ink* we tried to act as directors or outside eyes for each other, but it meant we could never work on scenes with all four of us and see it at the same time. Eventually we realized that we needed someone on the outside and hired our director, Jean-Pierre Cloutier.

A director or outside eye might also be able to push you further in certain directions to get the full potential out of a scene. Bringing in these people removes one hat for the artists to wear and allows them to commit more of their energy to the sole role of being an artist. But beware- if you're starting your own show it's likely you have an idea of what you want it to look like, and you could end up regretting handing over your project to someone if their taste or vision doesn't align with your vision. A director can be valuable, *if your visions align.* Your team has to have enough trust in them that if your tastes differ you will still be willing to go along with them, trusting that they will lead somewhere you want to go. Ideally this collaboration will lead to a result that is stronger than the sum of its parts!

While making *Crystal* with Cirque du Soleil, Sébastien Soldevila gave a speech about the 'Mystery Island' and the importance of trusting the captains. "We're all on the boat," he said, "and we're looking for Mystery Island." No one knows where Mystery Island is, not even the captain(s). It might not even exist yet. The captain is up on the deck with her telescope, telling the crew to go left, or go right. Everyone needs to row in the direction the captain is pointing. Maybe you might think the captain doesn't know what they're doing, but this process is the nature of exploring. Everyone has to row in the same direction or you won't get anywhere. But if you can manage to work together, and row as a group no matter which way you're going, or whether or not you have a captain, eventually the island will appear.

Enter directors, coaches, outside eyes and other creators.

All of these roles can be extremely valuable in bringing direction to a group. Whoever you choose to collaborate with, in the beginning you will want to communicate your vision of the show as best you can to them so that you're on the same page and feel comfortable trusting that wherever they lead you it is with the goal to accomplish the things you had hoped for with your show. To continue the Mystery Island metaphor, you need to do a good job describing to the the captain you hire what kind of island you're looking for, so that you can row your hardest and when he or she finally says "Land ho!" you're not completely surprised by the type of vegetation you see on the shores.

How do you do this before you know exactly what it is you're making? Doing a good chunk of exploratory creation work ahead of time can help, as well as doing workshops with potential directors before you commit to bringing them along for the full ride. When Barcode was making *Sweat & Ink*, we took the first couple of weeks of creation to explore ideas we had on our own and try exercises with friends that directed us for the day. When we started working with our director Jean-Pierre Cloutier, we already had some initial ideas that we could show him. He was then able to see what to grow, what to ignore that didn't serve the show's goal, what connections were possible, and what needed more exploration.

If you don't already have a director in mind this could be a good place to start, but you can also do this knowing your director from the beginning. The 7 Fingers will often do an exploratory week of creation months ahead of the big chunk of creation so that they can throw stuff at the wall and see what sticks, then make a plan for the 'main' creation block. Michaël Hottier, co-founder of Back Pocket, recently hired a director and wrote the outline of their next show *before* bringing in the cast at all! It all depends on how you want to do your creation. There's no right answer.

It can be confusing to want to make your dream show and then have to hand over the rudder to someone else to steer. Make sure you completely trust that person and enjoy similarities of taste with them before you commit. This is less of an issue with outside eyes, since those relationships tend to be shorter term, and usually differ in terms of how much control they have over the final product.

Regardless of who you decide to work with, a healthy dose of gratitude will go a long way towards making that relationship work smoothly. A card in the mailbox, an unexpected bottle of wine or homemade pie… these things of course in no way equal what people contribute to your project, but there is a lot of value in attempting to show how much you appreciate them, in a way that doesn't make the relationship transactional.

As discussed in the "Ask for Help" chapter, bringing someone in to fill these roles can bring a lifetime of experience to something you are only just learning. As Lewie West, senior acrobat and rehearsal leader for the Australian companies *Circa* and *Gravity & Other Myths* says, one of the best things you can do is to find someone that knows how to do the thing you don't know how to do, so you can, "ride the wave of other people's knowledge and funding and backing."

What follows is a summary of the different roles you might collaborate with, and some tips for working with each.

Key Takeaway:

• Leaders can be invaluable, but the relationship has to be built on
a foundation of respect and shared vision to make sure you don't
have a mutiny.

Sweat & Ink *Rehearsal. Photo by Eric Bates. Artists: Tristan Nielsen, JP Cloutier, Alexandra Royer, Eve Bigel.*

Directors

One of the strengths of having a director is having someone on the outside with a bird's eye view of the project. This will allow the creatives to dive in, get lost, put their heads down and row, trusting that someone is steering and watching over to make sure everyone is rowing in the same direction.

Throughout a creation you're going to have a lot of different people to please—yourselves, the other artists in the show, possibly producers, some combination of a scenographer, choreographer, light and costume designers...

Everyone will want to make the best for the show, but if they all have their own ideas of how to do that you might end up with ten different visions of the show instead of the one show you're actually making. Especially if you are an artist within your show, you won't be able to step outside it to make sure everything looks how you want it. A good director will know how to speak to all of these people in the languages they understand. As Lydia Bouchard (La Résistance) puts it, **"for everything to be in symbiosis you need to be a polyglot of your idea. You need to speak many languages."**

While the artists are training and figuring out the circus, a director can also keep an eye on other themes and concepts that bring a lot of power and relatability to a show. When Gypsy Snider (The 7 Fingers) directs, she looks for exercises that connect to human weakness and desperation.

"I love the pathetic emotions," Snider says. "I feel that they hold the deepest quality in terms of interpretation onstage. And especially when you're doing circus, which is the antithesis of pathos, if you can capture how fragile you actually are (even though you can do all these cool things), that's what I'm looking for. To a fault, actually."

Giving someone the power of final decision-making can help group dynamics by externalizing and streamlining a potential source of conflict. Yes, you want to be on the same page as your director, but having someone that can ultimately make a decision can prevent days of arguing. This is why it is so important to hire someone you trust artistically. This will allow you to convince yourself that even if you don't understand a decision they've made, from their perspective (and experience) they can see something you can't that will benefit the show. This, in turn, will allow you to keep moving forward instead of second-guessing yourselves.

It's important to remember too that directing is its own skill set. In circus especially, artists tend to self-direct their own acts: they learn tools to think creatively, and maybe even with a group of people, but there is rarely any sort of training on formally directing a show. For this reason artists can often forget that there is a skill to seeing the big picture and shaping the pieces accordingly, and that that skill set is different from being an artist within those scenes. Would you be surprised if you tried to design your own lights and found it hard? Of course not! Directing is the same.

If directing is something you're interested in, there are ways to practice and grow. You could assistant-direct a show. Help choreograph someone's act. Give workshops. Take workshops. Sit beside the choreographer or sound guy to learn how they do things, and what challenges they have and the tricks they use to overcome them. The director has to be familiar with all of these roles since they are all part of storytelling. Try to understand their thought processes. Build that muscle before you need it.

It can also help to clarify upfront each party's relationship and ownership of the show after it's made. Some companies want the director to keep checking in, other companies want ownership so they can evolve the show after they've premiered. Having everyone on the same page from the beginning about the director's role in the company both during and after the creation will help things run more smoothly.

While hiring a director can make a lot of things smoother, it can also add difficulties and is not a magic bullet. There can be money issues, and creative-vision issues. It can feel like you've added another person to manage. Err on the side of too many conversations early on so that once you dive in you don't end up second-guessing yourself the whole time and you can enjoy the experience.

Rehearsals for Midnight Circus: Photo by Eric Bates: Artists: Alexandra Royer, Mason Ames, Tristan Nielsen.

Coaches

Because often a new cast will not have all worked together in the past, or performed the required disciplines before, technical training is often necessary to acquire the skills needed for the cast to work as a cohesive ensemble. For this, a good coach is a game changer.

This could be a circus coach to teach teeterboard (as we did for Barcode's show *Sweat & Ink*), a dance coach for a new style of dance (like Cie XY did to learn lindy hop for *Il n'est pas encore minuit*), or a piano teacher (so the new casts of The 7 Fingers show *Traces* could learn to play!). A good coach will have a positive attitude, know from experience when to push and when to hold back, and bring a vision for getting you to your technical goals on time. Having a good coach, especially if you're integrating a new discipline into your show, will be worth every penny. Having someone else in charge of a training can also be a welcome break from the constant decision-making that creation demands.

A good coach provides you an opportunity to leverage someone else's knowledge. Especially if you want to integrate a technique that is outside your domain of expertise, such as a new dance or discipline, coaches can be the fast track towards making it look good, authentic and finding something that will work specifically for your team.

Edgar Zendejas, choreographer and artistic director of Ezdanza, said he puts a lot of trust into his coaches from the circus world, and even from other forms of dance he is less familiar with. He trusts them to show him the foreign disciplines' full ability and let him know what is possible, while he still keeps control as a director to craft it to his taste.

Coaches don't have to be just for the physical acts in the show though—the Australian company *Gravity & Other Myths* hired a business coach to help them organize themselves and keep them accountable as they put a new system in place. As you'll see later in the section "Keeping the Team Happy" on page 225, Barcode hired a group therapist to help work on our team's relationships. Good coaching is money well spent.

KEY TAKEAWAY:

• Coaches can fast track your team to looking good and authentic in new disciplines- even non-circus ones.

Outside Eyes

In the circus world, an 'outside eye' is usually brought in for a few short periods in order to give feedback, often later in the process. The creators then decide what to do with this feedback. This differs from a director, who is there for the entire creation process and will be the one making final creative decisions. Outside eyes can be most useful to help clarify the main theme/ line of the show when the performers in the piece are too deep inside it to be able to have objectivity, but don't necessarily want a director for artistic control or financial reasons.

In some cases in theater, but increasingly also in circus for bigger productions, the role of outside eye as explained above is covered by a different title altogether—that of *dramaturg*. As well as giving an outside perspective, a dramaturg will often also bring context to the production to help the director(s) better understand a play's subtext, or to help the actors better understand their characters. In the case of a play, this often includes helping everyone better understand the play's historical elements. In circus, this could also be helpful in identifying themes in your show and understanding those themes in contemporary society to make sure your show is relevant.

A dramaturg can also provide additional or different services for a show, such as creating printed material based on your show's themes. These could be placards about historical influences, or activities for youth groups, for example. These sorts of things can make shows much more marketable, and is a service that is often eligible to be included in grants for show creation.

How does one use an outside eye? Michaël Hottier (Back Pocket) says that the role of an outside eye is a funny position, and it's important to clarify what you're asking of them: "Outside eyes aren't necessarily there for base work, they're there for finishing work once the piece is already there." He says that he prefers to use outside eyes late in the creation process once the piece already has some shape. Outside eyes are especially useful to look at lights, or see the piece as a whole if all of the creators are onstage and can't see the effect from the outside.

Hottier reflects that, "When it's your first creation, you're insecure. You want someone more experienced that can help." It can be tricky to take the responsibility of making all of the choices when you've never done it and don't feel qualified. "Once you understand that it's not that hard, that helps," he says. "If you think a red balloon is good onstage, then put a red balloon. You're going to be happy with that. You don't need someone to validate everything."

Outside eyes are there to help you realize your vision, but they will also bring their own opinions, experience and perspective. In a best case scenario, their fresh perspective will allow them to tell you what they see and understand from watching your piece, then help you to clarify structure or pacing elements to better deliver your intended message.

When Cirque Barcode and Acting For Climate Montréal made *Branché* collectively without a director, we brought in an outside eye at the end of the process. What we found was that oftentimes all of the performers *thought* they were following the same guidelines (for example- "move your hands like moss growing on a tree") but it took an outside eye to realize that all of the performers had drastically different interpretations of the same idea, and the effect didn't feel unified.

It can be delicate to bring in an outside eye, because you're giving them permission to tell you what they think is good and what they think isn't working. You're asking for their honesty. Make sure you're on the same page about what you're trying to accomplish with the show, then have them tell you what they think. Whether or not you take their proposed solutions, listen to what they think needs work. Many teams find outside eyes especially helpful to cut scenes late in the process.

Hottier says in their first creation they had to have a discussion with their outside eye to make sure they were still creating the show they wanted to create and not let the outside eye turn into the role of a director taking the show in a different direction than the team's original vision.

For Cirque Le Roux's show *Deer in the Headlights*, they got stuck while writing the show because they wanted a cohesive narrative and were having trouble figuring out how to bring it together. In this case, they hired someone to help take their ideas and consolidate them into a story that the writer thought made sense, which was helpful because it gave them a starting point. Based on that draft, they ran the show as an improv to see where it got them, then made changes from there.

More often though, in collective creations outside eyes are brought in later in the process to give feedback and to see if the material created is reading like the creators hope it does. Sometimes these are professionals in your field (such as circus directors for a circus show), but not always. Having an outside eye from a different field (dance, theater, comedy, etc) can provide a fresh perspective since they might not value things the same way your community might, and see a fresh side of what you're working on that can add an interesting layer.

When The 7 Fingers created their first show *Loft*, they each acted as an outside eye for a scene. This recognized the need to have someone on the outside, but kept the collective spirit they were hoping for that incorporated everyone's voices.

Barcode has used a similar strategy, putting someone in charge of a scene or a warm-up exercise (albeit for shorter periods than The 7 Fingers did), but we will also alternate, having everyone try the scene even if it's not our discipline so the person whose act it is can access the same outside perspective on what they're doing.

Costumes, Props, Scenography, Music
While each of these roles can be extremely important to the result of your project, they tend to come later in the process than the other members of the artistic team. For this reason, we'll save further discussion about them until the section titled "Production" on page 201.

KEY TAKEAWAYS:

- Outside eyes are often used later in the process and for shorter periods than directors. Useful to make sure your show is doing what you hope it does when you can't see it yourself.
- Think hard about the people you recruit/ hire to help you—you will likely have differences of opinion at some point, so be prepared to trust those people's opinions over your own or trust that you will be able to work through the differences in an enjoyable way.
- Hire people more experienced than you that you trust. It could bring your project to a level you couldn't have gotten to alone.
- Listen to your instincts when deciding whether to work with people, and define the scope of your partnership. A show is a constantly evolving project that can have multiple iterations.
- Make sure the people you bring in to help drive your project know how long you expect them to stay in the driver's seat and when you expect to take back the wheel.

Exercises

- On your next few contracts, make it a point to talk to people with different jobs than you, from the makeup artists, to the riggers, the choreographers, and the directors. Ask them how they got into it, what they did before, what their favorite part of it is, what they get worried about, who they look up to, etc. Not only will this teach you more about the different theatrical disciplines and how they contribute to a show, it will also be the start of building a network of people that you can call on when you're making your show to advise or join you.

- Pay special note to relationships you have with collaborators that feel "light" (as opposed to "heavy"). These are the people you're going to want to continue working with down the road (if their work is good!). Continue to nurture these relationships, either by helping them with their projects or just reaching out once in a while.

- Ask other people that have made shows what their relationships with their directors and/or outside eyes were. What would they have done differently, or the same?

CREATION EXERCISES

Backbone *by Gravity & Other Myths. Photo by Eric Bates. Artist: Kevin Beverly.*

"Well, there you go,"

Claude said, turning to leave us alone in Cirque Eloize's empty creation studio.

"Have fun!"

We looked at each other. What happens now?

How do you actually create material? This could be the subject of its own book (for a few titles I recommend see "Appendix E- BOOKS" on page 347), but I will leave some ideas here. What will you actually do once you're in the room? How do you plan on making material? This chapter will talk about some of the exercises Barcode has used, as well as other companies' strategies. Many of the exercises used in contemporary circus come from theater creation techniques, partially as a way to break free from traditional act building dramaturgy and tropes. We have worked a lot with The 7 Fingers and they rely heavily on these sorts of exercises. At the end of the chapter, Gypsy Snider (The 7 Fingers) explains how she links some of these theatrical exercises to circus or movement.

Games Need Rules

A lot of creators stress the importance of rules in a creation. Games and sports have rules for just this reason—they're a framework within which you can be creative. Once you have a few rules in place, you can then either improvise within the context of those rules, or work in a more structured way.

Is it strange to have rules in the context of creativity? In his Ted Talk *Serious Play*, Tim Brown says that rules actually help us get out of our "old rules and norms that we might otherwise bring to the creative process." He's talking about the unspoken rules of society that tell us what are normal, acceptable or safe ways to act. Without new rules in a creation we might unknowingly play by the rules we've become accustomed to in our everyday life—the boring ones that make us not stand out or do anything different.

In the Australian company Circa, the company's director Yaron Lifschitz will give a rule such as "all acrobatics are going forwards and you can't break eye contact with the audience." Since this is not normally the way acrobatics are done, it leads to new discoveries as they break old patterns to try to adapt to the rule.

In the book *Grip*, Bram Dobbeleare of the company Ea Eo describes a scene in *All The Fun* where the rule was to exchange three clubs with his partner as they constantly circled around each other. Bram refers to these as "small frameworks", in which you're allowed to experiment and play as much as you like. He distinguishes this from completely open improvising—it's building something together, step by step, seeing what could come out of the previous thing they built, even if it's just three second phrases.

Sometimes a game is strong enough to make a whole act out of it, other times the rule or the idea is too vague and doesn't create as much material. In this case they still film it so they can come back to it.

Bauke Lievens describes in *Grip* that for her show ANECKXANDER they had a rule that, "the object had to function as a prosthesis." This led to many of the costume elements of the show: boxing gloves, a collar, platform shoes. These rules, "are the restrictions you place upon yourself, that you have to find a creative solution for. I think this very much structures the work process."

In a broader example of a "rule", Lewie West says the company Gravity & Other Myths structures their creation by doing "acrobatic nerdery in the morning", then "tasks in the afternoon"—for example, based on their theme of '10k hours to mastery', they might do an idea of 'How can we show the

Vice and Virtu *by The 7 Fingers. Photo by Sebastien Lozé. Artist: Eric Bates.*

progression of a skill, of one person learning a skill, but using all 15 people?' and they go and play with that for 30 minutes.

KEY TAKEAWAY:

- Rules give a framework within which to be creative, and can also serve to break us free of the habitual, unspoken "rules" imposed on us by society.

Exercises

Below is a collection of creation games I have used during my time with Barcode, Acting for Climate, The 7 Fingers, and more. Many of them come from theater, we'll discuss at the end of the chapter how they can relate to circus.

7 Minute Directing

Decide on themes without telling the others, either by writing ideas related to your theme on scraps of paper and putting them in a hat, or coming with prepared ideas you want to try. Then you set a timer for seven minutes. Each team member takes a turn as the "director". They have seven minutes to read the paper, create a short scene however they want using the others, then when they're happy with it, film it. Then it's the next person's turn to direct and the roles switch. This is a nice exercise because it lets everyone practice being both a leader and a follower, and experience the challenges inherent to both so they can improve at both roles and be more empathetic to people in the opposite role. It also takes some of the pressure out of 'directing' because it's such a quick exercise—it's ok if something amazing doesn't come out of it. It also makes people feel less precious about ideas. Ideas can come from anywhere, and you can flesh out anything once you've acted. It also forces people into action instead of just talking about the best way to do things.

Contrasts

I like this exercise because contrast tends to be fun. This might be a good place to start if you're finding that all of your rule-driven improvisations are making moody, depressing material. Jokes are often just a contrast between your expectations and what happens in the punchline. Here's how it works: Everyone teams up with a partner and gets a certain amount of time to find some detail that sets them apart from each other. For example, it could be how different their personalities or physicalities are from one another. They have 2-3 minutes to find something and figure out how to show it. Fast is good! No time to overthink or worry about an idea being too first degree. After 2-3 minutes everyone presents their little pieces and you switch partners until everyone has worked together.

The Supermarket

This is a nice exercise to show how natural it is for humans to build a story around a character, without having to overthink things. One person (the 'main character' of the exercise) is onstage, miming out some sort of pedestrian action—going to the supermarket, for example, but something with inherent movement. Whenever a supporting actor wants, she claps her hands to indicate to the main character to freeze, then based on that frozen position, joins the scene and starts a completely different scene that they then improvise together. This could be playing paintball, or cutting hair, etc. After it has run for a bit, the director or one of the other actors claps again and the supporting actor steps out, letting the scene revert to the main character once more doing their groceries in the supermarket.

Repeat with the other supporting actors joining the scene, but resist the urge to try to make the new scenes string together into a story of any sort. The "memory" scenes don't relate to each other, they're just unrelated moments in the main character's life. In fact, the more varied they are the more we will learn about this main character.

Once everyone has gone (or it has gone on long enough, if you're a big group), take a minute to discuss. What did we learn about this main character? How does she react under stress? Is she funny? What has her life been like? Happy? Depressing? Naive? If the scenes were in a different order, would they tell a story?

Step In, Step Out

This can be a fun way to work if you've established a game with rules but don't have an official director. The idea is you play the game (let's say, "the floor is lava", except you use bodies on the ground instead of furniture), and whenever someone wants, they can step out to watch the game, see what they like or don't like, maybe even direct the others briefly, then dive back into playing the game. This lets you keep evolving the game ("It looks good when there's more distance between people!" or "It looks good when the person walking on top doesn't use their hands."), but without stopping and starting constantly which can kill the momentum. It also lets everyone see the game, and make decisions for themselves about what they think is interesting from an audience's perspective.

Car and Driver

This is a movement-based partner exercise we've used with The 7 Fingers, the idea being that there is a leader (the driver) and a follower (the car). The driver touches the car (maybe lifts a leg, or uses their head to push an elbow, or presses on their shoulder to guide them to the ground), giving impulses or physical 'suggestions' that the car follows and flows with. If the driver stops touching them, the car continues the movement naturally but without further impulse will slowly come to a stop. One key to this exercise is that the driver is also part of the scene, and should be physically involved accordingly, not just a puppet master. It's best if they can also guide the car in a physically interesting way. Of course you can make plenty of variations on these rules—the driver has to stay in contact and the car follows like a magnet when the driver moves away, or the opposite. The driver can't use their hands to guide, or the role of car and driver can change. Start with one rule for a while, then try others. Just don't let it be a free-for-all right away, rules can inspire creativity!

5-Rules Improv

Define a set of rules. These will define what options you have during the improv, which is otherwise an open movement improv. These could be anything, but some suggestions that have worked for us: Imitate someone else in the group. Stillness. Repetition. Yell something you're scared of. Make eye contact with someone.

Then you put on some music and move, looking for opportunities to implement these rules, and see what happens. This can also be done with an apparatus.

Both Yaron Lipschitz of Circa and The 7 Fingers directors I've worked with will often do something like this, then give feedback and try it again. Sometimes a part of the day will be dedicated to working on moments that were found this way, then improvising again to slowly "sculpt" the improv (by keeping more and more of the moments that "worked" over the duration of the creation period) until it's at a place where it will be choreographed and no longer an improv. Or in the case of Circa, it might remain an improv but with stricter rules and guiding principles.

Emotions 1-10

This exercise can be done as a group but without relating to the others in the room. Everyone starts talking about a subject (maybe "how their morning went"), and the idea is to ramp up an emotion from one to ten. Gypsy Snider (The 7 Fingers) says this exercise is silly, but "ideally that emotional thing turns into gestures and movement, it's not just seeing someone lose their mind. It becomes very physical, and connecting to how to make the art of an emotion physically readable to the audience is super important."

Add On

This is an easy way to make choreography. The first person proposes a movement or eight count. Everyone learns it, then the next person continues it for the next eight count, and so on, resulting in a choreography that is a blend of different people's styles.

Tell Someone Else's Story

The group gathers in pairs around the room, and each pair tells their partner a story from a time in their life. Then the group gets together again and one person tells their partner's story to the whole group, from the first person perspective. You can combine this with movement by having a third person improvise movement to the story. The storyteller can play with rhythm and repetition, volume and emotion to influence the mover.

Take a Class Together

"We knew we wanted to make a show together," says Nathan Biggs-Penton, co-founder of Acting for Climate Montréal, speaking about working with some of his circus classmates at Stockholm University of the Arts (formerly *DOCH*), the circus and dance school in Sweden. "So to start the process we just took an eight-week [creative circus] class together. Whenever during the class we would have an assignment we would often do it together, and then at the end we had all this super nice material that was really relevant to us."

Le Discours Sympathique

Le Discours Sympathique is an empathy game where you pick an emotion, you talk about a subject (maybe related to the theme of your show somehow), another person hears what you're saying, picks a different subject, adopts your current emotion, then when they've fully adopted the emotions starts their conversation with the emotion the first person had. The first person steps out and the second actor continues, transforming the emotion to a new emotion. (Mad to sad, suspicious to enthusiastic, etc). Gypsy Snider (The 7 Fingers) says, "I use that one a lot because I feel like very often in circus we're not doing the emotional work, but there's so much intensity within circus—the risk and the fear and the cost that it takes to do circus are so intense... I think because circus is... incredibly emotionally charged with subjects like courage, risk, trust, danger, gravity... we tend to avoid in the creative process the empathetic emotions related to subjects that we're talking about."

Reading the Room, Stakes

Regardless of what tools you use, Snider says that the biggest tool that she uses as a director is, "being receptive to the needs of the room." She describes these as a mix of what the project is, who she has to work with, the space itself, what she understands of the project's goals, the energy she feels and how far she thinks she can push different people. She also has to personally evaluate her own intention, why she is doing the project and what it means to her, and what the stakes are for her. "The stakes can be what's at risk for the character of the people who are onstage, the characters onstage, and what's at stake for the art itself." She then pours these stakes into the work itself. Just thinking she's doing something good "doesn't charge me. And it doesn't help charge the people that are there."

Relating the Exercises to Circus

These exercises can be great tools to drill down to core concepts in your show, but how do they combine with circus disciplines? I asked Snider how she transforms them from acting exercises to circus exercises.

"So what do you do next?" I ask Snider. *"Put those exercises on a trapeze?"*

She laughs. "I take those exercises and put them on a trapeze. Let's say I'm working with [a hula hoop artist] and I really don't want it to look like a typical hula hoop act, so I set her in: her grandmother passed away and she's got the bed and the sheets and the closet, the old clothes, and every time she touches the hula hoop it's like she's looking in the mirror that her grandmother looked in. Does she look like her grandmother? When she puts the hula hoop over her arm it's like she's putting on her mother's old wedding ring. So you're doing all the things that you would do if you got to go into your grandmother's room after she died and just dig through everything, but the only actual object you have is your hula hoops." This results in the act having a texture that comes from a circus vocabulary built on what the prop was representing during the improv.

She'll improvise in this manner until they find things that seem to fit between the circus and the story or intention behind the circus. "Improvisation is my favorite thing in the whole wide world," Snider says. "I think it's the only way to access the uncontrolled parts of our body, our mind and our soul. I have a lot of structure around that, to allow for very extreme things to happen, without people getting hurt or emotionally messed up."

Snider prioritizes the story or an emotional beat first, then lets that lead to the appropriate circus tricks, rather than trying to do it the other way around. When done correctly, the circus then feels natural, like a reasonable and exciting way to express a story or a moment. Such methods allow the power of circus to physically reflect the power of those emotional moments. This is what lets it feel "real".

Snider warns that there's another phase after this construction where people will want to put in new tricks, their "signature moves," etc. Then it's a process of not ruining everything they found that felt like a natural extension of the theme just to put some random trick in. You need to give the right information to your audience; and in the case that you have a trick that is magnificent, you need to do the work to see if it can fit into the story you're telling.

Brent McCoy (Vermont Vaudeville) also stresses the value of improvisation, and clarifies that it is often more powerful when done in front of an audience of some sort (even an audience of your creation partners). "It's where the good improvs happen, the great jokes, accidents, the discoveries, those moments become clear when they're shared in their most vulnerable, raw, unpolished, not finished state. So finding someone that is that person, or several people that are those people, has been something [important to our creation process]."

These different exercises are all ways to poke and prod at your relationships, group dynamics and characters. Once a few sparks fly it makes you curious to delve deeper, but the hard part can be getting that motor started or finding the path. "It's a bit like throwing spaghetti on the wall to see what works in this dynamic of people and trying to find those moments of surprise magic that click," says Mason Ames. "Then going, 'Oh shoot, we lost it, what happened in that improv that worked and how can we make it work again?'"

You don't have to use any of the above exercises or styles when you create, they're just ideas. If you don't have a director or someone leading the creation when you get to the room you will be not only making material, but also making the *way* that you make material. It's worth considering how you have made material with other companies in the past, and that you have the opportunity to do it however you want in your own creation. Regardless of how you want to do it, having an idea or two before you get into the space can help keep your motivation high.

ADDITIONAL CREATION
ADVICE

Backstage at Midnight Circus: Photo by Eric Bates: Artist: Patrick Tobin.

Research is a process of exploring ideas and relationships you haven't seen before. It involves making a lot of material that doesn't necessarily "work" or fit what you want your show to be about, and discovering things that do. It might mean trying physical ideas you haven't seen before, or just figuring out what you're capable of doing with this specific cast given their aptitudes and experiences. As Einstein apocryphally said, "If we knew what it is we were doing, it would not be called research, would it?" For some companies this might involve a lot of sitting around and talking about concepts, others might do improvisations. Personally, when leading a creation I like to direct in action. It looks like this:

We try something, then depending on what is working or not working, we push further in the same direction until we find stuff we like. We have a scene in *Branché* called 'Hide and Seek' that's a good example of this. We started by trying to make bodies on trees that looked like moss. Everyone stood behind a tree and slowly let their hands worm out around the bark to try to imitate moss growing. We didn't yet have a way into or out of this scene, and it was slow for my taste, so I suggested seeing what it would look like to have everyone move to a new tree and then begin the 'moss', just to see what would happen.

Inspiration! I liked the movement between trees, the sudden flash of the woods filled with bodies, then stillness as they were once again hidden. Forget the moss for now! Let's explore this.

I began giving instructions to the group. "When I say 'Go' everyone switch trees and hide. 'Go!' Now let's try it as quickly as possible. Now sneaking. Now by doing cartwheels. Walking backwards." In this way the idea evolved from "Moss" to "Red Light Green Light."

It helped (in fact, it was critical!) to have one person on the outside that could look at the image that was being created to see if it worked, and to direct the others, because they couldn't see the image from within the scene. That said, the person in this director role can change from scene to scene, or even within a scene. Rotate out and get different points of view.

Another way this might play out is to direct everyone, all at once but each on their own, to find three movements, or an 8 count, on a chair for example, or involving whatever prop you're trying to explore. As the director you can see all of this happening, and see what you like. Then when you see something

74

that speaks to you, you can direct the group's attention to that one person's movement, and say "Yes, this quality, play with this everyone," then off you go again, eventually stringing together a few of these short sequences that you can have the whole group learn, or do as a solo, or everyone doing their sequences at the same time, for example. Put the group mind and the different styles to work, then pick out what you want and try putting it on other people's bodies. Turn it into a choreography of sorts.

The Deadly "Ors"

Don't get bogged down in the "ors". This is when you propose an idea and someone says, "...*Or* we could do this, *or* we could do it this way..." They might even say, "That's awesome! *Or* we could do it in a handstand!"

Do not get bogged down by the *ors*! Just do one of them as quickly as possible. While *ors* are perfectly natural, often stemming from each person trying to help improve an idea, *ors* drain energy. Acknowledge as quickly as possible that both ideas are good, then take a decisive action on which to start with and agree to try the other one next. Try both efficiently before going down the next branch of ideas, because you don't want to end up with one person not having their idea be tried because the first idea inspired a whole new string of ideas (or do this and follow the fun, it depends on your group). **Don't *talk* about ideas, *try* them!**

In *Grip*, Bram Dobbeleare, co-founder of EA EO, explains his companies' culture of receiving and parsing ideas. A large part of what makes them successful is that they are willing to try each others' ideas, no matter how cliché. "We've always been able to create a working environment where if anyone wanted to try something, everyone would be supportive of that idea, even if it doesn't fit that person at all. Trying out the idea will make them realize whether it works or not soon enough."

It's Easier to Fix Something Than to Make Something

Don't worry about making something perfect right away. The goal in the research phase is to get out of your head and into the physical so you have something you can actually start improving upon, rather than an abstract idea that might look different to everyone inside their own heads. Make *something*. Make *anything*. Do it 15 different ways. Have the "wrong person for the job" do it. In each of these cases you'll learn more about it, especially in the early phases of creation.

Simplify

When we get stuck (sometimes due to talking too much during our improvs, which is not our strength), what often helps is to simplify. Here is an example:

We were trying to figure out a scene with three people: an 'Angel' and a 'Demon' each trying to convince the main character to eat something that would be bad for them, but that would taste good. We started by having the Angel and Demon characters talk, highlighting the pros and cons of each option. It was boring, and lacked movement. We simplified the exercise to the "Demon" nodding yes and the "Angel" shaking their head no, which organically evolved into something much more interesting than us just standing there talking, as we took the movements and exaggerated them, and used more movement because words were no longer an option. Eventually this evolved into the food object being thrown around, the main character following it back and forth, juggling it—it organically evolved into circus.

Simplify first, then make it more complex if necessary.

"I think simplicity is huge," Brent McCoy (Vermont Vaudeville) says. "A lot of the times the ideas that happen up [in your head] are grandiose and perfect and immaculately thought out and they just make sense, and then you go do it on its feet and you have to be able to accept that that is too complicated or that it wasn't as grand as we thought or that instrumentation makes that music sound like garbage instead of joyful." You can still have grand ambitions, but starting simple and building them up as needed makes for a lot less wading through the weeds.

Gypsy Snider (The 7 Fingers) said she was talking to an artist that felt paralyzed by how big some of the themes they wanted to talk about were: poverty, COVID-19, climate change, they all felt overwhelming. "In cases like this," Snider explained, "I simplify. I focus on something small and simple. How do I feel about X (ex. Disposable coffee cups)? I try to make it about really simple, concrete things, and not about, 'global warming.'"

KEY TAKEAWAYS:

- Work in action.
- It's easier to fix something than to make something.
- Simplify.
- Keep digging before abandoning an idea.
- Try different methods of working.
- Decisions are hard, but you can't stand at the crossroads.
- Trying things is more productive (and less prone to argument) than talking about which things to try.
- Make something with what you have now.
- Knowing what you want to talk about can provide clarity for those decisions (thesis statement).
- Rules and plans don't necessarily take away from creativity, they can actually enhance it.

Keep Digging

As you deepen your research it is important to keep digging. Try different approaches to the same idea, don't just dismiss the idea as not working.

In Barcode, we often say that the creative process is like digging for dinosaur bones. They're out there somewhere. You're just not quite sure where. You might have an idea of where to look, so you mark out your site and start to dig. Sometimes you find nothing, but you don't give up, or go look somewhere else yet—you try digging another hole nearby. You try a different angle, or you dig deeper. You keep digging these reconnaissance holes, looking for clues, until you see something that lets you know you're on the right track. Then you get out the finer brushes, first in one direction, then the other, exploring the limits of what you've found, and finally you pull that thing out of the dirt, polish it, and put it on display. If an idea doesn't seem like it's working, you don't necessarily have to pack up the tools and go somewhere else entirely—you might just need to try nearby, with a different approach.

Here is an example: Alex had a habit of reading ingredients off of boxes on long road trips. (What the heck is even *in* some of the stuff we eat?) We had this idea of Alex reading the ingredients off a box of processed food to accompany a hand-to-hand number. Could it be interesting?

First we tried Alex reading the box while Eve and Tristan did hand-to-hand. Cocoa powder, magnesium carbonate, conjugated linoleic acid... Boring. We tried her reading faster, slower, adding emphasis: CONJUGATED *linoleic* **acid**. Didn't work! She played with different ways of using her voice to give Tristan and Eve something to play with acrobatically... nothing! Instead of abandoning the idea we tried a new approach. Alex did an improv with Pedro, she herself reading the box while doing hand-to-hand. Suddenly we had the beginning of something!

It was interesting to watch her try to read this box while being spun around, and there was something sweet about the attention Pedro had to provide to allow her moments of stillness in unexpected positions in order to read. It was interesting how both the physical and vocal combined to feel like reactions to each other. There was something in the twisted physicality of it that spoke to how complex the state of our food has gotten. We kept working it.

After the improv we said what we liked, and took turns doing the same improv with different pairs, sometimes waiting for the end to make suggestions, sometimes saying them while the improv was happening ("Only say the words on the box, no extra words!" "Have a conversation, using only the words on the box, with one of you being the boss and the other is an employee who's getting fired." "Whisper the ingredients to your partner like a lover to whom you're confiding sweet nothings.")

Once we found a bunch of elements we liked, we wove our favorite physical movements together with the favorite theatrical elements in an order that felt like it had a sort of progression or story to it, and... boom! We put it on stage that evening. This refinement process obviously can, and probably should,

The Thing-In-Itself *by The Chita Project. Photo by Eric Bates. Artist: Pablo Pramparo.*

take a lot longer... but the lesson is this: don't abandon ideas too soon. Keep digging.

Examine the Process

If this is your first creation, you might be simultaneously creating both material and the *way* that you create material. Because of this, Nathan Biggs-Penton (Acting for Climate Montréal) recommends that you take the time to write down the method you want to try. This way it will be clear for everyone in the group. You can try it 100%, and then check in about it and see if you want to try something else or not. "There are so many possibilities—every day, every second someone is making a new working method for a group. There's so many examples of group dynamics in office spaces, farming, etc... if your method is to do flow and just see what happens—that's a valid method, just as much as being really detailed in every minute of the day. Be clear all together and agree to try something for a while."

Maya McCoy (Vermont Vaudeville), who makes a brand new show for every performance, says that while "the production has gotten way better and more streamlined... the creative work is hard every single time... Even if we start well in advance, even if we have paid rehearsal time, it's always hard. But that's just part of the process. You have to get through that frustrating, 'What are we going to do, this was supposed to be a funny idea and now we've lost it all' phase." Their willingness to try new methods has helped them learn and grow and come to terms with the fact that there is no magic bullet for creative collaborations.

Decisions

Making a show is the process of making decisions. It's a million forks in the road, a product of an infinite amount of perfect, unmade shows out there that

80

can only exist in your mind. The show that makes it onstage will be inherently imperfect, it won't be able to compete with the unbounded power of your imagination. It's important to accept this so as not to get paralyzed at each decision. Try one thing, then the other. Usually one of the two will seem more appealing, hopefully to your entire team, but maybe not. The truth is, you can't stand at the crossroads forever, and sometimes even a "wrong decision" (or maybe just not your personally preferred option) will reveal a lot of beautiful possibilities later.

Constant Gathering

Brent McCoy (Vermont Vaudeville) is constantly writing down jokes whenever he thinks of them over the course of the year. "Sometimes it's an accident that happens in life, that if you find it funny and you put it in your character's world, that's enough to start a bit." Write everything down, don't worry about quality as much as quantity. Jerry Seinfeld had the simple method of writing a certain number of jokes every day. Every day he successfully completed his joke quota he put a big X on the calendar. Then his only job was to not break the chain.

Charlie Wheeller said that with his company Barely Methodical Troupe they also constantly gathered physical vocabulary together, regardless of the contract they were on. By doing this they ended up with a bank of material before they needed it, so that when they arrived in a creation they didn't have to build everything from scratch.

This idea of 'constant gathering' applies to music as well. Make a playlist for "music to try", with anything that catches your ear. Put a bunch of different styles on there so you have options ready to go when you get in the room to use for improvizations or testing out ideas.

The Cold and the Technical

Sometimes you need to get as simple as possible in order to get started. In *Grip*, Benjamin de Matteis says in their process they will write out the cold, technical sequence of tricks, then they find relationships and moments through improv that turn what would be a few seconds worth of tricks into a full act. When making a juggling routine I'll also often start here, laying out a basic order of tricks to give myself structure to fill and flesh out with the nuances, transitions and moments unique to each piece that give it life.

Making Something With What You Have Now

One of the exercises I liked when working with Acting for Climate was to make something *now*. It's easy to say, "This scene in my head is amazing, it's a 40 foot wall of books and then they all start flying and we do circus in the flying books." That scene never happens. So instead of thinking, "If only I had *this*, I could make *this*," start to build the practice of making something with what you have already available to you, then gradually expand from there. Paul Valéry once said, "A poet's function... is not to experience the poetic state: that is a private affair. His function is to create it in others." To do this you must move from the dreaming state to the working state and begin the messy reality of recreating your dreams with the imperfect clay of your body and your available resources so that you can inspire those dreams in others.

Similarly, if you have an idea—maybe to have dirt onstage, or a swinging hourglass that pours sand out onto the stage—get that thing and try it. Bring in dirt. Bring in a bag full of sand and figure out how to rig it to the ceiling. It's much better to try things than to just imagine them in your head. It forces you to see the reality of what you want to make, and maybe to be pleasantly surprised by how the object or research looks in real life, as opposed to what you thought it might look like in your imagination.

Where to Start If You're Stuck

What is your subject? Why is it interesting to you? Why is it important to you?

Let's say you have a passion for video games and want to make that the theme of your show. You could start by examining why you chose this subject to make a whole show about. What games did you love? What about them did you love? What about the whole "video game experience" did you love? Was it about becoming someone else? Escaping from something else in your life? Getting to hang out with friends eating sugar and being goofy until late in the night? Doing things you can't do in real life? Feeling good at something for once? The anticipation of getting home from school to play? Were the games ever frustrating? Did that one friend always drive you crazy?! What else was part of the video game experience? Snack breaks? Getting kicked outside to get some fresh air? Saving up money to buy a new game? Cheat codes?

Any one of these leading questions could reveal places to look for material.

You could chat until late in the evening about these things, and create a list of stuff to try. But the key is that you try things, in the room, with your body and circus disciplines. All the ideas in the world will not make a show if you don't act on them!

This could take the form of homework—write a story or memory about the theme, then go make a short solo section based on that story. You could then work on that piece as a solo or a group number.

Let's say you find something interesting. Perhaps a scientific article that's related to your show's theme... but how can it translate to circus? You'll have to examine the text more to understand what exactly about it piques your interest. Are you trying to teach your audience something? Or are you trying to embody your emotional reaction to this thing you learned? Or maybe the new knowledge you learned gave you new ideas for physical movements to try on your rope.

Alternatively, you could bring in stories or memories, or through conversations with your group find something that is interesting, and see if it inspires an idea to try together. Even if it doesn't seem to spark anything while sitting around talking (a common occurrence!), it's important to try something, anything, in action. You have to do some digging in order to find gold! Start with one idea and even if it doesn't produce an amazing, broadway-worthy moment, maybe it'll give someone else a new idea to try that sparks some excitement and gets your creative juices flowing.

Sometimes your starting place is specific: "I want to make a tree out of bodies."

This is easy. Start trying to make a tree out of bodies.

Sometimes your starting place is more vague: an emotion or a feeling: "I feel sad or depressed about the climate crisis."

This will take a little more work. What specifically about the situation makes you sad? How does this feeling translate physically? Does it feel heavy? Like you are carrying a weight around all day? Maybe this manifests as more and more people piling on top of you while you try to get through your daily routine. Or maybe it looks like people adding rocks to a backpack while you try to do handstands. Who knows!

There are lots of creation games in theater textbooks. Many of these take the form of improvisation games, and might be good ways to get you out of your head and into action. Some can even lead to interesting material to work with.

There's no one way to make material. You will have to find the way that you create best with your group.

CASE STUDY: THE 7 FINGERS

Let's look at some of the tools Shana Carroll uses when creating with her company, The 7 Fingers.

Creating a Thesis Statement

When in creation, Carroll tries to give names to acts or scenes that are like mini thesis statements for the scene. It helps get all of the artists (including lights, sound, etc) on the same page about what this moment is about, what the emotional essence of the scene is. It also helps her as a creator to stay focused, so she isn't distracted by flashy moments if they don't line up with the vision of the scene, and in the end detract from it.

In *Queen of the Night*, instead of calling the first hand-to-hand moment "Hand-to-Hand 1", she called it, "Love at First Sight." This is a simple change, but for Carroll, it made her feel more driven as she was creating it. "The point is, 'Let's project love at first sight,' not [let's just make a cool hand-to-hand act]."

She has expanded this concept to also having a thesis statement for her entire show.

She notes that this thesis statement is different from an elevator pitch. A typical cliché elevator pitch is something like, "Imagine the TV show *Friends* meets traditional circus in a boxcar." It's designed to quickly give the feel and experience you would have if you watched the show, and maybe a quick storyline if it's a longer elevator ride.

Carroll's thesis statement, however, is more personal. It's for the people in the show to get on the same page. When Carroll was making *Passagers* she explained that her thesis statement was based on two very personal experiences, ones that had also impacted a large swath of the circus community—the death of two performers and friends. "It was a few months after Raphael Cruz had died," Carroll explains, "and I was in bed and super depressed and I didn't want to get up, and Fletcher Sanchez had died the year earlier, and I said, "I want the world to go back to a place where magical things can happen and not a place where young men I love die."

Her husband, Sébastien Soldevilla, replied, "It's both."

"The thesis statement for *Passagers*," Carroll continues, "was, '*It's both.*' That captured the parallel tracks of all the beauty and magic and interaction and connection; and simultaneously all the loss and not arriving. With trains the acceleration and the stillness and the seeing your reflection and seeing the landscape, there were all these juxtapositions that were constantly being referenced. ...It meant something to me and I could explain it to the cast, but it would be hard to explain in an elevator pitch."

The Bones

Carroll says that for her, "the exercise of writing is often very reclusive and solitary." After working with a group she would try to put the show on paper, to write down the bones that they could work off of and exchange about. She would start with a pacing based on ideas, discussing things they'd talked about so they knew what the meat of the show was. She would write it down with big spaces in between to put in ideas for transitions, some of which stayed, some of which evolved into something else. Having this on paper gave them something to try, regardless of whether they used them or started from scratch. Note that this process of turning ideas into concrete decisions might be painful- it can be hard to nail down the beautiful and ephemeral ideas in your head with the messy tools of reality. The vision you had will almost certainly have to change and develop in order to fit practical concerns such as budget, artist abilities, costume materials, etc. While potentially painful, it is also an opportunity for these ideas to be transformed and grown by your collaborators, an opportunity for the collective nature of creation to surprise and delight you.

"Personally I would love to keep it in my head and make notes and make my own order and move things around, but often for the design team I have to create a whole script," says Carroll.

Survival of the Most Passionate

Carroll warns that a "Yes, and..." strategy, in which you incorporate everyone's ideas somewhat equally, can be dangerous because you may end up with something tame and polite, a lowest-common denominator sort of result. "One thing with The 7 Fingers that we're good at now, because we're not polite [laughs], is survival of the most passionate. Usually the idea that sticks is the one who's most passionate about their idea."

When employing this approach, be wary of doing it with negation though. Proposing lots of ideas can be great, but just saying no to other ideas is death to a process. With Barcode, our approach is to try things as soon as possible rather than talk about them. Like a great looking shirt in a store, you only know the fit once you put it on your body. Sometimes it's easy to imagine yourself wearing something that ends up being a clear rejection (or success!) once you actually try it on.

PLANNING YOUR CREATION

There's a lot you can and should do before starting your creation. Let's look at some of the ways to plan your creation to set yourself up for success in the room.

Reserving Space

Finding space for your project can be a bigger challenge than you might expect. Circus projects tend to have more needs (rigging, height, mats) than just an empty room, and while training spaces with these requirements exist, finding a private one for your team can prove difficult.

There are residency spaces dedicated to supporting artists' creations, but like theaters and gigs, they tend to book in advance. If you're hoping to make a project and not spend a fortune renting rehearsal and theater space, you need to plan well ahead of time.

That said, if you do plan ahead, it's possible to get up to a three week residency relatively affordably, or even for free. And believe me, that focused time in the same location where all you're doing is creating your show is much more productive than fragmented creation time.

When we did our first exploratory workshops we did an exchange for space at Cirque Eloize, and got a residency through En Piste at the National Circus School (ENC) in Montréal which gave us 3 hours a day. However, if we also wanted technical training time, we had to book that separately. This meant we would often train in the morning (bring our Russian bar, hoop, boxes and teeterboard down to Cirque Eloize), then pack it all up in my partner's car (if it was available!), eat lunch, drive across the city to ENC, unpack everything, bring it upstairs to the creation studio, set it up, train for three hours, take it all down, pack it back into the car and bring it to one of our houses for the night. Not ideal.

Sometimes we managed to schedule better to avoid some of this back-and-forth craziness, but we didn't always have a choice—we were tied to the available slots we could get. When we finally found a two week residency space, it was a blessing because we could focus uniquely on the show: all those space-related headaches of logistics, coordination and scheduling disappeared.

My top tip for finding a dedicated space like this (besides booking in advance) is something echoed by many of the creators I interviewed: **The best creation space for you is not always close to home.** What you sacrifice in the convenience of sleeping in your own bed will come back to you tenfold in the benefits of getting time to install somewhere and to burrow into your project.

After Eloize and ENC, we paid for 2 weeks of creation space in a barn up near Quebec City, then did 3 paid performances of our 'pre-premiere' in Fringearts Theater in Philadelphia (USA), where we were able to use their theater for 10 days before the opening (we got that one by having a booth at Montréal Completement Cirque six months prior). A year after that, we did a month and a half of creation (for free) in Jatka78, a theater located in Prague in the Czech Republic. Was it a big coordination effort to get over there, and did it cost money to ship our stuff over there? Absolutely. But it gave us a month and a half to dive into our project with zero distractions, and at the end of our residency, it gave us a paid opportunity to play for three nights to an audience where European agents and theaters could see the show.

Many theaters and venues have space they're willing to let people use, and often have various levels of other support like accommodation, tech, and money to offer to artists in residence. If you're looking for a place you can really install for at least a week or two, it's possible to find it if you look early, just don't expect it to be in your backyard. And book it now. Commit to your dream!

The main advantage of finding a dedicated space is that it's a distraction-free environment. Trying to get into a creative zone with people watching you or with other people training nearby, or where you have all your friends around may eat into your ability to focus on your project and to make huge strides.

Another note: Frequently you'll get into an empty space, and there's no *stuff* to play with. If you have ideas for your show, see if you can bring in elements to play with, at least prototype versions—if you need a table, find a table, if you have an idea to play with sand, get some sand. Figure out how to test your ideas so they don't stay in the imaginary realm.

Think also about the things you want to do, and how the elements you surround yourself with will change the story of what you're doing even if the movements remain the same. Doing a show in the woods, or on a stage covered in lentils, or in a single spotlight, or naked, or amongst the audience (hopefully not while naked!) will all change the perception of the thing you're doing.

Exercises

- You'll likely need a presentation file to apply for formal residency spaces. To prepare for that, consider what your project is about, create a file or a PDF with photos and video, ideally laid out in a pleasing way. You'll actually need this information for just about everything (grants, promotion, website, selling it to people, etc), so work on it early, and keep updating it as your idea is molded and clarified. Then start sending it out, and see if you get any bites.

Gather:

- Short "elevator pitch" description of your project- what's the most important thing to say about your project if you only had 90 seconds to make someone care about it? How about 30?
- Longer description and goal of your project
- Photos
- Video

Failing to Plan is Planning to Fail

If you don't plan ahead, you'll end up having to figure everything out in the room, which isn't an efficient use of time (or money if you're paying for the room).

This isn't to say you need *everything* planned out ahead of time, but at least have a few jumping off points. If you want to try an improv, what will some of the rules/ ideas for the improv be? If you have an outside eye coming in to work with you, what specifically do you want them to help with? If you have a residency coming up in two weeks, what can you do now to get yourself as ready as possible? Start researching music? Plan out some meals? Make sure you have the prototypes of the props you're hoping to try?

For an idea of a full creation timeline, see "Appendix A: Full Creation Timeline" on page 319. That will help you figure out what you'll be likely to encounter on your journey so you can plan accordingly. On that note, remember this: When making a show, everything takes ten times as long as you think it will!

Phases of Creation

"You don't do the 'writing a show' all day, you spend a part of the day writing and then a part of the day organizing a way to make that writing come to life. Once it has enough of a life then you can actually get a grant for it, or present something."
-Gypsy Snider, The 7 Fingers

I find it useful to identify what phase of creation you're in, both in a big picture sense and at the moment in the room. How you behave in an exploratory, research context will be different from when you're polishing material. How you behave when you think you're in an improv might be different from if you think you're rehearsing a choreographed piece. I've found it useful in my head, and to reduce conflict within a group, to divide up and identify the different phases to help the team be on the same page. Here are some of the distinctions I make:

Preproduction

- Brainstorm/dream- This is freeform letting ideas flow without worrying how you will accomplish anything or its feasibility.
- Figure out the *Hows*- This is the time to explore questions and decide if your ideas are achievable in the timeframe and with the budget you will or won't have. For example, ask your team things like, "Let's look online and see if that's a realistic idea/ would it be worth it to spend our entire budget on that? Is there a creative way we could do it for less?" There will be multiple phases of figuring out the *hows*.

Early creation days of Sweat & Ink. *Photo by Eric Bates. Artists: Eve Bigel, Alexandra Royer.*

In Creation
- Research/exploration- try more improvisation, surprises, new things.
- Rehearsal- take what you've determined you liked from previous improvs/ things you made and try to put them together.
- Polish- The routine is set, recreate the same piece repeatedly so you can clarify details and work on consistency. Determine if you are trying to push through without stopping or if something is off if it is ok to stop and address it.

Furthermore, it is likely you'll have multiple phases of creation blocks, often divided by when you have private space reserved. These will include general research blocks, meaning workshops without presentations, then later on workshops with presentations to small groups to get feedback, then eventually performing a part of your show (an extract of 20 or 30 minutes), before it is time to present the full show.

Our first creation block for *Sweat & Ink* was at Cirque Eloize's studio, during which we brought in outside eyes and generally did research on our own. We also did technical training at either Eloize or at the École Nationale de Cirque de Montréal where we also had a residency, or had booked training time. At the end of our residency at the circus school, we presented a work-in-progress to a small group of people, focusing on new material.

We later spent two weeks at a friend's creation barn, living together in his house and putting together what would become the first version of the show. We also had a week at the Fringearts theater in Philadelphia, where the show was to open as a 'work-in-progress' in front of an audience. Fringearts was able to give us a week in the space before we opened, during which we threw together costumes, created lighting for the whole show, painted the set, and worked with our director to finish the show.

Almost a year after this we went back into creation, this time for one month living in the theater *Jatka 78* in Prague with our director. During this phase we commissioned custom music, our light designer arrived to design the lights, we hired a local costume designer and we repainted all of our set design to give it a cohesive look. This, give or take, was the show that we toured for the following three years.

Research:

This is the first phase of the creation process when you're physically *in the room*, unlike pre-production which might take place in an office, your apartment, or cafés. You want to make a show about something, you haven't tried any ideas yet, so you get in the room and throw a bunch of stuff at the wall to see what sticks. You've talked about it enough, now it's time to try stuff physically. Some companies, like The 7 Fingers, will try to have a short research period months before their big block of creation so they have some early feedback on their initial ideas they can use to structure more of their big creation block. Barcode has also employed this strategy with *Branché*, doing a two week workshop in the winter before the big block of creation in the summer. It's useful to see what ideas show promise early, and work out and reflect on any initial bugs you might have with your process so you can improve it before the big block of creation starts. The main advice I have for this phase is: Make a lot of material, and film it.

Make a Lot of Material

Lewie West (Gravity & Other Myths) recommends making a lot of material that is vaguely linked to a theme. This can be something broad like "Strength" or "Ten Thousand Hours of Mastery", but it's specific enough that you can explore ideas that may be somehow related to each other. In general, you're going to make more material than can fit into the length of your show, which is a good problem to have because then you can just keep the best bits.

As you explore different facets of the theme, you're also getting a better idea of what the show itself is. In the beginning when you're digging for dinosaur bones—don't worry about putting the whole thing together into one big skeleton yet. But if you do find an idea that excites you, keep going. Darcy Grant (director of Gravity & Other Myths shows) recommends going the path of least resistance. Follow the fun. If you're getting roadblocked on something, work on something else and come back to it, or try it from a different angle. Maybe the momentum from another thing will take you through the idea you're stuck on.

In Grip, Bram Dobbeleare of EA EO says they will explore an idea, something as simple as, "Wouldn't it be cool if [a juggler] were surrounded by lots of people?" If it's a strong idea it will tend to create a lot of interesting material. If not, then you might find it wasn't strong enough, or you're coming at it from the wrong angle. In Barcode's creation of *Sweat & Ink*, we explored a lot of ideas with a sand timer and a slide projector as ways to express time passing and memory. Despite trying a lot of variations on both ideas, neither made it into the final show—they didn't have the visual impact we had imagined in our heads, or were too hard to make work from a technical perspective. We filed away the research for another day.

Some ideas might make it into the final show, some might just lead you to other scenes that are in the final show. You'll figure it out later. For now, keep making material and film it so you don't forget it when you get to your next workshop.

"Looking back we went about it all wrong, because we tried to structure the show and choreograph way too detailed and intricately before we had any material, and after that we made a whole bunch of material and then it was way easier to see what shape the show was going to be," Lewie West says, reflecting on the creation of his show *Fold*.

The more material you make, the more connections and transitions from one new idea to the next will start to take shape. You'll start to see ways that short moments can be combined.... You're making a lot of puzzle pieces, discovering how they fit together later (and which ones go where.) Don't fall into the trap of endless creation though! The goal after all is to refine your material into a show. One necessary step that will help get you there is presenting your work-in-progress.

Presentations

Presentations are a way to show a limited number of invited guests what you've been working on. Scheduling a presentation provides just enough motivation to get something together, but where you can control the amount of pressure you're putting on yourselves. You do this by controlling who comes to see it, inviting people you trust and that understand where you are in the process and that will give you useful feedback.

Even just the experience of presenting for a single person—such as a new outside eye for the first time—can have this effect. Even if you're just presenting for your neighbor, that difference can feel huge compared to working on a scene for an empty room. Presentations such as this give you a realistic view of where your creation is. Presenting means they won't see your ideas or your philosophy or your conversations, only what you've actually made.

Building a series of presentations into your calendar lets you keep taking the temperature of how you feel performing the work you've made in front of people, while you still get to control the people that are coming to see it.

Mason Ames, reflecting on his creation of *Deer in the Headlights* with Cirque le Roux, said, "One of the presentations we did was so dark, just overly creepy- not in a good way. In an awkward way that felt really terrible onstage. So we decided we had to make it more fun and lighthearted." You want to have these realizations in front of small groups of trusted people, not on opening night!

In Barcode's first *sortie de residence* (literally translated as "exit of residency", it's a presentation you often perform for a small group at the end of a residency to show what you've been working on), we put together a lot of the new material we had made focusing on only new material. We didn't present any of our acrobatic specialities. The one acrobatic discipline we did want to present was mini-teeterboard, since it was new for us. We didn't have any choreography or music or anything, just a series of tricks, but this brought a raw quality to the act that we loved: it was just us working together to do the tricks and support each other, and we liked it so much we pretty much kept that vibe for the final show. We added ambient supporting music and figured out the best order for the tricks, but the feeling remained the same. You can learn a lot by putting things in front of an audience. This controlled-viewing tactic is used at many stages of a show's roll out.

For Machine de Cirque's show *Ghostlight* they did multiple dress-rehearsal style presentations in the same week, sometimes changing huge chunks of the show. It's more or less standard practice for shows to have soft openings, which are basically performances in theaters that are not the official premiere, where you invite everyone (producers, programmers, newspapers, etc) to see it. Cirque du Soleil used to do months of pre-premieres before their 'official' opening. Broadway shows will typically play for at least a month in another city before they open on Broadway. On a smaller scale, some theaters will request official premieres since it gives them prestige, so to preserve those dates there's nothing stopping you from calling any prior showings a "work-in-progress" or a "pre-premiere" if you feel you want time to keep working things out. It gives you the opportunity to keep improving the show but still get that vital audience feedback. Sometimes shows will open in smaller fringe festivals in order to try out material in front of an audience who have lower expectations and might be willing and interested to watch something you still consider a work-inprogress (regardless of how you bill it).

Adapting during performances

You made it through your workshops, sorties de residences, performed your 30 minutes, and now you've made a full length piece, right? Now it's time to perform it! Presumably you've had this date in mind for a while, if not, you might be in for a wait. Oftentimes the official performance, even if it's a pre-premiere or however you want to brand it, comes on the back of a residency in a theater, so you have time to figure out your lights, sound and staging for the first time. If you're looking for somewhere to rehearse your show, many venues might be able to give residency space in exchange for a performance, or on the condition of a paid performance at the end. Some theaters even have money to support residencies as part of their mission.

If you have the luxury of helping to decide your show schedule, it can be really nice to have a day in between performances to work stuff out, like Cirque le Roux did when they pre-premiered *Deer in the Headlights* at a circus festival in France. "A day off in between shows really gives you a day and a half, since you'll have the morning of show day as well. At the end of the creation process that was dynamite," Ames said.

Vermont Vaudeville said that as they did more shows they fixed problems and improved their process and their humble cabaret improved each time, slowly becoming more and more like their original vision of it. However, in the beginning though, "We cared about the aesthetic, but we weren't precious about it," says Brent McCoy. "We did that first show with like four lights. No production value." Ten years later and they've now done over 23 original productions (each show is completely original material), tweaking and defining their aesthetic each time. Perfection is a moving target. It's a goal you can work towards but never achieve. **Don't think everything needs to be perfect before you can start.**

Make 30 Minutes First

Of all of the people I interviewed, many specifically mentioned making 30 minutes before you make your full show. Héloïse Bourgeois, co-founder of Cirque Entre-Nous, said at first that they didn't know if they could make a full show with only Chinese pole as a discipline. After making 35 minutes which they sold as an outdoor show she said, "Because that worked, because it opened a lot of doors for us to work with theater, music, etc, we decided we would make a full show." See if your idea has legs! See if it's a theme and a group dynamic that has the potential to go the distance.

"I think putting 30 minutes in front of an audience really lets you know what colors are working, where you want to take things," Mason Ames says of his first presentation with Cirque le Roux, "and it's extremely helpful because there's so much doubt in the creation process. There's only so many times you can argue it back and forth between yourselves. Putting it in front of an audience and seeing what's working, what's not working, what's coming to life, what are the surprising moments—it's essential. And also, it forces you to get your shit together because otherwise you can be in a room for two years by yourself and if you don't have that pressure, you don't get your shit together."

Production value is not the goal here. As we'll see in the "Successful Shows" section, audiences are interested first and foremost in the human performance element. As a physical artist, the physical material is the foundation of your show and that means the concept and how you explore it. That's what you

101

want to put onstage for 30 minutes. A small group of artists, for example, could make material together and start finding opportunities to perform it in other people's shows—in cabarets, or within the context of a bigger show, and eventually growing that material to the 30 minutes that you present as a stand alone piece.

You could present this 30 minutes at a more official platform like Circus Next, or Montréal Completement Cirque, or in someone's hometown theater or church, or in a festival, or as a part of a local cabaret… basically put it up anywhere that you can get eyes on it. Barely Methodical Troupe made 30 minutes by themselves and performed it at the Young Choreographer's Platform, at which point producers came to them, asking to produce the show that eventually became *Bromance*. Take note though: sometimes these festivals refer to "presenting" as talking about and selling your show rather than performing it. Make sure you know what you're getting yourself into!

KEY TAKEAWAYS:

- Identify which phase of creation you're in and what is important for you to get out of it.
- Presenting your work can be painful, but it's a necessary step. It can be extremely valuable to get audience feedback, too.
- Film your work, and organize it so you can use it easily later.

Exercises

- Make a music playlist of "one day" music. Anything that catches your ear that you think might work for something eventually. You could also save playlists that surprise you. Film soundtracks, other languages, various beats per minute, well known songs or very niche songs. It can be helpful to know a song well, and it can be helpful to never have heard a song before and be surprised by it in an improv. Having a big collection of music with different emotion and grandeur can really feed a creation if you're the sort of group that likes to improv to music.

- Make a list somewhere (maybe in a shared online folder) of exercises to try that can help you create material. There are a lot of games and exercises out there—don't limit yourself to resources specifically for your discipline: many theater or dance or circus exercises can work interchangeably with a little creativity.

- Make a list of the physical things you need to try ideas you have, and their costs (or at least prototypes). If you're approaching a creation period, and your budget allows, get those things.

- Talk with your team about the roles you see yourselves playing. See what you can automate/ set up before you need it (measurements, important documents, CVs, information on the members, etc).

- Plan a sample creation week. To try to make a realistic schedule, keep in mind transportation time, food shopping/prep/eating/ clean up, creation time, and meetings.

Embracing the Digital Age with Video

Many creators listed video as a useful creation tool in the room. This section will talk about video as a research and creation tool, but as we'll see later in the book, it's also indispensable for promotion.

When in creation, taking video of moments you find can prove invaluable. A thorough research video allows you to save good ideas and come back to them later without losing track of everything or having to spend time 're-finding' movements, tricks or moments you've already found. It can help everyone get on the same page by being able to see and point to the exact moment they're talking about. It can help you build a scene.

For research video, it's not extremely important how you film (any phone's camera will do nowadays), but it is important what you do with the clips. At Barcode, for both *Sweat & Ink* and *Branché*, we organized our videos in a cloud storage service such as Google Drive or Dropbox. Vermont Vaudeville puts their videos on a dedicated external hard drive as well. Label the videos, or at the very least drop them into some sort of organized system of folders. It can be organized by date, residency location, scene or discipline; depending on what works best for you and will allow you to retrieve an interesting tidbit you only faintly remember a year later. Try to edit the clips down to the good stuff while it's fresh—you'll save storage space and it will make it more likely

Filming of Sweat & Ink: *Photo by Stefanie Fournier. Artists: Tristan Nielsen, Alexandra Royer, Eric Bates.*

that you'll actually use these videos later since you won't have to wade through endless material to find what you were looking for.

One common technique during creation is to pump out a lot of material. Try everything. As acrobatic coordinator for *Gravity & Other Myths* Lewie West attests, filming and classifying ideas means that as the show develops and you get a better idea of what exactly the show is going to be, "you'll see which things you've developed speak more strongly to that theme and that idea, so you can go back and find that thing—that maybe at the start it didn't seem like it fit, but now it really fits. You can bring that back out and interrogate it a lot more and expand on it."

Héloïse Bourgeois (Cirque Entre-Nous) would make short montages of all the most promising research they found under one idea or theme, sort of like a highlight reel for the idea. In the book *GRIP*, Pia Meuthen, founder of Panama Pictures, explains that she does a similar thing. After a creation period she will go through all the research videos and edit pieces together into something she thinks will work, or will show her what she's missing, like a dynamic part, or a group scene. Then she can take this to the artists in the next creation block to help her transmit her vision of what the scene or show will be.

Also in *GRIP*, Christian Coumin, artistic director of the French circus school Le Lido and other companies, warns to be careful not to lose too much time rewatching video, and not to rely too heavily on video since it "is a distorted image" of what happened, especially if it is at the expense of remembering the actual sensations felt when doing an improvisation.

When we created *Sequence 8* with The 7 Fingers we also used video extensively—it was helpful for directors Shana Carroll and Sébastien Soldevila to be able to show us specific moments that worked in improvs so we could do the improvs again, trying to work in the moments they liked, until we had something close enough to an act that they could choreograph it.

However you choose to use it, video can be a valuable tool. Just remember to keep it organized if you want it to be useful!

A final benefit to well documented research: You will undoubtedly end up with loads of material that is good but doesn't make it into the show. Having this unused material on film means it can serve in other projects down the line: ideas or sequences you might have loved but that didn't fit in your current project won't be lost forever. When you see these a year from now you will marvel at them and wonder how you ever forgot them, and they will possibly spark new lines of research as time gives you a fresh perspective.

Performance Space

A number of the creators I interviewed performed their new creation (or creation-in-progress) for the first time in venues in either their current hometown or where they had grown up. Not only is this a good way to get an audience, but it can be a blessing to test out material in your show in a friendly, low-visibility setting so you can work out the kinks.

Another option is inviting people to a *sortie de residence*. It can be a good way to get eyes on your show without the pressure of a "premiere" where everything has to be finished and it feels like a tour depends on it. It lets you test ideas you're not sure about to see how people react.

Creation spaces will often encourage some sort of showing at the end of a residency– either a performance they sell tickets to, or at least a short presentation to which they can invite a handful of guests such as people that donate to the space, for example.

Mason Ames (street performer and freelance artist) says it's nice to have residencies that are just for your team to explore and experiment with working together, then to have other residencies where you have what he calls "get it together time" to make decisions in order to present at the end. An ideal strategy might be to time those different sorts of residencies not too distant from each other so you don't have to spend the whole "get it together" residency remembering what you did last time. Remember: recording video of your research can help!

Making a short presentation forces you to make decisions and try ideas, but it will require spending time to put together a draft of something that likely won't resemble the final show. This might feel like wasted time, and indeed it is a compromise, but on the whole a necessary step to make your ideas concrete. For a sortie de residence, don't worry too much about transitions (unless you are specifically interested in trying transitions) because people will understand if the presentation is a hodgepodge, and you can usually say something before the presentation to that effect if you feel self-conscious about it. Focus on what is important for your team to get out of the experience. If you're doing a more official presentation of 30 minutes that you're hoping will look like something and presenting it as such, obviously then you should invest more time in the transitions.

Tackling Imposter Syndrome

Many of the artists I interviewed for this book mentioned imposter syndrome. It is common for artists to think to themselves, 'Who am I to make a show, or to tell people what to do, or to do anything?' According to the 2019 study "Prevalence, Predictors, and Treatement of Imposter Syndrome: a Systematic Review" (*Journal of General Internal Medicine*, 2019), as many as 82% of participants reported feeling imposter syndrome at some point in their careers. In my interviews for this book, many of the successful creators quoted in these pages mentioned, unprompted, having felt it when they took on new projects.

I notice this tendency to feel like an imposter in Barcode members as well, especially when we made our first show—an experience which was new to us despite our years onstage. Because we always want to do better and see where we can improve ourselves, we tend to undervalue our work, or make excuses for it to people who didn't ask, when what we need to do is assume our artistic choices and stand behind them. Just because you see every detail in the show that needs improvement doesn't mean that other people do! It was only after I talked to many creators that I realized how common a feeling this was. Many creators felt similarly critical of their own work and would criticize and downplay it when we discussed it- work that had touched me immensely as an outside spectator. You have as much of a right to make a show as anyone, and know that any feelings you have as an impostor will not be unique to you, and may only go away with years of work, or may never go away!

Recognize that you will have things you are good at and things you are less good at. You don't have to be good at everything before you can start a new project!

The reason why people say "fake it 'till you make it' is because until you do it the first time, you will never have done it. If you wait until you're "qualified" to do something, you might be waiting a long time. So *make* it until you make it. Keep making stuff. Dive in.

When I have doubts about what I'm making, and the imagined voices of what other people must think of me start to rumble in my head, I try to remind myself that the simple act of doing something new and challenging for me is in itself a success. There may be more work to do, but that bar for success will always continue to move higher as your skills grow, so don't discredit the work you are currently doing. You're already succeeding by doing it.

On the other hand, if you don't know what you're doing, don't hesitate to admit it and to ask for guidance! People like honesty, and will help you if you're straightforward about where you're at. No need to pretend to be anywhere other than where you are in your journey. If you're putting in the work, you're no longer faking it. You have earned the right to ask for help.

Asking for help is part of the creative process. Don't be afraid to admit what you don't know, but also don't let not knowing something stop you from trying to figure out how to do it.

Taking on any sort of proactive role in bringing your project to life is kind of like transitioning to being an adult. As you grow older you realize that there's no qualifications for being a responsible adult (or a creator!)—everyone is just figuring it out as they go. One day you find yourself in a place saying, "Shouldn't somebody do something about that?" and you realize that person is you. Sometimes the only qualification you need is the assumption of responsibility.

That said, there are ways to learn before you get yourself in over your head. Shana Carroll (The 7 Fingers) spent a lot of time helping other people to choreograph their acts, and acting as an assistant director before she ever directed her own show. James Tanabe (Cirque du Soleil) recommends doing your first project on a very small scale. One of his first projects was a $750k behemoth, and he says he got really lucky that it worked out. If he could do it over again he says he would do a $10k project with five sponsors coming in for two thousand dollars each.

Strategies such as this will help you grow more confident in your ability to carry off a bigger project when the time comes. This is another reason many artists suggest making a 30 minute piece as a first step.

So get out there and try to do something to the best of your ability and make those genuine mistakes, mistakes that come not from lack of trying, but from when you tried your hardest and just needed more experience. That's where the real learning comes from, and everyone that looks like they know what they're doing now felt that way at one point too.

Leading vs. Following

I had an interesting conversation with Jerome Hugo, an acrobat who worked with Cie XY, a collective in which all decisions are made collectively amongst the 24 cast members. The gist of the issue was that there were people who naturally liked leading more, and others that preferred following/ supporting. The 'leaders' felt that they were doing more of the work since it was up to them to organize and prepare more. Having led myself, I understand the logic to this side of the argument. However, Jerome explained, there is also an art to being a good and supportive follower. He pointed out that those 'leaders' could have stopped taking the lead and instead supported someone else's lead if they felt it was too much work, but often they were unable to be open to how other people led—they always wanted to have their say which inhibited other people from leading successfully.

The moral of the story is a good one: both leading and following is important, and both can be done well or poorly, and everyone will have to do both in a creation. In a creation process, I believe that clearly defining roles of leaders and followers, even if only temporarily or for a single aspect of the creation, makes things go smoother, *but* it is important that everyone experiences the different roles. Not only will this allow more input from the naturally quieter 'followers' (which is equally valuable input), it will also let everyone experience the challenges of each role, so that they can be more understanding and supportive regardless of which role they find themselves in most often. A supporter can support more successfully if they know the ins-and-outs of why their role is important and how their efforts produce results, and a leader can lead better if they understand what it's like to try to follow someone else's ideas.

Take an honest look at the people that comprise your team, and how they like to work in a group. As Mason Ames says of his experience working in multiple collectives, "I think a lot of people want to say that they're a 'natural leader', but if you have a team full of 'natural leaders' it's not a good team. It's a difficult team, it's a high tension team. Everyone is fighting for their place and their ego, and it can be tough. In circus, there are a lot of fragile egos and that can be a lot to deal with... and in smaller situations that can raise a lot of tension because you can't just brush it off."

Ames says it's important in any situation to understand as a group how decisions will be made. If there is a clear director/ group in charge of the project that has hired the artists that might make it obvious, but in a collective situation it can be less clear. If you're a small group, Ames says, "you can talk around the table a million times." Once everyone's said their piece once or twice, it's good to have a plan for how you will move forwards that everyone agrees to.

During Barcode and Acting for Climate's first creation period for *Branché* we had up to three or four people lead each day, with one person leading each exercise or block of time and usually at least one other person in a supporting role during those blocks. This has become more or less how that show's creation process works. Sometimes the day leaders can be invited guests, or members of the cast, or members of the core team. Trying out different roles, even temporarily, may also help you to better understand how each of the team expresses themselves, which might reduce friction in other contexts.

This core team in *Branché* is made up of anyone that wants to come to the meetings often enough and assume those responsibilities. This puts them in the natural position of leaders in charge of *Branché*, but they also delegate responsibilities to people within the group, both in creative situations and in other situations (assigning grant writing, calling people, social media posts, etc.) There are more meetings for the core team, but the work that everyone does is invaluable to the success of the project, and this in turn reduces the core team from being overloaded so they can continue to lead and delegate.

With *Branché* we've also used exercises to learn more about each group member's style. For example, we do regular check-ins to see how people are doing emotionally, and talk about character traits people are self-conscious of at the beginning of a creation process so that we can better understand each other during the creation.

Leaders don't have to have all the answers to do their job well. In fact, acknowledging how much clarity (or lack thereof) they have for their idea can give those interpreting it the liberty to try something and not get it 'wrong'. This might come across as saying, "I want to try it *exactly* like this," or it might mean saying something like, "I'm not really sure what I'm looking for here, can you try something like that and I'll see if I can clarify as I watch?"

When Lydia Bouchard (La Résistance) is in a leadership role and *does* have a clear idea, she explains the process of getting the rest of her team onboard with her vision. "Before my show is a good storytelling piece, I need to storytell 2,000 times around the room in order for people to understand what I'm trying to do. Otherwise people are like 'What is she up to? What is she doing?' If they don't believe in what I'm doing, if I'm not pitching to every single person on my team properly, I believe it won't be a show that has a good cohesion."

Bouchard says when everyone understands and is excited about her vision, it makes them invested in the show with her. "The more invested people are in the piece, the more generous they will be with you."

You want people to understand your vision so that they can bring their own magic to it. As a leader you want to walk the line between staying true to your vision, but also allowing it to grow to the size of the abilities of everyone around you.

"Insecurity is a very poor friend with leadership," Bouchard says. "Because the more insecure you get the more you try to control everyone around you, the less people will feel safe, giving you the best of what they've got, or getting out of their comfort zone. But when you're touched and people can reach you with human qualities... I don't believe you can do that by controlling people. I think honesty and openness brings artists and creators there."

If you're working in a collective creation, one strategy you can use is to have different leaders for different sections. This was something interviewees mentioned over and over again as a useful technique. Maybe one person is in charge of all of the technical training, while another is in charge of directing improvs, and another in charge of making rehearsal schedules and finding training space, or someone is just in charge of keeping the group on schedule throughout the day.

For their creation of *Loft*, The 7 Fingers had each member of the cast direct a workshop for a week, then later had each member act as an outside eye for one another's acts.

Leaders frequently do work that gives choice and responsibility to other people. For example, the leader will give each person 7 minutes to direct a scene, or they will direct everyone to create a count of 8 in small groups, or they might ask someone else to look at an image/ scene and direct or choreograph it while they work on something else, or they might ask someone to lead the writing of a grant with a small group. Leading is about using your strengths when you're the best person for the job, and getting other people on board when they would be better suited to do something.

Another positive effect of formally assigning a leader for an amount of time, section or task is that it can be motivating because that person knows they will be in charge and thus want to prepare something good. As Emilie Fournier (Machine de Cirque) notes, "If you're going to have artists or employees that are bored, they're not going to stay, so it's important to keep on challenging people and giving them responsibility."

It's best to keep things transparent and clear, says Mason Ames who recommends, "Clearly defined roles of who's taking care of what and how to structure things, even if it's just one person is doing this on this day, or having a rotation of who's in charge. Having your expectations be realistic is very important. If any dynamics or power hierarchies are in place, for that to be clear. Or who's in charge of what, for that to be clear so you can properly manage your expectations."

Key Takeaways:

- Both leading and following are skills, and it's worth having everyone experience both roles so they can know the challenges of each.
- Good leaders frequently delegate tasks to people better suited for them.
- How will final decisions be made in this group?

Cirque D'Hiver. Photo by Derek Scott: Artists: Eric Bates, Alexandra Royer, Tristan Nielsen

SECTION 2: ORGANIZATION

Backbone *by Gravity & Other Myths. Photo by Eric Bates. Artist: Jack Manson*

START A COMPANY, PUT ON A SHOW... OR BOTH?

Do you need to make a company to make a show? The general advice people gave me while I was writing this book is that if you have a vision to make multiple shows over your lifetime, a company might be good for you. As former artistic director at Cirque du Soleil, James Tanabe says succinctly: **"You don't need a company to make a show, you need a company to sustainably make shows year after year."**

That said, it is entirely possible to make a show without making a company. Barcode made our first show *Sweat & Ink* and performed it in the US and in the Czech Republic six months before becoming an official OBNL (Canada's version of a non-profit organization). In total, we had worked on the show for a year and a half and performed it in two countries before integrating as an OBNL.

A company isn't just a name, or an email, or a website—we called ourselves "Barcode Circus Company" long before we were any sort of legal entity. The truth is you can have the trappings of a company without being one, or be a company and have no one know it. The main distinction is in the eyes of the government and how other companies (like the theaters that will hire you) will interact with you. Depending on the country you live in there are different rules regarding companies, nonprofits, sole enterprises, collectives and so on, each with their own advantages and disadvantages.

Are there advantages to having a company? Yes. Let's explore them, but first we must ask 'What is a company?'

Promotional postcard for Sweat & Ink *by Cirque Barcode. Photo: Eric Bates.*

There are multiple legal structures a company can take (sole proprietorship, non-profit, general partnerships, co-ops, corporations, and more!) that we won't get into here. For the sake of simplicity, I'll refer to all of these and their variations as "company", but know that they are legally different things that you will undoubtedly have to get acquainted with if you're thinking about getting serious with your future show-making ambitions.

From a philosophical standpoint a company (or one of its variations) is something you can grow together as a group of people that is separate from yourself. Having your project linked to a company that is separate from yourself might protect your personal finances. Companies also require hierarchies and roles, which will force you to organize your team. Having a company can also simplify how other companies interact with you by paying you one lump sum as a group instead of individually, for example.

The main advantage to legally incorporating relates to taxes. The biggest downside is that there is a lot of strict paperwork that goes into anything involving the government's money, which is why for a first show (or a small show), I don't recommend starting a company unless that's the sort of thing that gets you excited.

When I talked to Tanabe he said that the main advantage of having a company is that you can deduct your creation expenses so you won't be taxed on the money that was spent making the show. Every country differs in their approach to taxation and what support is available to the various entities, so make sure to do your own research, and don't take this book as legal advice!

"To clarify," Tanabe says, "I'm all for paying taxes. But if you receive $50k in your personal bank account, even if you spend it to make the show and don't actually profit from or keep that money, you can be taxed at a higher income rate which may cost you a lot of your personal money to pay in taxes."

This happened to us when we made *Sweat & Ink*: we filed the grant under our only Canadian member's name at the time since she was the only one that was eligible, so the money went into her personal bank account. This caused big problems at the end of the year when the government thought she made $50k more than she actually did, and it took us a while to unravel how much it increased her personal tax burden and how to sort that out. So tread carefully if you're filing grants under one group member's name!

Tanabe's recommendation is that if you have a project on the horizon, the budget of which represents a significant amount of your revenue that year, then you should start a company. I think this makes sense, because I know from experience that if you try to start a company at the same time as you're in the middle of getting the show off the ground it can be overwhelming. This brings us to the disadvantages of starting a company.

Starting a company is not easy for the untrained—it comes with fees, paperwork and accounting—lots of headaches and challenges that might take away from your excitement and ability to make the show in the first place. These challenges might also present opportunities to land yourself in hot water if you take too much of a 'laissez-faire' attitude. If you need to hire people to take care of those things (which you likely will, unless you happen to be a performing artist who also studied accounting and/or tax law), the show you make will also have to make enough money to pay for the people who will do those things, plus the initial fees and investments that opening and registering a business requires.

If it's your first foray into making a show, and you don't foresee an enormous budget that can accommodate paying for a company's infrastructure (even if it's just one person), I would say you don't need to be a company yet. It can be tough to have people be dependent on you, and taking care of all that infrastructure can suck your energy away from making the actual shows. Conversely, doing everything yourself without those people can also suck your energy away from making the shows. Catch-22 right?

My advice is this: if you are interested in being a company and have a decent understanding of what that entails, make a company, ideally before you're also in the middle of your creation. If you're on the fence about the company part and are excited about making the show, focus on that (and actually, make just 30 minutes first! See earlier chapters), and afterwards, like Barcode, you can decide about the company. This is especially true for people with a mission-driven approach, rather than looking at it purely as a financial opportunity. In the meantime there are options such as fiscal sponsorship in the USA that let you piggyback on another company's 501(c)(3) status while you're getting your show up. Afton Benson, Managing Director for CLIMB Theatre, Treasurer for the International Jugglers' Association, and Accountant for Bindlestiff Family Cirkus, recommends US-based artists look into fiscal sponsorship. This allows you to apply for grants through another company that is already registered as a 501(c)(3)—but without the legal ramifications of having to set one up yourself. This strategy can allow you more options to fund a show without having to establish a full blown company.

How this generally works is that your fiscal sponsor will receive and hold any money you get from grants or charitable donations, then when you need to use that money to pay people or for props they'll pay it directly, or give you the money for you to pay out. For this service they generally take an annual fee and a percentage of the money you receive (which you build into your grant budget). **Making a show is a big endeavor, so you might want to see how much you enjoy just that part of things before you commit to making a company that plans on doing it year after year.**

Sophie Picard, who has either worked at or helped pretty much every circus company in Montréal before co-founding Cirque Barcode as general director, says, "You can create a show without a company—no problem. See if you enjoy working together first. If you do, and you then decide to create a company together, you'll need someone who is not an artist that understands all the roles and responsibilities that come with making a company." Just as shows have directors (someone on the outside, looking in), companies often have directors too, someone that makes sure things are organized and sees the big picture.

This strategy of making a show first worked well for Barely Methodical Troupe, who made their first show, *Bromance*, before having a company. Actually, they made and performed 30 minutes of what would eventually become *Bromance*, at which point another company proposed to produce them. Here they invited Di Robson (owner of *Dream* and independent cultural producer and consultant) a producer that they had worked for before and trusted, to come

Credits: Elemen'terre Project: Photo by Eric Bates: Artists: Tristan Nielsen, Eve Bigel.

to the meeting with the company to ask the right questions (a strategy Barcode also employed when we faced a similar situation in the beginning of our creation for *Sweat & Ink* when Eloize offered to produce us, meaning basically to deal with money, help organize the production and sell it through their channels). After the meeting, Barely Methodical Troupe decided to reject the company's proposal and work directly with Robson as their producer. This strategy (teaming up with an existing production company that they trusted) allowed Barely Methodical Troupe to focus on the parts of the job they liked and were good at, without having to focus as much on all the rest. Also, the producer's existing connections and relationships opened a lot of doors for them, so they were able to grow quickly.

Companies, as opposed to independent contractors, have multiple hierarchical roles. This starts with the executive roles, such as CEO, that tend to focus on big picture questions and goals for the company. Below them are managerial roles, that receive instructions from the executive roles and manage the people underneath them on the operational level. Examples of operational roles can include accountant, graphic designer, sales rep, or performing artist.

Where it gets confusing is that as an independent contractor, you will often be in the operational role of performing artist when you work for other companies, but at all other times you are a company of one, responsible for your career goals, marketing, accounting, time management and so on. We'll discuss this further in the section "The Problem of Hats" on page 214.

As we'll see throughout this book, **one of the main challenges in making a show comes from repeatedly having to answer the fundamental question:** *How are decisions made in your group?* **and** *Who is responsible for different tasks?*

Assigning clear roles that have decision making power and responsibility in your company, or in your group if you're not officially a company, can help resolve these questions.

Afton Benson (CLIMB) says a good exercise is to look up 'how to write a business plan for small businesses', and start there. That will lead your team to ask itself the right questions to see if they're in a place to know if that's what they really want to do. This will help them define their end goal, and all of the steps along the way: What are your skills? Who will do the marketing? Who will run the numbers? How will decisions get made? This process will help you identify gaps in your team's abilities that will make things challenging. Then you can decide whether someone will learn it, or that it will be an expense you need to hire out.

Keep in mind that regardless of whether you establish an official company or not, you will still have to do most of the same administrative tasks a company does: you will have to deal with budgets, insurance, organization, scheduling, paying people, taxes, promotion, emails. Not making a company doesn't mean that all of those things go away.

Having a company, however, does require certain things by law, which will change from country to country. Because a large advantage of having a non-profit (or being fiscally sponsored by one!) is tax related, a lot of these extra responsibilities revolve around paperwork and strict documentation of finances. For this reason, among others, many US troupes and companies follow the for-profit model that can feel less cumbersome. Benson says that in most circumstances she does not recommend people start non-profits, and recommends using the fiscal sponsorship model to apply for funding or receive tax-deductible donations.

To add to the confusion, many companies around the world will have both a non-profit and a for-profit branch that hire each other. Ask around in your local communities for the advantages and disadvantages of both.

Additional examples of an established company's responsibilities include:

- Keeping minutes on every meeting you do
- Building general rules for your company and amending them if ever you change them
- Yearly meetings with the whole administration
- Extremely tight bookkeeping

If you're not at the point where you can pay someone a salary to do the administrative work yet, there are other models. One model Barcode has experimented with involves paying people a commission on projects, similar to how agents are paid. We also work with outside companies that act as 'offices for hire' (sometimes called production companies) that will take care of the administrative work for a fee or percentage.

It can be tempting to look at some of the bigger grants that are only available to companies (at least in Canada) and think, "If only we were a company we would have access to that." Besides the fact that for many of these grants you are required to have been a company for a year or more in order to apply, it's worth considering that if your only reason for becoming a company is to access bigger grants, you might not want to be a company in the first place—and the companies that *do* want to be companies for the long haul often depend on those grants to stay in business. It is easy to be cavalier and say they should have to keep duking it out like the rest of us, without knowing the effort that goes into keeping an arts company rolling year after year. If you just want to make a company to hop into the grant pool and hop back out again, you might not want to take the plunge in the first place.

Pros of legally incorporating your company:

- Possible tax advantages.
- Bigger grants available than for individuals.
- Some venues will only work with incorporated groups.
- One cohesive "brand" (although we called ourselves "Barcode Circus Company" before we were a company).
- Ability to make shows that don't necessarily involve yourself as an artist.
- Building something that can live on after you.
- Legal protections. If someone gets hurt, if a venue sues you, etc – it's the company that gets sued, not you as an individual.

Cons of having a company:

- More paperwork.
- Careful monitoring of legality.
- Less flexibility.
- More responsibilities.
- As you get bigger more people will rely on you.
- Once incorporated, it is still possible to disband—though there are additional tasks and financial matters to consider if you decide to close up shop.

CHOOSE THE TEAM

CASE STUDY: THE 7 FINGERS

Who They Are

The 7 Fingers, world-renowned contemporary circus company. Since their founding in 2002, they've made dozens of successful shows: including stationary and touring shows, broadway productions, cruise ship collaborations, special events, and even choreographing for the winter olympics and the Oscars.

How They Started

In 2002 a group of seven circus artists wanted to do something different. They had all performed for Cirque du Soleil and were thankful but tired of the experience. They had performed the same show eight to ten times a week for years, made money, met partners, but no longer felt they were growing as artists. More importantly, they wanted to make something different, to rethink what circus could be.

Many of them had never worked together. Some hadn't even met each other. Even knowing this, they bought plane tickets to San Francisco, agreeing to talk about what founding a company and making a new kind of show together might look like.

Hand to Hand in Montréal. Photographer: Eric Bates. Artists: Kyran Walton & Oliver Layher.

"We had our first meeting," explained Shana Carroll. "We all went to San Francisco and we were in my mom's living room and we were all talking about our vision and dreams for the company on a life level—where we were, the type of impact we wanted to make, the type of life we wanted to live... and we were so on the same page. It was amazing, you could tell it was really this fortuitous [meeting]... seven people that all wanted the same thing."

Day two, however, was different. "Day two of the two-day meeting," Carroll continues, "we said we'd talk about ideas, we'd talk about artistic visions of the show. And I walked out of there like.... *What are we doing?*"

Their ideas and visions were all over the map, the cohesiveness they had experienced on the first day suddenly felt very far away. This is normal in the creative process—**dreaming is easy, hammering out concrete details is hard.** Yet, they prevailed.

These seven artists, of course, went on to become The 7 Fingers, the world-renowned, Montréal-based contemporary circus company that revolutionized what circus could be, "telling human stories with superhuman skills."

How did this somewhat random collection of artists work so well? On paper, while it's clear that all of the artists were high-caliber, and eager to do something innovative, there was no guarantee that they should have been great together. They had no proof of past successes together, some of them had only just met each other when they decided to form a company together.

It feels like they rolled the dice and got lucky.

Here's the thing: many people roll the dice when they build a team. They work with their friends, people they kind of know from past contracts, people who volunteer to help them. Making a show and touring it means practically marrying your partners, only without the ceremony. It often means living together, traveling together, cooking together, tying your financial success to each other, working and socializing together, making a million decisions together, and ultimately, creating something that didn't exist before together. Was it really luck that got The 7 Fingers through all of this?

Putting in the Work

What isn't always told about The 7 Fingers' success is that despite their unlikely start, they worked hard to get to know each other in the beginning.

They invited in collaborators, "kind of these Buddhas," Carroll remarked, "that grounded us so much.... They didn't do a lot in terms of imposing anything artistically on us, but they did a lot in terms of getting us to gel." They invited Jan-Rok Achard, the then-director of Montréal's National Circus School, to work with them. He hosted sessions where they talked about their goals, their ambitions, their values; they got to know the people they would be working with.

"Jan-Rok put us through several exercises where he would ask us questions and we would fill them out on index cards privately and afterward we would see where our intentions aligned. Everything from how much money do you see yourself making to what are you trying to achieve with this show, with this company... It was huge," Carroll said.

Some of Jan-Rok's questions The 7 Fingers currently use are available as exercises in "Unifying the Vision: Jan Rok's Questions" on page 229.

They also did one month of workshopping together, in which each team member took a week leading a workshop for the others. "It's one thing to sit in a room and hear [someone] talk about his ideas, it's another to have him play with them for a week in front of you and be his tool. It crystallized what each of our styles and methods of working was. Informative in both positive and negative ways, but super informative," Carroll explained. "A lot of great material came out of it. For me, that was one of the richest times. **The fact that we took turns leading avoided the painful anarchy when you're in a collective.**"

How many teams do you know that put in work like that, in a structured way, before diving into the huge commitment of making a show together? And how many teams, despite the constant pressure of producing and touring, continue to do that work? The 7 Fingers still hold annual retreats to check in on their evolving goals and priorities as individuals to make sure the company can continue to align with those goals. It's one of the things that has allowed their company to grow with them and held it together for 20+ years.

When you're creating the team, take the time to find and get to know the right people. This goes for both the artists and the administrative team. You want to make sure everyone's values align or are at least complimentary. You want to make sure you get along. As Joseph Pinzon of Short Round Productions says, "You need to like the people you're going to work with. Even if they're the best person for the job in the world, if you don't like them, it's going to be a miserable process."

The 7 Fingers did have one final hurdle to get over though: despite having learned to gel creatively (Carroll described it as a sort of "culture shock. Like, oh my God, *that's* how your brain works?"), they had neglected the administrative side of things.

The Missing Piece

After performing their first show, *Loft*, to wide acclaim in Montréal, they received their first offer to perform it overseas. It was at this point they realized that the custom set they had built for the show which was made-to-measure to fit into the circus school where they were performing was not very portable or tour-ready. They would need to build a new set, and as a kicker, they would need $360,000 worth of road cases to transport it.

Many creators I talked to noted that the things that were difficult for them were, unsurprisingly, the things they had *not* studied to do—administration, accounting, etc. They stressed the importance of finding people that could fill these roles as well as the 'creation' roles.

How did The 7 Fingers solve their dilemma? The artists had already put all their time and personal money into the creation of the show, and they certainly didn't have an extra $360k. Their project might have died then and there, had it not been for the connection of one of their brothers, who introduced them to Nassib El-Husseini, political science PH.D and lover of the arts, who, after seeing and falling in love with their show, helped to produce *Loft* and became the company's CEO. They had found a crucial member of their team, and he's been part of it ever since.

One of the best parts about building a team is that you can work with people that are much better at things than you could ever be alone. You get to make something that is greater than the sum of its parts. Take the time to get to know your team members' strengths, outside of what they do onstage, then do the work to get on the same page early and often, and you can build something more wild than you'd ever imagined.

Shana's Excavation Questions: A Series of Team Building Exercises

Shana has a whole bunch of questions that are meant to dig into your team's strengths and weaknesses. She uses these to get an honest picture of how everyone sees the collective, and where they see it going together—for the full list, head to **page 327**.

Reach Out to New People

Here's some good news for making connections: Everyone is reachable by the internet these days. For the most part there are very few barriers to contacting the person you're hoping to work with or talk to. But be smart about it—you want to be respectful of people's time, and ideally also bring something to the table, even if that is just you bringing them the feeling that they are competent and someone you look up to.

Here's a few tips for reaching out to people you don't know by email:

- Focus on the benefits. If you're reaching out to someone you don't have an established relationship with, it can be helpful to show how you might be able to help them. Again, this might be as simple as saying how you respect and look up to their work, and they're someone you'd love to learn from if they have time for a couple of questions.
- Reciprocate. If you can offer a way to help them, all the better, but it shouldn't come across as transactional, such as "I'll help you in this way if you answer my questions." A better approach might be to think about how you could genuinely be able to help them: *"I just saw your post that you're looking for a great videographer. I just happen to know someone I think you'd love. Let me know the best way to put you in contact with her if you're still looking for someone."*

- Keep it short and sweet. You don't need to lay it all out in the first email. You want to provide enough info to pique their interest, but still be respectful of their time. You can elaborate later on the phone or in a follow up email if they respond positively.

- Be specific. Being clear about what you're offering and what you hope they can help you with will make it easier for them to help you. This starts in the subject line.

- Be nice. Emails tend to be interpreted however the recipient is feeling, regardless of how you wrote them, so it pays to make an extra effort towards the positive when you're writing. Don't hesitate to celebrate something about the other person, as long as it's sincere. Here's a good example of this: One of our contacts at Barcode was frustrated because we were slow to respond to his emails. Did he get mad about it? No. He made a meme about it. We got the message, and were careful to reply as promptly as we could after that, largely because he had made us feel good where he could have made us feel bad.

- Be clear about your timeline. If you need a response by a certain time, be clear and honest (and polite) about it. "If you're able to, I'd love it if we could find time before Thursday to go over this grant request together so I can submit it by the deadline on Friday." Don't expect the other person to be on the same timeline as you—if you ask them to get back to you at their earliest convenience, it won't help you if it's after your deadline. If you make this clear in your email you might get a quick response saying they won't have time to help you, but at least that will give you time to find someone else who can.

- Provide action steps. Your email should have a clear action step for the recipient to take. This could be a question for them to answer, or a next step you suggest the two of you taking together.

Hiring the Best: How We Hired Sophie

When we were first kicking around the idea of creating a show we reached out to Cirque Eloize to see if we could do an exchange to use their creation space. We had worked with Eloize many times before and had a comfortable relationship with them, and someone in the upper tier of their company got wind of the news that Barcode wanted to make a show. They called us in for a meeting, saying they would be interested in producing the show. We would make the show, they would get to use the big administrative machine they'd built to run it. Win-win.

We had reservations about this meeting, not sure what we were getting into, so just like Barely Methodical Troupe calling up Di Robson, we called up Sophie Picard: a friend who had managed one of the first projects we'd ever done with The 7 Fingers nearly eight years prior. We asked her if she could come to the meeting and make sure we asked the right questions. She came (Eloize tried to hire her on the spot), asked helpful questions, and we left the meeting feeling like it had gone ok.

However, after the meeting Sophie turned to us and said, "You know, I don't think you should work with them, since they want artistic control of the project and you want to do your own thing. I think you should just start a company yourselves. I'll run it for you." Our jaws hit the floor. Sophie said her choice was a combination of factors- she believed in our skills and stage presence, but also she connected with us when we had worked together at The 7 Fingers. She also wanted to give us the opportunity to pursue our careers when we could no longer perform onstage and learn how to manage a company and a team.

True to her word, Sophie co-founded Barcode with us and is still the driving bureaucratic force behind it to this day. We would never have had this opportunity if we hadn't asked her to that meeting with Eloize in the first place.

Be Honest

It's ok to not know what you're doing yet, and in fact this vulnerability can be an asset, as long as it comes with an enthusiasm to learn. Being honest about the situation you're in is empowering to the party you're asking to help you because it shows them respect. It shows that you're not trying to manipulate them. You lay out the situation, the good parts and the bad, and let them decide. Transparency is key in a 21st century organization. Here's what Joseph Pinzon (Short Round Productions) said to his potential cast for his first creation:

"Do you want to go on this crazy-ass journey with me? I will pay you, not that much, because this is what I have, but it's going to be a wild ride. These are the people you're going to be working with, and the process will be fun. It's going to be hard, but it'll be fun." Almost all of them said yes.

"But wait," you say. "I can't ask qualified people to help me for free or less than they're worth, even if they are my friends!" That's a good point, and in general I'd agree with you. However, consider this: money is a tool for people to get the things they want, and there are also things that can't be bought with money. Engagement, working with specific people, creative liberty, performance opportunity and specific experiences can all be strong motivators. Being willing to work together at the start for less money could also lead to more money down the line. The most important part is to be upfront and honest with what you're offering. If you're transparent in your request, it's their free choice to help you or not on the terms you're able to figure out together.

Because this might make it sound like Barcode exploits the people we work with, I'll take a second to point out here that of all the grant money we received creating *Sweat & Ink*, none of it went to ourselves—it all went to our collaborators, props, sets and rehearsal spaces. Money is a handy tool, especially in the short term, but you're going to need to be more resourceful than that in this game. You're in it for the mid/long term. The folks who are coming in to help with specific parts are often there for the short term.

Here's a few thoughts, and examples, on that:

In *Rich Dad, Poor Dad*, Robert Kiyosaki recommends going from an *"I can't afford that"* mindset to a ***"How** can I afford that?"* mindset. This might mean finding ways to pay people through grants, subsidized accompaniments, matching programs, or figuring out what the other party wants and seeing if you could find a way to get that for them directly. For example, when creating *Sweat & Ink* we needed a creation space and Cirque Eloize needed performers for their next corporate event. Normally, both of us would have charged each other a lot for these services, but we also both had the option of giving them for free. Neither service cost either of us anything, so while on paper they might not have been a perfectly equal value, everyone was happy with the exchange and we built on our relationship in the process by collaborating.

Getting More, a book on negotiation recommended by James Tanabe (Cirque du Soleil, 51/49 Productions), talks about trading items of unequal value so that everyone wins. It might take you two seconds and cost you nothing to fix someone's excel spreadsheet that is driving them crazy, and they might be able to offer you something valuable in return that also costs them hardly anything, or that they enjoy doing. Not all transactions have to be monetary, or 'equal'. Keep your ears open to how you can help other people, and who might be the right person to help you.

One thing to watch out for though, says Gypsy Snider (The 7 Fingers), is if you invite people to help you move your train forward, make sure you clarify how much of that train then belongs to them, and how long they will be along on that ride with you. A lot of people will try to help you once you start. Don't get in too deep with anyone until you're sure you are comfortable in the relationship and your roles are fairly well defined, since it can be hard to backtrack after people have invested a lot of themselves into your project.

For example, when we talked to Cirque Eloize about making the show that became *Sweat & Ink* they wanted to have artistic control of the project. We were happy to exchange creation space for us performing in their events, but not to give up artistic control of our show. However, for other people this might be a great trade—if what is important to you is working with your friends and doing a new creation, but you have no interest in running a company, such an arrangement might be very much to your benefit.

Another friend I know got a grant to make digital assets. He began talking with a company that had experience in this domain, hoping to collaborate with them. As the discussions continued however, he realized that they were suggesting that they would use most of the money and also keep the rights to the result of the project. He decided that because he didn't like these terms, he would prefer to not continue together so that they could remain friends and collaborators.

How you deal with these sorts of situations is up to you, but the earlier you can define the sort of collaboration you're comfortable with, the easier it will be to avoid uncomfortable conversations down the road.

- Figuring out *who* can help you rather than *how* you can do everything yourself will drastically improve your chances of success, and reduce burn out.
- Asking people for help while acknowledging their competence is flattering. Don't be shy to ask.
- Be honest. If you give people an honest picture of where you're at and what you're asking for, they can choose to help you or not. No harm in asking if it's done respectfully.
- Consider trading items of unequal value. Not all solutions need to be monetary.

Exercises

- Make a list of what it is you need help with, then brainstorm who knows how to do these things, or who might know someone that does.
- Make a list of your best skills. What are you good at that others could benefit from? Who do you know that you could confidently recommend to people?
- Try to have clear questions to approach people with, even if one of those questions is "Is there anything I'm missing here, or have forgotten to ask you?"
- Write down the reasons you initially wanted to make this show and what you were excited about. Keep this list somewhere so that when you're nervous to ask for help, or are discouraged, you can remind yourself of why you took on this massive project in the first place.

Division of Tasks

When we established Barcode as a company we were five people—four artists and Sophie Picard. At first I thought, "This is great! We'll each do 1/5th of the work and we're off to the races!" In reality, it often felt like we were doing five times the work. It took us a long time to figure out each of our strengths and things we liked to do, and build the trust to let those people do those things without feeling the need to double-check on them. People also sometimes need help and support so they don't feel alone in those things, and figuring out that balance also takes time. How do you make sure it feels like everyone is contributing equally to the team without everyone having to do everything?

Focus on strengths

In general, every creator I talked to recommended focusing on people's strengths and nourishing the positive traits in your partners. Emilie Fournier, international touring manager of Machine de Cirque said, "Take people's strengths and push them towards this. Give them responsibilities in what they are good at. I've seen a lot of people trying to do everything, or want to do everything, but it's not true that everyone is good at everything. You have to pinpoint the strengths of everybody and make sure that everyone knows their place and has a place. If you don't have any responsibility you're just going to get bored and if you have too many responsibilities you're going to get overwhelmed."

Division of work

This one is tricky. Which is more valuable in a team—writing a grant, talking to dozens of producers that might book your show, designing a poster, dealing with cargo, doing music research, accounting, or organizing schedules? In truth, they all have their place and they all help to make a team successful, but they often come at different times in the process of a creation and different people enjoy and excel at different things. So how do you balance it so it feels fair?

My perception of fairness once hinged on everyone chipping in equally on certain tasks—all hands on deck! In reality there are situations where different people's talents will be better suited to the occasion. The balance won't always be a mathematical equation. It will be up to your team to figure out amongst yourselves if the work everyone is contributing feels fair and enjoyable.

Some companies record their hours and balance it that way. How much time does a job take to do? Or if we had to hire someone, how much would we pay them? For Barcode the thought of having to record our hours sounded more painful than our current system, but for some companies it was a useful solution, and the result was an imbalance of hours, but with appropriate pay.

Another strategy is to delegate some of the tasks to other team members that are doing less. The difficulty here is if that person doesn't do it as well as the original person, the temptation will be to say, "Just give it to me, I'll do it." The better response is, "How can I help you?" This takes time, but will eventually free up the first person. Also consider that "not doing it as well" might actually just mean "doing it differently".

Having regular meetings also can reveal who is doing what. Not everyone is constantly announcing the work they do, so when you're swamped with work it can be tempting to focus on your own feelings of frustration and being overwhelmed, and to feel bitter towards others on your team you assume aren't doing enough, instead of assuming they might also be working hard at something different from you. Regular meetings can reveal if the workload is severely unbalanced, and allow people to help.

Raphaël Dubé, co-founder of Machine de Cirque, told me some good advice that helped them—either you get in there and do the work or you shut up about it. As your company grows to a certain size, you can't do everything yourself and criticizing other people's work without knowing the constraints, compromises, reasons and consequences that led to how a team member made a decision is a good way to piss off someone that has put a lot of hard work into something. There's always a way to work together with them with appreciation and humility in your knowledge of what they've been working on, but remember to tread delicately, and think twice before diving into casual criticism of someone's personal project.

SECTION 3: FUNDING

See You Down the Road *by Cirque Barcode. Photographer: Nikola Milatovic.*

Artists: Eric Bates, Tristan Nielsen, Alexandra Royer, Mathilde Jimenez

MONEY

There are a lot of good ways to make money in show business. Doing ten shows a week in Las Vegas, performing at special events, and even street performing can all provide a comfortable lifestyle. Creating a show, at least in the short term, does not top that list. Will you learn a lot and grow as an artist? Absolutely. Will you get to make something that will touch and inspire people? Heck yes. Will you make a ton of money quickly? Unlikely. Making money is probably not the reason most people want to make shows in the first place, but if you're coming from the gig economy, it's definitely a good thing to know that it's not a get rich quick scheme. I'd be lying if I told you that before we started making a show I hadn't at some point thought , "Heck, we're already basically doing the entire show for other people, think of all the money we'd make if it was our name on it! Let's cut out the middleman!" Turns out there is no "middleman". Everyone *in* the process *is* the process. There's a lot more to running a successful show than just the acrobatics you see onstage!

That said, in favorable circumstances circus can be a fun, lucrative business as a performing artist. If you're one of the fortunate people that works steadily as a performer on other companies' shows, the financial struggle of making your own show might come as a shock. As Gypsy Snider (The 7 Fingers) puts it, "You need to have a very healthy relationship with what you do that is independent from the money you earn doing it." It can be easy to justify to yourself the artistic and societal merit of the shows you are hired to perform on as long as they also pay the bills. Believing in your own project, still vague and incomplete, can be made harder still when in the short term it will likely be costing you money. **Knowing why you want to make this show other**

than for short-term monetary gain is a necessity to get you through the challenges that will inevitably arise.

At the same time, "You need to have a plan to make your money back," says Joseph Pinzon (Short Round Productions), "because if you don't, it's not an investment, it's disposed income."

Part of what makes the creation of a show difficult is that it is a similar but different skillset to the tools that make up the career of a 'performer for hire'. If you are also performing in the show you are creating, you will maintain all of the responsibilities of being a creative acrobat while adding a host of new challenges related to the business of creating a show– challenges you haven't experienced before and haven't been able to anticipate- because you didn't know they existed!

This depth of involvement does come with a bonus, however: it will be humbling and make you much more mature and agreeable to work with as an artist on other people's projects, knowing all the work they are doing behind the scenes.

When creating a show, you're going to have fixed costs such as renting space, buying props or costumes, hiring directors, outside eyes and coaches, other artists, etc; and you're going to have opportunity costs, meaning you will likely have to turn down other paid work in order to take the time to make your show.

For Barcode, we were working regularly for other companies when we decided to start making our show, and it was hard for us to turn down work. My conclusion at the time was that if we couldn't say no to paid work we were going to have to find a way to pay ourselves to make the creation. Knowing this struggle, Joseph Pinzon says the same thing: "One of my philosophies is to not do projects if I can't pay. I always put the artist first." The solution that I saw at the time for Barcode was to get a grant.

In retrospect, I think this was what we needed to get started, even though in the end, none of the grant money went to us—when you're making a show, you will pay everyone else before yourselves (at least, this is my ethical recommendation). There is often more that you want to do than you have money for (especially if it's your first show and you're still learning the magnitude of the project), and because you can't cut the compensation of the people who you have asked to be on your project, you tend to cut your own.

Gypsy Snider says she doesn't even associate getting a grant with paying yourself—she associates it with making the art, and you are investing in that process. Then if the art 'works' and people want to see it, that is when you get paid.

Granting bodies differ from region to region, industry to industry, and country to country. For some, it's expected that the applicant earmarks part of the funds as compensation for their own time. Other organizations will reject applications where the artist reserves a portion of the money for themselves, rather than the project. If possible, it can be very helpful to look for (or ask to see examples of!) successful grant applications from others. On that note—if your application is rejected, ask them how you can improve for the next time!

For Barcode's second creation, *Branché*, which we made with the group Acting for Climate Montréal, we took a different approach. We spent almost zero money, at least for the first year. Everyone that came to the project knew we would pay them if we got a grant, but at first they were inspired enough by the idea of the show to volunteer their time for the initial research phases (and it was 2020, the beginning of Covid, so everyone had time to spare). For some of them it was their first creation in which they had been there from the very beginning, getting in on the ground floor, and there's power in that. It's exciting to build something from the ground up. Also, like Barcode, most of the participants were also members of Acting for Climate Montréal, so they were also in the startup phase of forming their company during which they put a lot of sweat equity into their project.

For *Branché*, for both ecological and logistical reasons, we decided to make a show that required no props, no lights, nothing. Not even a theater! These 'limitations' were also freeing because they helped us rule out a lot of possibilities immediately, and that let us work a lot cheaper.

Lewie West (Gravity & Other Myths) described his take on the power of constraints on creativity to me like this: "You get to be creative as an acrobat with those constraints, which is really helpful because sometimes in creation it's too broad and too big, so having someone say, 'You have to fit these rules', that unlocks a bit more possibility because you don't get so roadblocked by the openness of everything." I agree with this premise, which can also be applied to financing a show. **Limits can be great for inspiring creative solutions.**

One of Acting for Climate Montréal's specialties is finding 'rescued food'— traditionally known as 'dumpster diving.' For almost every one of our creation periods they were able to feed our cast of 8-10 people for a week for nearly no money, using perfectly good food that would have otherwise have been wasted, often by simply asking at local places if they had any food that would otherwise go to waste. Constraints can unlock creativity—in this case overcoming the constraint of a limited budget with a creative solution for how to feed everybody, in a way that also fit their mission of being less wasteful.

Nathan Biggs-Penton, cofounder of Acting for Climate Montréal, and one of the co-creators of *Branché*, says that in North America we're used to seeing shows with a big production scale. When he was attending circus school in Europe he saw a lot of small shows with very minimal sets that were also beautiful and touching. Doing your research and seeing more shows can remind you of all of the ways there are to do performances—and how making a great show is possible at any level of budget. An expensive show is not inherently a good show, as many a failed multimillion dollar Las Vegas production can attest!

It can be easy to think "I can't start until I have *this*." That's a common trick your brain will play on you in order to procrastinate the hard work of making physical material for your show. You think of making a show and you think, "If only I had [a complicated acrobatic rig, or a budget to make crazy magic tricks, etc], I could make my great idea happen." Try to train yourself to think in terms of what you *do* have, and start with that.

Finally, take heart in this:

When James Tanabe worked as Senior Director, Business and Creative Strategy/Senior Innovation Consultant for Cirque du Soleil, he studied circus shows from geographies across the world to see what mattered most to audiences. Was it the costumes, the music, the effects, the theater, the technology, the acrobatics? He had access to 15 years' worth of exit surveys, plus he went to 30 circus shows from 19 other non-Cirque du Soleil companies, three circus school graduation shows, three different international circus festivals, and interviewed 20 industry experts both inside and outside of Cirque du Soleil. What did he find after all of this?

"At the end of the day what we found was that **the human performance elements were still the number one driver of audience satisfaction for the shows,** and we actually found out that the technological elements of the show had zero correlation to the appreciation of the audience except when technical elements directly enhanced the audience's appreciation of human performance."

Creating great work can be difficult, but audiences come to live performances to see *people*. You don't need a big budget to start. See the appendix on page 357 for sample budgets of various sizes.

PUTTING A PROJECT TOGETHER

Sweat & Ink *Creation Meeting. Photo by Eric Bates. Artists: Eve Bigel, Alexandra Royer, Tristan Nielsen.*

Putting a project together will likely take a combination of many of the types of funding already discussed. Please remember, not every show needs a million dollar budget. It can be easy to see big shows with high production value and think that that's the only way to do things, that that's the only way to make a "real" show. Try to stop thinking like this and to start where you are. James Tanabe (Cirque du Soleil) spoke with me and broke down his approach to funding big projects. As previously mentioned, Tanabe studied hundreds of shows and thousands of acts in his time as an advisor at Cirque du Soleil, and the number one influencer of audience appreciation that he found was the human elements of a show. So don't fall into the trap of thinking you can't make something until you have a big budget. Start making something, then the money will come.

Story of the Elephant

James Tanabe compares putting a project together to the fable of the blind men and the elephant. Three blind men come across an elephant for the first time, and they each touch a different part of it to try to figure out what it is. One man touches the trunk, and he says, "Oh, it's a snake." Another holds the leg and declares, "It's a tree!" The third touches the elephant's side and says, "It's a wall."

Your project is the elephant, but to each of your potential funders, you should present the piece of the project that interests them. When Tanabe was putting together his $750k elephant of a project, he went to the National Theatre of Taiwan to see if he could interest them in funding part of it. They wanted the 'snake', so he had to talk about the 'snake' elements of his project- Half of the creative team and performers had to be Taiwanese. As long as they had that, they had fulfilled their mission and were happy to help him get the funding to make his project happen.

After that, he went to the Canadian embassy, the French Embassy, the US Embassy, and the CALQ (Conseil des Arts et des Lettres Québec-, Quebec's granting board). In the case of the CALQ, they cared about the aspect of the project that aligned most with their mission/mandates: Canadian multimedia content, Canadian performers, and a Canadian creator. They also liked that it was happening in China. By presenting the different Canadian 'legs' of the project, the aspects of the elephant that best reflected "a tree" he was able to land three grants for $25k each.

"All of that was just us figuring out what part of the elephant to put forward. And once we had our money, and as long as we didn't do a bait-and-switch and bring a Russian choreographer instead of a French choreographer, they all got what they wanted …and the show we put onstage was the exact same goal we wanted to put onstage, but it was not the show we pitched to each of those different pieces," said Tanabe.

Use your creativity to deliver the show on paper that works for everybody, but still leaves you freedom once you're in the studio to do what you want onstage. The creative parameters that come with it might actually help your creativity. This strategy of Tanabe's came from him having tried numerous times, unsuccessfully, to push his creative vision without thinking about what the people with the money might be interested in. When he opened himself up to being the person that brought the team together instead of trying to force his team down someone's throat, the process got easier. This didn't mean he still couldn't make the show he wanted to make, but it became more of a collaborative process than a one-sided affair. Tanabe credits that experience as being the one that made him fall in love with being a producer and creator.

In the case of his collaboration with the National Theatre of Taiwan, he had a long conversation with them where he asked, "What's in your mind? What are the things that are interesting to your artistic director right now, what are the things that are resonating with the Taiwanese government right now that if we were able to bring to the stage of the National Theater would help the National Theater make the case that they should get more funding next year?"

They told him there was a huge cultural bridge being built between Taiwan and France, so having French creators would help. He looked at their list of

French creators they were interested in, picked out ones that worked for his purpose and called the French Embassy to ask them to help support bringing a French artist to Taiwan.

"We took all of those constraints and we made them the creative and artistic givens in terms of the team. And we were very committed to the belief that we would do a better job creating by pulling together the team we needed to have and then finding a way to work than if we said "ok what's our dream team" and then "lets go find someone to pay us to bring all of that together."

Piecing the Funding Together

"Let's accept that no one is going to give us our $100k," Tanabe clarifies. "I had to beg and scrimp for $1,500 on a flight grant, $2k for this, $3k for that, $1k for this. You get to $250k through a lot of one thousands, two thousands." Once you've scraped together enough small donations that you have a decent amount, then the door starts opening to bigger potential donors such as the Canadian and US Embassies. There is an element of luck and timing to this whole process, so do your best to use your creativity and open-mindedness to find ways that your project can work within the current artistic and political landscape. "It's not easy," Tanabe says, "but it's definitely creative and it's definitely empowering."

Three-Year Goal

Let's say we want to start building our big show. Project X! How do we start? Tanabe explains that any 'big dream' sort of project should have a three-year timeline. He'll plan that show for three years from now, then figure out what projects he needs to do along the way to make that happen. In Tanabe's case, his Project X was making a show happen at the Tohu in Montréal. He started by directing a street show festival in Taiwan, while simultaneously mentioning to the Tohu that he was creating a show in Taiwan, and would they be interested in bringing it in two years? His directing the street show festival made him connections and gave him the opportunity to direct (and perform in) his dream show. This festival in Taiwan then transformed into a Canadian circus festival the second year. The year after that, the Tohu theater brought the opening ceremony show from that festival to Montréal.

For you and your Project X, this might look like finding projects to do together with the cast you see yourself making a show with. This will allow you to start creating material together. If you have an idea for a director you'd like to work with, maybe you could see if they have any short-term projects like a summer show or winter cabaret that you could be involved with, or you could suggest their name for another project.

Big companies and projects, like big ships, can take a long time to change course. An advantage of having a smaller show is that you can be more nimble and flexible. Bigger projects and incorporation methods might require waiting for meetings and consensus between more people before a project gets a green light. We've tried to have multiple year goals with Barcode, and it surprised me to discover that some of our team wasn't wired that way, and in fact, there's a good argument for not pinning yourself down so you can be open to opportunities. Opportunities often arise by simply going out and doing things; not just sitting around waiting for the phone to ring. Proactivity is a character trait that all the members of Barcode share, regardless of their opinions on long-term goal setting. So if a three-year plan doesn't work for you, flexibility and one foot in front of the other with some long-term goals might get you through the first show and give you true feedback on what is a best practice for your company."

There's a saying that luck is when opportunity meets preparedness, and going out to make your own projects happen is a great way to learn about the industry and prepare yourself for whatever comes next. It's also a great way to meet people, learn humility and talk to a lot of other people about their own projects. One of my biggest takeaways from making a show was that the artist is a smaller piece of the puzzle than I initially thought. It is very humbling to learn how much work goes into a show before the artists arrive at rehearsal.

Funding Momentum, Getting People Onboard

There's an old trope in arts administration that goes, 'people want to fund work that's already going to happen one way or another– and make it better.' People want to back a winner! Keep this in mind as we discuss funding throughout this book. Although creating a show is less of a strictly linear process than a series of overlapping phases, you'll have a better chance of success if you already start to make something and *then* try to get funding than the other way around.

In the funding phase of the project, there will be a lot of meetings, and it might feel like a long time before you actually get to make the show. Tanabe says to expect a series of at least three meetings with the "friendly" leads, such as the embassies he mentioned earlier—people that want to say yes but have strict rules about how they can support something. He tells them "I have this project, it's super strong and super flexible and we can adapt it to meet your needs."

After Tanabe assures the embassies or funders that his show will meet their funding requirements, he asks for a letter of intent from them. If you have their promise in writing, depending on the conditions they set, you can take that to your next funder and show them that you already have $10k committed if they come onboard. Maybe since you have German artists you ask the German Embassy if they could cover the cost of flights. They say no, their program doesn't allow them to do that. So, Tanabe says, you ask, "Do you have any contacts with Lufthansa?"

Tanabe would then go to this contact in Lufthansa (or Air Canada if he had Canadian artists, etc) and convince them to donate plane tickets. The seats cost the airline nothing, or very little since the plane is already flying, but Tanabe can attribute a dollar amount to them based on normal ticket prices. This then allows him to go back to the first contact and say, "Look, Lufthansa just donated $20k worth of travel expenses." This $20k 'unlocks' their earlier letter of intent promising a certain amount of money that was contingent on him gathering enough other funding.

"It's just this process of going through, finding out what everyone needs, what everyone has to give and what everyone needs to get to be able to unlock it. Then you just start getting the low hanging fruit, putting it together, then you come back to those people, always with good news. 'I've got great news! We've raised $50k so we can finally work together!' And they're never, like, 'Ah shoot, now I need to give you that money,' they're, like, 'Ah, thank goodness, I thought I was going to lose that money again this year if I didn't use it.'

This is something you can already start doing. Identify every network you're a part of, and why they should care about the work that you're doing. It's all about finding the right angle to sell a story and getting people to care.

Tanabe's rule was to never walk out of a meeting without two more people to call. Have those meetings before you need them. Call them up, tell them about the project you're currently working on, but also ask what sort of project might excite them in the future. File that response away in the back of your mind (or with an organizational tool,) "because once you get five or six people vibing on the same idea you can bring those people together for the next round."

Projects can take a long time, and to use Lydia Bouchard's analogy, it's okay to have a few different pots on the stove and see which one gains momentum. When that happens, put the others on simmer and focus on that one. Just remember to not tell everyone just how many projects you've got on the stove at once, since when it's time to turn up the heat on one of them you need to be able to focus on it, and convince people that you won't be boiling over elsewhere.

Country-Based Creation

Tanabe also recommends "country-based creation"—basically working with artists from a country different from yours with the creation taking place where they live. This might be more feasible if you're a producer or director, but we've been pitched this option as well with *Branché* where someone asked us to take the time to teach or incorporate local artists into our show. This could take the form of social circus, but not always: for one of his creations, Tanabe worked with former members of the National Wushu team of Taiwan. He described them as "extremely skilled athletes who loved hip hop, loved everything that was contemporary."

He says when you have a strong pool of talent like this and you're able to be creative with who you want to bring into the project, things get cheaper. After all, they only have to fly YOU out to them, rather than flying their entire company to wherever you are! If the cost of living there is also cheaper, you save again. More importantly, you might find tons of incredible people that would be interested in collaborating with you, plus it makes it easier to get support from both sides. Economical and cheap to pitch to funders.

Budget

Joseph Pinzon (Short Round Productions) watched many shows before he made his own. Every time, especially when he watched a show he didn't enjoy, the question he asked himself was, "Who put these up?"

"They couldn't have put them up all by themselves because that's a really hard process. So someone in the world said, 'I believe in you, and I believe in your concept, and I'm going to give you money and I'm going to help you to put your thing up. And they did, and those things that weren't fully formed went up somehow. So it all just takes convincing someone. If you have an idea, no matter how good or bad it is, someone is going to believe in you. It's not easy to find that person, but you will find them, and they will help you."

A last word of advice: Don't forget to budget a little extra on your project for promotion after the premiere. Once you're off the runway, you still need gas in the tank to fly the plane. Give yourself a little more room for promotion, buying a stand at conferences, getting good video, reworking lights, etc. Sometimes you can find this money later, but another round of granting or fundraising will slow your project down. If you're able to raise the money sometime before you premiere it will help you gain momentum out of the gate.

Exercises

- Watch a few trailers of shows by Dimitris Papaioannou, and make a list of which scenes or images you could create today with little or no funding. Many of his shows are built out of interesting images with very little—hair, chairs, bodies, sticks, cardboard boxes, boards, a sheet of plastic. Do you think he was able to make 30 minutes of interesting material before he got the budget for a set?
- Make a list of people and organizations you would be interested in working with whose missions or skill sets overlap with your vision for your show. Try to make connections with these people or organizations by seeing if you can meet them or find ways to help them before you're asking anything of them.

Funding Solutions

When looking to create a show, many people's first thought is, "How can I get money to fund my show?" Money is an extremely useful tool to get things, but think—what are the things you actually need to make your show? Creative material? Training space? A director? A set? Many of these things can be acquired without money having to change hands. Money is just a tool to get the things you actually need: identify your real needs first, and see which might be able to be solved without the need for money.

You will find that there are a surprising number of resources available to artists, and people wanting to help you make your project happen. There are free spaces out there, specifically to help artists, some of which even come with housing or a rehearsal stipend. Other rehearsal spaces will happily exchange the use of their space for an event or coaching time, or even just a showing of your "work-in-progress" at the end of your residency. Many people are willing to volunteer or donate their time and expertise.

Generally anything you do will require a balance between your time, money and the energy you can put into it. Everyone that joins your project, even as a volunteer, will require (and deserve) your time and attention- both of which are finite resources. As you get strung out between all the things you'll have to do, remember to give all of these people the appreciation they deserve. It's one of the best currencies out there, and it's free to use.

"I definitely think you have to make something without money before the money will come," says Gypsy Snider (The 7 Fingers). This, she explains, is the conundrum of *creation* versus *finding money to create* that each circus artist faces. "You know it feels great to get a trick. It feels great to work for hours and hours and hours to do a trick that very few other people in the world can do. But then if you want money to turn that into a show, you need to put that into the context of something that is relatable to someone who's never done circus before." It's important to remember that the people with money to fund shows aren't often people with a strong background in the circus arts – you need to put your creation in context.

One of the things we came to realize when we were still talking about making a show was that it was going to be very difficult for us to turn down paying contracts to do an unpaid creation. It was hard to say no to work. Now this might not be an issue for you, but it might be an issue for artists you want to work with—it will be hard for them to turn down better paying opportunities to do your creation. Which brings us to the topic of the next chapter: funding.

Besides providing for all the other costs a show might require (space rental, costumes, set, administration, music rights, light designer, advertising, etc), funding can also allow you the opportunity to pay your artists (and yourself) rehearsal fees. There are numerous ways to do this, and most projects will end up being a combination of these options over their lifetimes:

- Ticket sales
- Grants
- Social funding campaigns
- Private funding
- Out of pocket costs (which may or may not be reimbursed by other sources of funding or profit if the show is a success)

Dessa *by Creative Sovereignty. Photo by Eric Bates. Artists: Alexandra Royer, Mason Ames, Stefanie Fournier. Laser design by Adam Hummell.*

FUNDING STRATEGIES

Ticket Sales

If you're self-producing (more likely in smaller venues), you might be able to pay for the project with the revenue from ticket sales themselves. This has always been the approach of Vermont Vaudeville, and there's something fair and immediate about it. Similar to street performing, how much you and your artists earn will depend on the number of people that come and how much they are willing to pay.

Maya McCoy from Vermont Vaudeville said that when they first started they did shows for years where they split the door to pay themselves and their artists. "In the beginning we did a favored nations approach where you get a share based on basically your stage time, we did that until 2014 when we became an official business." This allowed them to get their feet under them and **build a consistent audience**, then once they were more established they evolved their system. "Then we started selling tickets online so we had to shift, we started telling people what they'd get paid in advance, because we were getting consistent ticket sales. Then we brought on four sponsors for each show, so we have some corporate funding, and we've gotten consistent grant funding. It's primarily ticket sales, and a little bit of supplement from sponsors and grants."

Maya's husband, Brent McCoy, also a cofounder of Vermont Vaudeville, says that at the beginning he had no idea if they made any money. "We literally counted at the end of the night, the producers got a share for producing, we each did our acts, you got half a share for traveling, etc. We gave people an envelope at the end of the night and it was always transparent and fair and immediate. Once we started selling out and we had to turn people away, we decided we needed to pre-sell. Then the money started to be less thinly spread, because it actually started to generate some revenue."

Brent and Maya both agreed that at the beginning they put a lot of sweat equity into the project, for years, before the show produced any revenue for themselves that reflected the amount of work they had to put into it. 'Sweat equity', meaning unpaid contributions of labor and time that benefit the company or project, will undoubtedly make up a large part of your initial investment to get your show started.

The obvious danger of relying on ticket sales is that in the beginning it might be slow to grow your audience, and therefore you might not make much money. That said, it might be gratifying to know that the strength of your shows (consistently, over time), and the work you do to advertise will have a direct impact on what you can charge and how many people come to see you. It will also let you work a lot of the kinks out with less exposure and expectations. A small audience can be a good thing at first, although it might not feel that way if it's made up entirely of people you know in your town.

The ticket-sales approach will likely work better for people that have a consistent audience, or where they are well known. Even for big companies, self-producing in theaters can be a big risk that is not taken lightly if they have lots of expenses to cover with every show.

Fundraising for a Cause

Another strategy that Vermont Vaudeville uses is to raise money for the local theater in which their show is performed.

Maya says "It's a good way to get people on your side, to do fundraising for something. And to not have that fundraising come out of your bottom line,

Midnight Circus Setup. Photo by Eric Bates. Artists: Martavious Owten & Dominic Cruz.

but to generate it from your audience." People like to support things that make them feel good or altruistic.

By doing a "hat pitch" at the end of their show for the theater, rather than having it come out of the ticket sales, they were able to keep ticket prices low, and still allow those that had the means to provide additional support to donate to their local theater. This strategy was important to them because they wanted to keep their show accessible to their entire community, not just those that could afford high ticket prices. It also gave their show a mission that was bigger than themselves, but that still aligned with their goal of providing quality live entertainment for their local audience.

Zander Howard-Scott, director, composer and co-founder of Creative Sovereignty, has made some of his biggest shows by combining forces with a fundraising event. In an effort to woo potential donors for a fundraising campaign, charities will often put on lavish events such as dinners and shows:

167

get the potential donors in a happy and emotional state, and they might be more inclined to open their checkbooks. This might sound a little coldhearted and calculated, but the result is people having a good evening, the artists getting to put on a good show, and a charity for a good cause benefiting. Win-win!

The key, Zander stresses, is thinking of "how you can elevate someone else's effort." By aligning your interests with the big objective- raise money for their charity- you can use your talents to improve the smaller objectives within that goal: in this case making an evening that will be more exciting, memorable and creative than if you weren't there.

Branché *by Cirque Barcode and Acting for Climate MTL. Photo by Alex Galliez. Artists: Anne-Marie Godin, Agathe Bisserier, Stefanie Fournier, Heidi Blais, Nathan Biggs-Penton, Adrien Malette-Chénier, Eric Bates, Tristan Nielsen.*

Social Funding

Social funding relies on numerous private donations, and is nowadays often run on social media. Generally this will be done on a platform such as Kickstarter, GoFundMe or LaRuche. The obvious advantage of this is that many people that know you or your work will be likely to support your dream through donations, and it will also serve to get the word out about your project, which can start a ripple effect of people seeing what they can do to help. Disadvantages are that those platforms might take a small percentage, and it might make you uncomfortable to ask your friends and family for money. Some platforms are also "all or nothing", meaning if you don't make your goal, even if you're just five dollars short, you get nothing.

One strategy that Joseph Pinzon (Short Round Productions) recommends is to get a kickstarter coach. A social funding campaign isn't just something you put online and hope for- it can take months of planning ahead of the moment where you actually launch the campaign to be successful.

"Money attracts money. People see success happening and it draws them to it. They say, 'What about that is successful?' It's all about getting people hyped up, not for the project, but for you to cross the finish line," says Pinzon. John Teasdale (Kickstarter Coach) agrees with Pinzon that potential investors need to feel confident that the project will be successfully funded. But how can you build that confidence? He says you need to lay the groundwork so people are just waiting to support it. Teasdale accomplished this before starting his crowdfunding campaign by reaching out through polls, receiving feedback in comments and getting people to sign up for his newsletter. Afterwards, he felt confident that people would rush to contribute, and it worked!

Social funding can also take the form of individual donations outside of the context of a specific campaign. If you are a nonprofit or if you partner with a fiscal sponsor these donations can even be tax deductible for the donors. Afton

Benson (CLIMB) says when she's nurturing relationships with donors she tries to get to know individual donors and learn why they volunteer or donate to her organization. She learns what they like about it and why it makes them feel good so she can give them more of that feeling. You will have to promote yourself or ask directly somehow, which not everyone loves, but remember that it can make people feel proud to contribute to something they believe in, to support a good cause. You won't know if you don't ask!

If you go the private donation route, be on the lookout for ways to tie your project to events people are already familiar with. Holidays, or days such as Giving Tuesday can be good moments to run campaigns since people already associate those days with generosity, and might be already in the habit of giving money at that time of year.

Private Funding

In this section I'm referring to 'private funding' as individual donors or decision-makers for a private company or charity that have the financial power to finance an entire creation themselves. Zander Howard-Scott (Creative Sovereignty) has funded multiple ventures this way, and he says there's an art to successfully forming relationships with these donors and making the experience a win for all parties.

Zander says that while he was deliberately looking for people that could help fund projects, his primary goal was to develop solid relationships and friendships before asking for anything. "I think the idea that you just go and find money from whoever to fund your project is wrong," says Zander. "The only way it's going to work and feel good to you without compromising your heart is to make sure that you actually can see eye to eye with that person. That gets revealed over time. It doesn't just happen in one instance." He spent months getting to know the partners he eventually ended up collaborating with.

He says that no one wants to feel used, neither artists nor those with wealth, and that he believes wealthy people are constantly being asked for favors, and it's exhausting for them. The worst thing you can do is make them feel objectified. This might be a hurdle you have to get over if you didn't grow up with wealth—the temptation to put those with wealth on a pedestal, or demonize them, rather than thinking of them as people first. One analogy he sites is the relationship between artists and nobility throughout Western history:

"I think all throughout history, there has been a relationship between the artists and the nobility, or the musician and the court. That is an exchange that works really well, because each party has something that the other doesn't have. It's a logical sort of trade. Those who've made their money can't buy the talent themselves, because they've made their money elsewhere. They haven't devoted a lifetime to a craft. But they can bring some of that magic into their world, and then have the artists be supported. And then the same way, the artist has often devoted their entire life to their craft, [rather than building wealth]."

Each has something that is valuable to the other.

From here what really unites them is a sense of purpose. "People reach a certain point where they've solved their money problem. They're looking for more meaning and more exploration in their life. That's an important thing to keep in mind when you're looking to raise money."

Whether this is working to use your artistic magic to support a charity they've started, or showing how your project embodies ideals they share, you have an opportunity to create something that supports their sense of purpose and making the world a better place. **If you believe that the show you're making will improve the world, there's nothing saying that your goals and self-interests and someone else's goals and interests have to be mutually exclusive. They can align.**

For individual donors there might also be a status element involved, because it might make them look good to discover and introduce unique, interesting people to their partners. We tend to lose sight of this being constantly immersed in the arts ourselves, but the artistic world can seem like a foreign and mysterious place to those that don't inhabit it. Just like the business world can be intimidating for artists, so too can the arts be for business folks. Someone that is able to bridge this gap and rub elbows with artists, bring them in to share that magic can gain status in their own circle.

Zander's last piece of advice is that for private investors like these, price is a detail. It comes after the purpose, and the dream. Numbers that might seem intimidating to you and me might not be as foreign to people that regularly work on much larger financial scales in their businesses. Zander says that when one of his clients first asked what he thought an event like the one he was proposing would cost, he was very intimidated. But he had made his calculations and threw out a number, $25,000. "At the time it felt like the most astronomical number," he said. In the end, with all of the catering and everything, the event cost upwards of $100,000- four times the original budget. However, the event managed to raise nearly a quarter million dollars in donations for the charity. It was a huge success! Seeing this changed some of his previously held concepts about what was possible, and he has since gone on to work with budgets nearly 10 times that amount.

One of the main advantages of private funding is that it allows you to negotiate. You can have a conversation with your investor- asking for more funding, or different sorts of support, or equity in a project, for example. It also allows you to understand what people are looking for, what the incentive is, on a human level. Negotiating can be intimidating to those that have less experience with it, and Zander recommends thinking of it more as storytelling. "When you start to learn about negotiation, or sales, or closing, it feels like a parody. Those concepts need to be integrated and put into your story, and that story needs a cause." Storytelling can be the link between art and business.

Disadvantages of private funding can be that you feel indebted to a person, and that they could possibly want more artistic control of a project than you're willing to give. Zander says he never had any problems with this, but it's always why he wants to get to know anyone before going into business with them or asking anything of them. **Capital isn't just capital, it's a relationship.**

Out of Pocket- Additional Funding

"If you aren't willing to put money in your own project, how can you expect someone else to?"
- Joseph Pinzon (Short Round Productions)

While other people might help you make your show, either financially or in other ways, it's possible you will end up having to put some of your own money into creating your show. Personal financial stability is a prerequisite. This means building up enough of a financial safety net while working on other contracts that you can support yourself for the amount of time you will be working on your show, since you won't be able to take on other jobs during that period.

Gypsy Snider (The 7 Fingers) says that they were only able to make The 7 Fingers because they collectively invested money into it- money that they made while working for other companies first. "We had all worked extensively for professional companies where we had minimal rent and bills, got per diem

173

and/or were fed every day, and almost never paid our own travel. Thanks to that career, I own a house, and was able to invest time and money into a company. I completely stabilized myself financially first, then built a company, bought a house and had kids. Since then it has been nearly impossible to accumulate savings."

Since this is money you're hoping to pay back to yourself one day, treat it as if it's a loan and incorporate this loan into your show cost when you eventually sell it. Just remember to keep immaculate records so there are no issues with your partners and investors when you go to pay yourself back!

While funding a project out of pocket is likely not many creators' first choice, it does have advantages, as well as a certain number of drawbacks. The money you put up out of pocket will make you especially conscious about what it is you're doing, and how you plan to make it back.

The positive side of this method is that it's your and your company's money, so you can do whatever you want with it! No one is looking over your shoulder telling you what you should or shouldn't do, and you won't feel guilty or pressured using money you gathered from friends and family via a social funding campaign.

For other, obvious reasons, using your own money can also be a disadvantage— one common difficulty is that you may begin to second-guess your artistic choices when you have to balance them against your financial limitations. You might think you love an idea, but do you love an idea enough to pay $740 to try it? What if it doesn't work? It's good to take some risks- so long as you're financially stable enough to survive if they don't pay off.

While this can be a concern with other forms of financing, it can be especially hard when it's your group's personal cash on the line; and if you have to justify trying an idea to other members of your team. It can also be hard to know when to stop spending—you need a new costume two days before the premiere? It can be hard to not solve every problem with the money hose if you have the means and you're not careful. You also have to watch out for the 'sunk cost fallacy', the phenomenon where you might be reluctant to give up on a strategy or course of action because you've invested heavily in it, even when it is clear that you'd be better off abandoning it.

One recommendation to overcome this is to set a finite budget and stick to it. This establishes a parameter for you, which can help in creative situations. Take the budget as the 'rules of the game', not some person telling you NOT to spend money. If you run out of money, that's it, you'll have to find new, creative solutions that don't require more money, or you'll have to do without. This way you're free to try the ideas you want (at least with the money you dedicated to "Creation" out of the total budget for your show), without feeling guilty about having spent money on something that didn't make it into the final show. And if you need something but there's no money left in the budget, try to overcome it creatively or trust that you can do without. It's part of the process. Budgets, too, can be used as a creative parameter.

Selling Merchandise

Another way to add to your bottom line is selling merchandise. This can work well at places like Fringe festivals where every dollar counts. Selling merchandise is similar to "hatting" an audience for a common cause in that it can be a fun way for people to give more if they have the means without having to raise ticket prices. But do consider where that merchandise comes from—think about the impact merchandise has when it comes from halfway around the world, and if there's a creative alternative you could come up with to reduce your impact. With Cirque Barcode and Acting for Climate's show *Branché* we

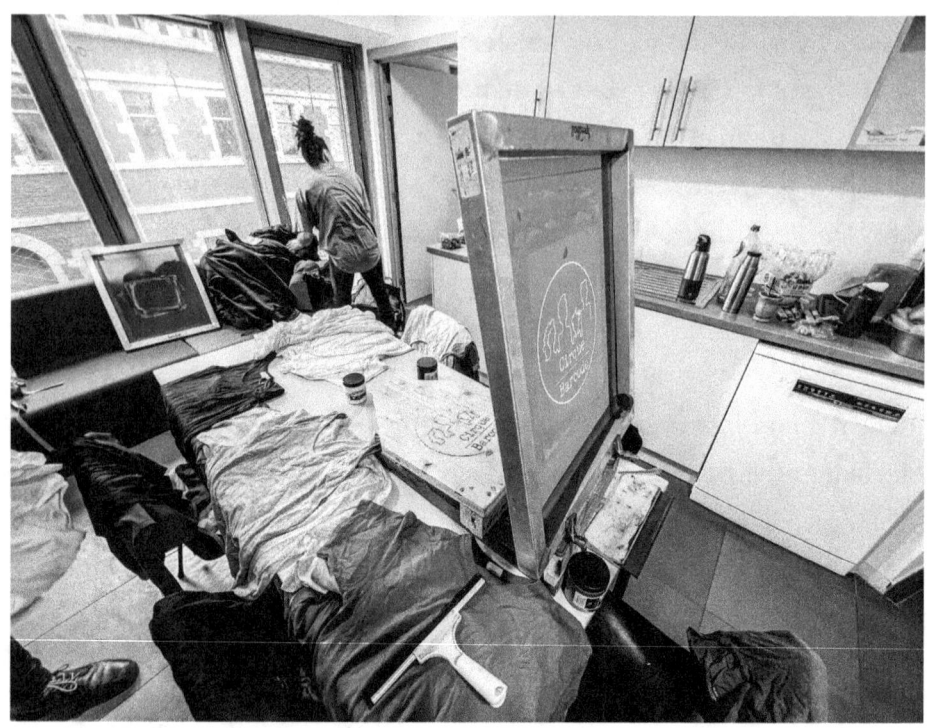

Making merchandise. Photo by Eric Bates.

silkscreen all of our own shirts on upcycled shirts, or allow audience members to bring their own that we screen for them. Cheaper, and less impact!

Street shows sometimes sell postcards or posters for a price or by donation after their show as a way to supplement the show's income. In the case of Héloïse Bourgeois's company Cirque Entre-Nous they will either hire a photographer themselves, or when people take photos of the show (common in an outdoor show) they frequently offer to let her use them for free—she just has to be professional about following up with them and tagging their photos with their information when they send them.

Charitable Gambling

This is a funny one. Some states in the US and certain provinces in Canada (and elsewhere in the world) allow for 'charitable gambling.' Charitable gambling is a form of giving, where a charity, rather than a municipality or private casino, oversees gambling activities such as lotteries, raffles, pull tabs, even meat raffles, and uses its proceeds to further its charitable aims.

Because the rules are so strict around this and involve regular audits, Afton Benson (CLIMB) recommends partnering with an organization that already does this, by selling their raffle tickets and taking half the proceeds, for example, rather than setting it up yourself. By partnering with an experienced organization that takes responsibility for it you won't have to worry as much about the legal ramifications.

Co-Commissions

When making their second and third shows, Di Robson (producer of Barely Methodical Troupe) approached different theaters around London to co-commission the creations. This basically means that the theaters put in money, in tandem with other arts organizations, and in return, Robson says, they got prestige. "Having their name on the bill of these shows that go all around the world, audiences see that and the theaters gain prestige and points with the arts council for being 'diverse', creatively."

"It's 'soft power'," Robson explains. By supporting a successful show that travels around the world carrying their name on the program, the theaters grow a reputation for having good taste and vision, which can build their reputations in turn and make other people and organizations want to support them.

This sort of arrangement would be hard to pull off as a first time company. Robson's long time career as a producer with good taste, and relationships with many of these theaters allowed her to nourish this sort of partnership.

"It's all about dialogue," Robson says. During their first show *Bromance*, she would travel with the company, especially when they went to places where she didn't know the people that ran a festival or a theater that she was interested in. This enabled her to have those dialogues with them so she would know them and understand them better. Or, she says, she would take the show there because she already knew the people at those places, and this allowed her to "keep having a chat."

"That's another role of the producer, that you can assemble a coalition of people that can help to make work. It's good for the theaters or festivals themselves, [to co-commission pieces that are well regarded]."

GRANTS

The Thing-In-Itself *by The Chita Project. Photo by Eric Bates. Artists: Anna Kichtchenko, Pablo Pramparo.*

"So let me get this straight..." I ask Tristan, while working on our third grant application of the year. "We're going to do all the work of writing the grant, and then at the end we get a lottery ticket that MAYBE will give us money to pay OTHER people?"

"Yes, but that is planning we have to do anyways, budgeting we have to do anyways, and money we would have had to come up with somehow to pay our collaborators anyways. And, we get to make our show."

"I guess. It's just hard."

It is hard. Grant writing can be frustrating and exhilarating and confusing. But it can also force you to take concrete steps towards making your project happen.

> *"I don't get it!" I cried, "I need to prove I have a residency confirmed in order to get the grant, but I need a grant to be able to afford to pay for the residency! Where do I start?"*

Oftentimes when artists think about getting money to make their shows they think about applying for a grant. In Montréal we are lucky to have a great network of support for the arts. Conseil des Arts de Montréal (CAM), Conseil des Arts et des Lettres de Québec (CALQ), and Conseil des Arts de Canada (CAC) all have programs to support physical, performance and digital arts. In the US there is less support—especially for circus—at the federal level. Many circus companies, though, have had success applying as theater or dance companies. More support can be found from state and regional arts councils, sometimes in categories as broad as "performance." A quick online search for your region and "performing arts" and "grants" may yield potential leads.

The People's Money

While grants are indeed a great way to finance your project, it's important to remember that grants are not "free money." Here is a quick word from Gypsy Snider reminding us that government-funded grant money ultimately comes from the people around us, the people we ride the subway with.

"You don't get the people's money unless you can prove that you have something of value to give back to the people. So wrap your brain around that first. You can't just say, 'Hey, I'm a cool, creative person, give me money so I can make something cool and creative.' It is a responsibility to create something that you believe will bring something back to society. And only then do you have the right to go ask for people's hard earned tax dollars."

So keep that in mind when you go down the grant-writing road. Art can contribute a lot to society, both socially and economically, so it's important not to be frivolous with these amazing funding opportunities. To be frivolous with the money is to be selfish- and the point of producing a show from the beginning is about sharing.

How do you start writing a grant before you know exactly what your show is about? This is a common problem. You have ideas, but you need to do the creation to clarify those ideas and see what will work. The truth of the matter is that a lot of what you put in your grant might not make it into the show—it might be a good starting point, but if the ideas you wrote about don't work in the creation, don't feel like you need to be tied to them. Obviously, don't do a "bait and switch," where you claim that the project is something it's not that you never intend to create, but you can take some of the pressure off of yourself because you're not submitting the final draft of the show when you write a grant.

"In the first version of the dossier, we are more vague," Christian Coumin explains of their grant writing process in Zinzi Oegema's book *GRIP*. "We talk about the intentions we have. We talk about the team. We talk about the history of the company. We look for co-producers or residencies. Sometimes we have to write more, especially for subsidies, because the vagueness will not be enough to ask for funds."

What you *should* submit are the reasons it is important that this show is made. This goes back to what Snider was saying. *Why* do you want to make it? What do you hope to achieve with it that will impact the lives of the people around you? Why is it important to the world that you make this show now?

In the book *GRIP*, Bauke Lievens explains her grant writing process. "I often write about the actual background, from which a certain idea or concept arises. You can also add a lot of external literature to that and that always looks good in a dossier. I always try to link that to a wider context outside of the circus, as well...*Why is it important to create that show today?*" She says it's important to convince the reader of the grant why this subject fascinates you and why it's needed, and says to do it not only with personal arguments, but with arguments that are shareable, understandable or comprehensible to an outsider.

Grants can also act as a clarification tool for a project. A main benefit to writing grants, besides the obvious objective of obtaining money in order to make art that will impact society, is that it makes you clearly define your action steps.

Where will your creation take place? Who will direct it? What do you plan to do with the time and money? What is your artistic goal? How will this project help both your company and the culture in which you hope to play it?

This practical exercise alone is useful for the realization of a project, and whether or not you receive a grant, they are questions that you should answer in order to move forwards. It will also likely lead to you getting the word out about your project as you ask people to look the grant over, gather pictures, video and other supporting material, and as you contact the places you hope to rehearse in, and so on. Then, at the end of this, as a bonus, you might also get money to bring these (now better organized) dreams to life.

Success Breeds Success

Something that looks good on a grant (and to any potential donor) is that the project will happen with or without the grant.

"That's a strange statement," you might be thinking. *"If it looks like the project will already happen, wouldn't that show the granting committee that I don't actually need their money?"*

Bear with me.

John Teasdale, who has run multiple successful kickstarters for card games, board games, and books, says in his article *10 Kickstarter Commandments*, "Nothing says, 'you can trust me with your money' like a lot of people trusting you with their money."

This is a phenomenon known as 'social proof', wherein people copy the actions of others when choosing how to behave in a given situation. We see this effect in 'canned laughter' on TV shows, where according to Cialdini's 1993 study, "the laughter of others offers "social proof" that potentially humorous material is funny," leading to higher humor ratings and overt laughter from the subject watching the show. This effect is also found in social media—the more followers a user has, or engagement a post has, the more they are seen as trustworthy and reputable. We can apply this same effect to garnering support for your project.

Psychologically, people like to support a winner. When you're submitting the grant, they want to see that you have already sold your idea to other people, and that you've put in the real work it takes to make a project happen.

These resources you've managed to gather might come in the form of donated time, space, or money. If you can show that you already have 50% of the project's budget/ requirements met, it will give a jury confidence that you won't be wasting the grant money and it shows that you are serious about putting in the hard work to actually make your project happen. People like to get onboard with something that will succeed, but also, people like to get onboard with a project where the people involved aren't afraid to get their hands dirty and beat the pavement before they come asking for cash. Asking for money before doing any work can read as off-putting and even entitled.

When we first made *Sweat & Ink* we personally invested money into the project, but we also received many contributions that were "in-kind" forms of support: goods or services rather than actual money. What's nice about this is that you can put a monetary value on these things in your grant application. If you get donated rehearsal space, you can list what it might normally cost to rent it. If you have someone offer to make you a promo video you can ask them what they would normally charge for their services, or find an equivalent service's pricing online. All of these things you can list in your grant application's budget as support you *already have*. This way, for example, instead of saying you're asking for $50k and you have $0 out of the project's total budget of $50k, you can show that it's really a *$75k* project, but you already have the equivalent of $25k or more in support. That sort of momentum and proof that you've already started to gather support is encouraging to people deciding whether or not your project will be a worthwhile investment.

Motivation Through Failure

While working on this book I filled out an entire grant application to try to get support to write it. I had written successful grants for Barcode before, so I thought I knew what to do. I uploaded all of the interviewees' CV's, wrote the objectives of the book, compiled my supporting documents, etc. Because I was stuck in quarantine, I also began doing some of the interviews before I had submitted my demand (usually you're supposed to wait until you've received the grant to begin a project, but I bent the rules... quarantine).

184

During these interviews, some of the first creators I interviewed recommended that anyone that was applying for a grant should get someone to help them with it. Figuring I should follow their advice, if only for the sake of researching this book, I called up a friend that specializes in grant writing, and the first thing she told me to do was to call the CALQ (Conseil des Arts et des Lettres du Québec) and see if my idea was eligible for their grant. If not, to ask why not, or if I could apply for another grant that might be a better fit.

After a ten minute phone call I learned that my idea was *not* something that the CALQ supported, but the man on the phone kindly gave me other organizations that might be more suited to my demand. While I was frustrated that I had filled out the whole CALQ grant for nothing, I was more motivated than ever to write this book, since the advice I'd learned in the interviews had already proven useful!

Phases of Writing the Grant

There are multiple phases of grant writing:

- Finding the grant
- Writing the grant
- Correcting the grant
- Budgeting for the grant
- Reaching out to potential places to train/ perform etc.
- Submitting the grant
- Improving the grant application

Finding

Step one is to find grants that you're eligible for. You can break this task up between your team members. Go to grant-giving websites together and decide between your team who will read each grant summary and decide if it is a good fit for your project. It's not worth trying to apply for grants you're not a good fit for. Don't try to fit a square peg in a round hole, you'll just end up wasting your time and energy, and the program's time and energy.

Afton Benson (CLIMB) recommends calling the organizations when you find a likely match to make sure you're eligible, and to get a feel for the organization and their goals. It's an extra step, but it sure beats filling out the whole application then waiting a couple of months only to receive a rejection letter because your project is 'non-admissible'.

On this call you can try to figure out what they are really looking for. "I saw on your website that you want to create more art opportunities in your community. What does that mean to you?" To you that might mean bringing a circus show or performance to a local park and making it free for everyone, but maybe you'll find out that actually the granting body prefers that you charge for tickets. If the organization's mission is to show that art has value to Texans, they might believe that the proof of this value is that people are willing to pay

for it. Learning nuances such as this can help keep your application in line with the granting organization's values.

Any grants that you are eligible for, write down important dates (due date, date the grant is awarded) and bring them back to the team. You'll likely find you just missed a good one

Sweat & Ink *Set up. Photo by Eric Bates.*
Artist: Mathilde Jimenez

by a day or two, or it's due tomorrow—this always happens. Put the dates in the calendar for next year or the next period. I'd recommend giving yourself at least a month to write a grant, especially the first time, as you will need time to collect letters of confirmation, CVs, and other information from collaborators and rehearsal spaces. Plus, a little more time will give you the chance to get feedback on your first draft.

If you don't know where to start, or where to find grants, start making calls until you find people that do know. Pretty much any arts school or company in your industry will be able to point you in the right direction.

Writing

First drafts don't have to be perfect, they just have to be done. Whoever likes to write in your group, let them at it. In general, some of the questions will be self explanatory, but others will be more broad. For example, "Describe your project specifying your objectives and highlighting your artistic choices." Where do you start?

One obvious starting point is to state the problem you want to correct, the injustice you want to address, or the inciting incident that touched you enough you want to make a show about it. In one of our successful grants for *Branché* we opened by talking about how there's an ethical dilemma between the positive values of contemporary circus and all the international travel it traditionally requires to share those values. As people worry about the climate crisis, how can we reconcile our art and use it to talk about the climate crisis without also contributing to the problem?

From there we talked about what we concretely wanted to do: make a show outside that challenged this traditional model, and the concepts we would base our research on: "Egoist pyramids", "Melting", "Reconstruction", elaborating on each to show how they reflected concepts important to our main goal of the piece, and where we would begin our research: "We'll try to build tall [human] pyramids without making sure there is a strong foundation, going as far as to abuse or disrupt the people on the bottom of the pyramid."

We went on to talk about the structure of our creation period, where it would take place and with whom we would collaborate, the goal of the workshop (creating a first draft of a show, and exploring how this format would work bringing the audience into nature), and our values.

In general it's good to balance **why** it's important to you to make your show, **how** it will contribute to society in general, and the **concrete** means by which you'll accomplish these goals.

Correcting

Here's where you get into the nitty gritty. Clean up sentences, show it to people, get their feedback. You can do this on a sharable platform like Google Docs that allows multiple people to edit at once and/or add comments; or send someone a copy and meet up afterwards to talk in person. Having a small circle of friends that gives each other feedback on their respective projects is a common practice amongst freelancers. Some employ ground rules such as 'you can send anything to the group and expect notes back, you just have to respond to other people's requests within 48 hours,' or something similar.

If you didn't have someone write it for you, strongly consider hiring someone to look the grant over for you. You can ask around at organizations established to help artists like En Piste in Quebec to help find someone. In my experience writers will charge by the hour, so asking them to write it will take longer and cost more than say, having them look it over once and give feedback after you've already done revisions on your own.

Budget

The number cruncher might not be the same person that's doing the "Writing" section of the grant. Basically, you need to go get dollar amounts for the things you need (or in-kind services that have already been promised to you as donations).

Example

- Mini teeterboard: $2,000.
- Two weeks of training space at The 7 Fingers (donated): -$10,000
- Six decorated coffee cups from the local thrift store: $6.09
- Outside Eye: 16 hours at $50/ hour= $800

It might feel tedious, but this is stuff you will actually have to do to make your project happen anyways. The granting committee wants to see that you're willing to do this work, to really figure out what it's going to take to make your show. This section will be done in conjunction with the next step.

Reaching Out to Potential Sources of Help

As you start to clarify your idea for the show, you want to lock in resources that can help. This will include coaches, outside eyes, training spaces, possibly donated projectors or cameras, props, etc. What's tricky is that you're going to have to book these things and people well in advance, often before you know if you have the money from the grant to actually afford them. Talking to these people will let you know what they cost, or what value they can donate, which you can apply to your budget section. You can also make it clear to the people you're asking to participate that it might be contingent on you getting a grant, and making sure that they're comfortable with those terms.

Submit

Send in the grant! Don't save this until the last hour of the last day, it would be a shame to be ineligible after all that work because your internet went down at 11:50pm.

Improve

If your grant wasn't successful, use it as an opportunity to learn. Oftentimes granting boards will have a phone number (or an email address that you can write, from which you can get a phone number), that you can politely call up and ask what you can do to improve your grant. They won't always be able to help you, and that's ok, but sometimes the improvements they suggest might be as simple as tweaking a few key things and resubmitting. Afton Benson said she had 3 grants that were rejected, but that after calling the board she was able to resubmit with minor tweaks. All three were accepted in the following round, without her having to write three completely new proposals. Not a bad return on a short phone call.

KEY TAKEAWAYS:

- If you live somewhere that grants are available to you they can be an amazing tool to get your project off the ground. The exercise of writing a grant for your project will take you through many of the steps you will already have to do in order to realize your project, with the added benefit of possibly resulting in funding at the end.

- Government grants come from taxpayer money. Be sure to show that you will be giving something back to society when you use their money!

- Showing how you are putting in the work, and how other people are supporting you can help convince new donors to come onboard.

- Call up the granting board to make sure you're eligible and to understand their mission to make sure your application aligns with it

- In your application, balance why it's important to you to make your show, how it will contribute to society in general, and the concrete means by which you'll accomplish these goals.

Edith, in the makeup chair. Photo: Eric Bates. Pictured: Audrey Toulouse & Edith Collin-Marcoux.

FUNDING ADVICE

Gating

"Phase-gating" is the idea of dividing your process into multiple phases. This allows a sort of check-in at each phase both for yourself and potential investors. This makes it easier to calculate the risk factor for everyone involved throughout the process. It makes it less scary for an investor to support a certain phase of the project before going further, rather than to give a huge chunk of money away not knowing if it's likely to come back.

The things typically checked at each "gate" or phase are: quality of execution, business rationale and action plan. While it's not necessary to use this terminology, it's helpful to know because these checks are processes you're going to go through anyway in grants or while convincing people to give you funding. Let's look at these terms:

Quality of Execution: When you're applying for funding, people will likely want to see what past work you've done that shows you will be able to competently use their investment. This could be done with a CV or video showing examples of past work, or written examples.

Business Rationale: From a business perspective does your plan make sense? This could include the cost of creation vs. whether you'll be able to make your money back by doing shows (and in how much time), and that you have a plan for the next steps in the creation/selling process so you can take it to completion. Some companies consider a project financially successful if they've recouped their initial investment after one year of touring. Others consider a project a financial failure if it doesn't generate a profit in the first two years. The important thing is that you have a plan that is achievable that you're happy with following through on.

Action Plan: This could take the form of a calendar or Gantt diagram (discussed "Pre-Production" on page 210) outlining your projected dates for residencies, works-in-progress showings, marketing deadlines and premiere dates. Showing you've thought ahead through these steps will reassure investors you understand the scope of what you're undertaking.

In Canadian grants you'll typically see these "gates" in the form of certain grants for "research and creation" with no stated goal to produce anything concrete, then later grants for "production and touring" with the goal of touring a show that tends to build on the previous grants. This way they can effectively phase-gate your project by doling out the money one step at a time instead of giving giant lump sums before you've done anything yet.

KEY TAKEAWAY:

- Split your creation into manageable steps and look for funding for the different phases, rather than the whole thing. As you'll see in "Appendix A: Full Creation Timeline" on page 319, you will likely be in one of the previous steps while figuring out the next step, but that's ok. Like driving on a foggy road, not seeing all the way to the horizon doesn't mean you stop driving, it just means you go the appropriate speed for how far ahead you can see.

CASE STUDY: 51/49 PRODUCTIONS

Who They Are

International Events Management Company that provides strategic, production, and creative consulting services for global live entertainment leaders including Fortune Global 500 companies, national governments and international arts organizations.

The Issue: Bringing Circus to Rural Japan

One strategy that James Tanabe, co-founder of 51/49 Productions, uses when putting a project together is to work backwards. He told me the story of a client that wanted to bring circus to rural Japan.

His first step when talking to his client that wants to make a project happen is to use the technique of the 5 Why's, a technique first described by Taiichi Ohno, founder of the Toyota motor corporation. The idea is to drill down to the core of why someone wants to do something by continuing to ask *"why?"* until you can go no deeper. When Tanabe explored the whys with this client, they determined that the client was interested in revitalizing rural Japan and giving jobs to the elders there in hopes that people would learn from and respect them when they came to visit the shows.

Strategy: Turn It Upside Down

At this point Tanabe researched the biggest social challenges affecting Japan that the Japanese government and the OECD (Organization for Economic

Co-operation and Development) agreed on, and indeed the aging population and the decimation of the population in rural Japan were on the list. His client's idea to bring circus to rural Japan was actually in resonance with a major problem that the Japanese government was already spending tons of time, resources and money to address. He had an angle.

Tanabe then read all the reports he could find on what the Japanese government and the OECD said was working and what wasn't working to solve this problem. He brought this list back to his client and told him, "Out of the 100 things you want to do, the OECD and the Japanese government have said, "[these ones don't]" work. Let's take these out and see if we have anything left that *does* work. It doesn't mean you can't do these things, it just means it shouldn't be what we're pitching forward to them."

He took the elements that the Japanese government was already interested in, then worked backwards until he arrived at his client's idea. The pitch looked something like this: "Japan is facing this major problem of rural flight and aging population...We know that live entertainment is a major driver of tourist initiatives, and we know that circus is a form of live entertainment that has had enormous success internationally because it doesn't rely on the spoken word."

Tanabe calls this process "turning it upside down"—start with the big problem that the client is interested in, then work backwards from there until it arrives at how your show or vision might address those issues.

The Result

Tanabe put together a nine-page document that outlined their project description, the social problem they were addressing, the results of their research (which showed how their solution would effectively address the social problem), their company's expertise, the positive impact the project would have and their potential partners both foreign and domestic.

In the end, the project was aborted due to a catastrophic mudslide that destroyed large swaths of the area. However, in 2023 after the mudslide and the pandemic, the first people they contacted about revitalizing rural aging communities was 51/49 Productions because of the conversations they had and the relationship they had formed. At the time of this writing those discussions are still ongoing.

There is a saying that when people go into a hardware store, they aren't looking to buy a drill. They're looking to buy a hole in their wall. When putting together your project (your drill), you need to show your potential funding partners why it solves their problem (the hole in the wall they're trying to make). In the world of theater performances this might mean showing shots of a happy audience, or putting quotes on-screen from rave reviews. "Turning it upside down," by working backwards from your funders' perspective and goals, is a way to ensure more success for your project.

Turn it Upside Down: Theoretical Example- The Alien Show

Imagine your company wants to do a show about aliens, perhaps due to a lifelong personal fascination with them. You also happen to think this theme could be physical and fun, while also providing an opportunity to show off that weird new apparatus you've made but you're not sure exactly what it is yet. How do you get it funded?

Upon looking at the grants page you see that there are research and creation grants, but also grants for digital technology and work made for younger demographics. You call up the grant organization and learn that indeed, these are priorities for the organization and they've released a new program this year with a big new budget specifically for anything that combines the two. Would weird, out-of-this-world noises made by digital technology live onstage fit well with your alien show? It might! And could your show be a good fit to bring this technology to a younger demographic, while also showcasing amazing live performance and a message of learning how to find your place in a strange world? Almost certainly.

Separately, you find that another organization is interested in helping artists research new apparatuses, and they themselves have received a grant and rented a space dedicated to this purpose and are looking for artists! You contact them and count their space as an "in-kind donation" towards your project.

A young costume designer you know is eager to cut their teeth and would love to make you some alien costumes as long as you provide the material. You put their fee in the budget anyways, because part of the granting body's mission is to pay artists, and you reach out to a non-profit that recycles costumes to see if they'd be interested in coming on as a sponsor if you put their name on the project. They are, and you count the donation of their materials as in-kind donations as well. In the end, you get your alien show, the granting body supports the digital technology for young audiences they are interested in, the other space fulfills their mission to help develop new circus apparatuses, your designer friend makes their first costumes and the recycled costume center gets their name on your program that will tour around the world.

KEY TAKEAWAY:

- See if you can work backwards from your client's goals and priorities and see what aspects of your project can align with them.

SECTION 4: PRODUCING

PRODUCTION

Setup at Midnight Circus. Photo by Eric Bates. Rigger: Eric Anderson.

Production Value

Production value is a measure of the level of quality and skill that was used to make your show outside of the human and story elements such as acting, directing and script. It is the amount of care taken to create the product that your audience is paying to see—basically, does your show give the impression that it was cheaply made, or expensive to make? Production value is the level of detail, sophistication, technical excellence and cohesiveness of a show. While the quality of the writing and acts in the show obviously matter a great deal, production value refers more to the elements of set, props, lighting, costumes and sound design.

In the end, it's a big-picture term that is used to talk about the perceived quality of a show. While this doesn't necessarily have to do with budget—maybe you have some very talented friends that are willing to help you out for free or a discount—the important part is the impression that the audience gets. Does the set and costumes look cheap or shoddy or well made? Quality work is often expensive both from a materials and talent perspective, which is why production value is often related to budget in people's minds. But you can do great things and have good production value regardless of the budget!

There are many ways to make a great show, or a bad show, regardless of budget. You can manage to have good production value without the stage needing to look expensive. Take Cie XY's shows- they always have many acrobats, which is inherently expensive (rehearsals, show fee, per diem, hotel, travel), but the set design and costumes tend to be simple- usually an empty stage with clean but cohesive costumes and simple but powerful lighting.

The type of show being made will also influence whether the production value seems good or not. A show such as Cirque du Soleil trying to look spectacular might feel cheap if they had costumes from the thrift store, whereas for an underground grunge cabaret this could even enhance the desired feel of the show. In fact, if the costumes looked too 'designed' or clean, it might even hurt the perceived quality of the show, by detracting from the goal of it feeling 'raw'.

Think about the sort of show you're trying to make, and what will be most important to your show looking like it has succeeded in that goal.

In Barcode's first public presentation of *Sweat & Ink*, I'm embarrassed to say that we had costumes bought from Walmart. Many of our props came from the thrift store. We painted the set ourselves in four different colors with our director JP Cloutier (thankfully a jack-of-all-trades), who also helped design the lights in the last days before the presentation.

In our second round of creation in Prague, we had costumes designed and custom-made by Kristina Záveská. We again hand-painted the set, but this time we took days to do it, meticulously projecting images onto the set and tracing them out in pencil before finishing them with paint. We painted a screen that was used for projections in the show in a matching style, and programmed custom projections throughout the show, including videos we filmed in the new costumes specifically for the show. We took weeks in the Jatka 78 theater to program new lights, including new images using a projector we didn't have before. We repainted all the props to create a cohesive overall look. We had custom music made. We re-recorded voice tracks that were played in the show in different languages for all the countries we would play in. Overall the show went from looking like a work-in-progress to a cohesive, professional looking show ready to play in the biggest theaters around Europe.

Building Your Production Team

The following section will cover the various roles besides your performing artists that you will have to fill. It's possible that you will do some of these positions yourself, at least for a while, in which case it's good to know what you're getting into!

Producers, Managers and Administrators

While producers, managers and administrators are not technically the same role, in small-company circus many of the responsibilities tend to be performed

Midnight Circus Setup. Photo by Eric Bates. Artists: Mason Ames, Tristan Nielsen, Eric Allen.

by one person, at least in the beginning. We'll look at some of the distinctions below, but for now, assume that some people will use them interchangeably, and that regardless of the title, the duties they perform will be vital to your success!

Chris Lashua, founder of Cirque Mechanics, says that "Unless you're a circus person that loves the business, you need to outsource the production tasks to people that are better equipped, better skilled than you are to do this. And almost anybody is better skilled to sell circus than us!"

Ideally this person will have business acumen, and also be a lover of circus.

A *producer* is somewhat of a unicorn in the circus world, known only through hints and whispers as a mythical being that can make all of your administrative and financial worries go away. As we'll see, sometimes this term is used interchangeably in the circus world with administrator or manager, and while there are technically distinctions in the titles, what's important is what the person *does* for your show.

I called up Di Robson, owner of *Dream* and independent cultural producer and consultant, who has, among other things, brought Barely Methodical Troupe's three shows *Bromance, Kin* and *Shift* to life, and asked her to help me define the role of *producer*. Robson described herself as an "engineer of the imagination."

Poetic, but not exactly the clarification I was looking for. I pressed her further.

"I see my job as bringing ideas that I like and I think are interesting and worthwhile to the public...When I started working we were all called 'administrators.' But very soon I came to realize I was involved in every aspect of the work– what the posters looked like, the marketing, the content of the show, how it was talked about, how it was delivered."

What became clear throughout our conversation was that while many of the administrative tasks of creating a show might remain similar, the role and tasks of a producer can vary wildly from company to company or even project to project. One might describe Robson as a *creative producer* because she involves herself creatively in the work onstage from the beginning of a project, as opposed to a *manager* or an *administrator* that focuses more on the (albeit still creative) behind-the-scenes tasks. All of these terms could theoretically be interchangeable with "producer" depending on what agreement they reach with the company.

"I'm a professional audience person," Robson says, "I've seen so many shows that I know which shows work and which shows don't."

In summary, a producer is a person or company that deals with the managerial or financial aspects of creating a production, and might also deal with bringing in investors as well as other needed talents to the artistic team—maybe suggesting a director, light designer or marketing agency. Again, this can be flexible, they could take on only a part of this, and might also implicate themselves in the creative process as well if that's the agreement you come to with them.

How to find a producer

Barely Methodical Troupe started as three friends that wanted to make a show together. Before they thought too much about touring, producers, advertising, or logistics though, they started by making a simple 30 minute piece. They were pleasantly surprised at its positive reception- a company even proposed to produce them. Not knowing much about this world, they brought in someone they trusted, Di Robson, the aforementioned producer who had mentored some of them in school. They trusted her to ask the right questions in the meeting, and they were glad they did. The terms offered by the company were unfavorable to the artists, and in the end Robson herself ended up becoming Barely Methodical Troupe's producer with her own already-established production company. Charlie Wheeller, co-founder of Barely Methodical Troupe, said this situation worked really well for them, it let them "focus on what we were paid to do. That's the best thing about working in a well-structured company. We're never required to do something we're not good at. Our strengths are really drawn out. We don't rely on strengths that don't exist."

The key element that made this happen, Robson emphasized, was that they got along. "They were green as grass," she said, but she could tell they had something special. "As a producer you have to sort of fall in love with your artists. You have to believe that what they've got is special and can make something special happen."

As an artist you need to feel the same way about your producer. You will be committing to working together for a good bit of time if you decide to make a show together, or even just to tour a show together if the show is already made. Being able to have both the exciting conversations and the hard conversations together is important.

"Companies that want to make a show need to go and talk to a number of producers," Di said, "and make it clear that they're talking to a number of producers and they're looking for the right fit. Find the person that loves your vibe. It's a love affair in a way. Find someone that really likes what you do." You can do this by thinking of companies whose shows you love and looking at their website or poster to see who produced them, or by reaching out and asking.

It will be hard to find someone that will trust you enough to give you "carte blanche", meaning they would do all of the work on their end, fund your project and still leave you complete artistic freedom and choice of collaborators. If you bring on a producer, you will have to give up some control or money, or likely a bit of both. Again, these arrangements will have to be worked out with the person you find—whether they take 15-20% like an agency, or whether you split up the work and risks and rewards equally among your members, or you pay hourly, or some other arrangement.

One way or another you will end up paying this person or company, which can feel difficult when you're just starting, but like in the case of Barely Methodical Troupe, it can be worth it to allow yourself to focus on what you're good at and to use the producer's skills and connections and reputation to springboard yourself out into the world.

At what point in the process should you take on a producer? "If you want someone that will help you shape a show," Robson said, "someone that will add value by understanding the market and having contact with the venues, etc.—if you want that kind of shaping, building, growing relationship, take on a producer as early as you can in the process and make them part of what you do, make them love you, because they will have an investment in you."

Of course, she says, some producers (or administrators, or management, as Robson would call them) would rather take on work that already exists. They might be happy to do all of the nuts and bolts, put the infrastructure in place, do the logistics and scheduling and booking and touring, but not want to have an artistic dialogue.

Many companies I talked to made at least the first version of their show through self-producing—finding all the funding themselves through various methods, choosing their collaborators, and making a show in their own vision. It was only once they had this first "proof of concept" that other people came on board.

Back in 2002, The 7 Fingers self-produced a first version of their show *Loft*, but had not considered the logistics and financial implications of touring it when they started to get offers for the show overseas. They were out of both money and favors at this point, and that might have been the end of The 7 Fingers had they not met Nassib El-Husseini. In *Loft* he saw the power of the team's innovative creative vision and supported it both financially and by providing managerial vision as the company's CEO.

Festivals can also act as producers. Sometimes festivals or venues will provide development money for a show, maybe in exchange for the rights to the world premiere, for example. They might provide residency space, pay or other forms of support.

Circus festivals around the world do these things to attract popular shows and foster up-and-coming companies, but they are also part of the machine of programming. There is a small corps of programmers and producers in the contemporary world who attend all of these festivals and talk to each other about which shows to book. Once you get into the network, and one festival books you, (excluding fringe fests—unless you are 'produced' there like with Underbelly at Edinburgh) you are in the booking cycle for most of them.

Fringe festivals, while often a financial risk, do have advantages—they often work with venues to get cheaper rental rates, and many underwrite/cover some portion of the venue rental. They might get a reduced rate on booking the theater but take a cut of the ticket sales. This means the initial outlay of money for the company can be lower than if you wanted to rent a space outside of the festival. That said, it's still considered "self-producing" since the artist/company has to cover all of those initial expenses and take on most of the risk involved.

Producers and feedback

The balance with working with producers as an artist or as the director of a show is that you want to maintain control of your project, but your producers, especially a 'creative producer' like Robson, will have experience in the business and will also want to have their say. This unsolicited advice might not always be welcome if it's not the creative arrangement you understood. When this happens, Shana Carroll (The 7 Fingers) says, "You know in your heart when there's something you have to listen to," and other times when you don't believe their advice is in the best interest of the show. In either case, it's important to listen respectfully before figuring out how you want to solve the issue.

Carroll recommends listening "to their observations, not their suggestions." She talks about one instance where she created a Chinese pole act in *Cuisine & Confessions* in which Matías Plaul talks about the kidnapping of his dad by rebels in South America. "In the beginning it was like 10 minutes long, maybe more, and he was crying while he was telling it, and people were really uncomfortable."

She kept getting feedback telling her to add music in the background, cut different sections… all sorts of advice that didn't fit her vision of the act.

Carroll says it's a skill to let them feel heard—it doesn't mean you have to take their advice. "As long as you've solved it in some other way, they don't really care." Also, she says, sometimes they're right. "That moment of checking your defensiveness and going, "Maybe I could actually take this comment and make something better out of this moment."

In the end, Carroll did shorten the act substantially, but she kept it with just Matías talking, no backing track. Just Matías talking about this emotional, terrifying time in his life while climbing and contorting his way up and down the pole, giving a visual, acrobatic metaphor to the story. It turned into one of the most poignant, intimate moments of the show. The producers were happy.

Pre-Production

"Pray to God but row for the shore."

\- Russian Sailor's Proverb

'Pre-Prod' is all the stuff that you can do before you actually start creating in the room. This means finding the creation space, writing grants, building a prototype of a set, talking to people that can help and support the project such as directors and coaches, planning ideas to try and how you want to try them. Ideally, this sort of work takes place at least six months to a year ahead of time, since all of the elements you will need (space, people, grants) tend to book well in advance and not on a day-to-day basis.

Light Check Sweat & Ink. *Photo by Eric Bates. Artist: Tristan Nielsen.*

Save time with a Gantt diagram

A Gantt diagram is basically a timeline working backwards from your premiere date. It takes into consideration what elements are dependent on other elements being completed, and what elements can be worked on simultaneously. When figuring out what you'll need for your creation and when you'll need it, this can be a helpful tool to clarify how much time things will take, and your order of operations. Figure out all the tasks you'll need to do, then organize them by what tasks are dependent on other elements and what can happen simultaneously.

An easy example of this would be: a dress rehearsal needs costumes. So you'd figure out when you want your dress rehearsal, say you need costumes by that date, then figure out how long it will take to make costumes before then by talking to your costume designer. While those costumes are being made, you could simultaneously be working on light design which will also need to happen before you can do a dress rehearsal.

Since you likely won't yet have a premiere date at the beginning of your journey, I would recommend basing your approximate timeline off of "Appendix A: Full Creation Timeline" on page 319. Many of the companies I talked to listed similar rough timelines, and it will give you an idea of everything that needs to get done and by when so you can anticipate things in advance.

That said, you can break your entire creation down into pieces- what do you need to do before your first ever workshop? What do you need to do before you get into a residency where you plan to present at the end? What do you need to do before you get into a theater residency? You will likely have time between each of these phases, and that time is when you do Pre-Prod.

To reiterate from earlier, before your first block of creation, you'll likely want to think about some of the following things:

- Music (for improvs, for potential acts—start making a "one day" playlist of anything that catches your ear)
- Improvs to try/ how you're going to make material
- Food/ cooking schedule
- Schedule of regular meetings: Emotion check-in meetings (Checking in on how the team is doing and making sure everyone is getting along: see chapter in "Keeping the Team Happy" called "Emotions Meetings" on page 231), creation process meetings (where you sit down with your team and talk about how you're liking the process of how you create material. If this is your first show, and especially if you're doing a collective creation, you will likely be figuring out your creative process together along the way and it's worth reflecting on specifically!), administrative time (administrative work specific to the show such as grants, getting materials, booking spaces, but also time to do other work like responding to emails for other gigs.)
- What will you need to bring to the room? If you want to try an idea with dirt, or with an overly large shirt, get that stuff (or a prototype of that stuff) before the workshop starts so you can try it.
- If you plan to have a set, especially one you hope your performers will interact with, get a prototype in place for them to experiment with. (Note: if this is not possible, be creative about it! For The 7 Fingers show *Psy* they had a vision of a three-story structure in their show. Before it was ready they took the whole cast to an olympic diving tower so they could see what tricks might be possible off of the three and five-meter platforms. Fun!)
- Book outside eyes, coaches, and/or a director.
- In your PreProd phase, you don't have to have everything known already—jumping off points are a good place to start. Remember, a good idea by itself will not necessarily translate well physically, at

least at first. There's going to be work to do and many phases the idea will have to go through to make it work. **PreProd isn't about removing the magic of creation, it's about doing everything you can to launch you into those exciting discoveries in the room** so you don't waste time sitting around looking for music to try, or sitting around with the clock ticking saying, "Well, what should we do today?"

While Gypsy Snider (The 7 Fingers) says she likes to go into projects already knowing her beginning, middle and end, she still says that, "What I always described to the designers and to the cast is that no matter how clear I am and how solid I am with my opinions, I still want to be surprised by the product at the end... Which is very contradictory of course, because as a director, you have to be thriving, pushing and clear in your forward thinking. But ideally every day I'm just completely surprised by what I see. The way that I achieve that is that I create the structure and then I also create a structure in which the performer can improvise."

The Problem of Hats

"Eric, did you see this email about the cargo?" Eve asks from the mats.
"Kind of busy!" I call, as Alex lands on top of me off the teeterboard with a thud.
"I think they will pick it up from the storage on the 8th," Tristan says, pulling in slack on the safety lines, "We'll call in the car."

Training finished, we load the teeterboard into the car, strap the Russian bar on the roof, plop the sandwiches in our laps while driving across town to our other rehearsal space for that afternoon. Eve has her giant laptop open in the backseat. Alex is calling CALQ with questions about grants. I'm trying to make an instagram post while fighting off motion sickness.

214

"Can we leave the board at ENC tonight?"

"No, we have training at Eloize tomorrow morning."

"Can we borrow Stef's car again?"

"I'll ask."

One of the problems you'll run into as you transition from being an individual artist to being the creator of a show is *the problem of hats*. When working for another company, the only thing you have to worry about is making good art (and you had likely trained a long time to do this, with a minimal amount of logistics that you were responsible for). As you create your own project, you will now have to worry about grants, accounting, logistics, hiring, PR, communication... In short, you will acquire many new "hats" you may not have much experience in.

"I think we did the same mistake that everyone does at the beginning," says Héloïse Bourgeois (Cirque Entre-Nous). "We didn't have much money so you think you can do everything but at the end you realize that it was too much, and at the end it brings your artistic level a bit lower. But I learned a lot."

What does this look like in real life? It means doing emails in between teeterboard jumps while you're in training. It means talking about grant options while you're warming up, answering emails and calling people in the car as you drive between training spaces. For Bourgeois, it meant, "At night instead of watching videos [from rehearsal] and thinking what we could do differently the next day, or looking for music or thinking about ideas... I only had time to write the next project for the next place to rehearse and make sure we could buy the mats on time and make sure the person that would do the costumes would be there or buy the train tickets."

There are many books that have talked about how to make a company, but one solid piece of advice I've come across is to sit down and define all of the roles you will have to play, all of the hats you will need to wear. This is a useful exercise because even if you don't want to be the accountant, someone will have to do it, and until you hire out the job to someone else, it will remain your team's responsibility.

Here's a quick list of some administrative and tech roles to get you started:

- Accountant
- Email response and delegation
- Travel agent
- Logistics (with theaters and transportation)
- Prop creator
- Costume designer
- Project manager/ scheduling
- Space reservation
- PR (Social media manager, outreach)
- Cook
- Setup and teardown
- Video filmer, editor and archiver
- Website designer
- Director
- Funding/Grant writing and follow up

These jobs might not be what you signed up for when you dreamed of becoming a circus artist! Gypsy Snider (The 7 Fingers) says that, "You have to love what you do and therefore you have to love everything you have to do to do what you love. And you have to have a very, very healthy relationship with what you do that is independent from the money you earn doing it."

If you're on a team, you're going to want to figure out how to divide and conquer. If you don't, instead of doing just the part of the work that you're each best at, you'll all end up doing *all* of the work. Of course, not every role will be everyone's favorite job, but remember that some people's passion *is* accounting, or finding solutions for shipping cargo. If you can figure out how to get the right people on the bus, and in the right seats, it'll make the ride a lot smoother.

A few years ago, I talked to a three-man team that toured Europe with a circus tent. I was lending a hand helping them to take it down, and noticed that the large porter of the trio wasn't there:

> *"Where's John?" I said.*
> *"Oh, he doesn't do set-up or teardown."*
> *"What?" I was baffled. The biggest guy didn't help on the teardown, the thing that in my experience everyone always helped with? This was an "all hands on deck" moment! Where was this slacker?*
> *"Yea, he didn't like doing it, so he just does all the accounting and promo. And we're all fine with that."*

This was a big "A-ha!" moment for me. It sounds stupid, but not everyone has to do all the work. A mistake I made in the beginning was thinking everyone had to help with every single aspect of getting the show off the ground and trying to hold myself and my team to that impossible standard. As we evolved as a company, we learned to trust each other's decisions more, and to let people handle things. Even if they're not done exactly how you would do them, that doesn't mean they're done wrong. The caveat here is that these arrangements have to be mutually agreed on and explicit so that resentments don't fester. Clarity is important!

Talk with your team about all the things you're going to have to do, then make a plan for who will be in charge of what. Follow your interests. There might also be things no one is interested or qualified to do, in which case you might need to find someone that can help with that task. Look at the list of tasks above and decide who will do what, and what will be outsourced. Then do your best to focus on wearing one hat at a time!

For an example of Barcode's organizational charts, see "Appendix C- Organizational Chart Examples" on page 331.

Regular Production Meetings

Regardless of how you divide the work, regular check-ins are recommended between team members to balance the load. Regular check-ins might reveal that one person is getting swamped while another team member has nothing to do, which happens fairly frequently depending on the work phase you're in. For example, if one person is overwhelmed writing a grant that the others didn't remember she was working on, someone with nothing to do might be be able to revise it for them, or collect the press articles needed for it, or work on the budget for it, or call up creation spaces to get a letter of support/ interest. Regular check-ins also means less things are likely to fall through the cracks due to a lack of accountability.

There are apps, programs and software suites that can help with this. Any new tool will take some time to get used to, but if your team is able to stick to them they may help better define who is doing what. The key is that they make life easier for your team. Everyone has their own workflow; these are tools that might help, but might prove less natural than a system you make yourself, and that's fine!

Alternatively, you could make some version of this yourself in any spreadsheet program. We'll discuss these more in "Appendix D- Organizational Tools" on page 337.

Imbalanced work loads are a problem that every small group ends up facing, so the better you are about consciously identifying everything that needs to get done and deciding together who will do it—plus asking for or offering help when needed—the stronger your team will be.

Day-to-Day Planning

When diving into a block of creation, it's worth taking some time to think about what's realistically possible in a day. Here I'm referring to a chunk of time dedicated exclusively to working on the show, during which you'll often be working together every day and maybe even living together depending on where your residency is. You will likely have part of the day dedicated to trying new ideas and part to training technique, but there are a lot of other elements that take time out of the day. Forgetting to include these can lead to unrealistic expectations and an unnecessary sense of rush. Joseph Pinzon (Short Round Productions) says that **it is reassuring to the artists that you have a plan, and by sharing it with them, they can help you accomplish it.**

Things to think about/ plan time for in your creation:

- Transportation time.
- Time to warm up.
- Time to shop for food, cook it, eat it and clean up.
- Short breaks/ quiet time (Unless your team is composed entirely of 100% extroverted people)
- The creation time itself! (Improvs/ experiments/ new stuff)
- Technical training time (practicing specific tricks/ disciplines)
- Group administration time (other potential contracts, emails, etc), to do during your "downtime".
- At least one emotions meeting per week

In Barcode, we have tended to use the same structure we used when creating *Sequence 8* with The 7 Fingers—improvs and creation of new stuff in the morning, technical training in the afternoons. This was not a hard-and-fast rule, and changed depending on the day or coaches and outside eyes' availability, but it was a way to divide the day that worked for us.

Costumes, Props, Scenography, Music

When working with all of the other people you will likely work with to make your show happen, not only can you not control everything, you shouldn't try to. You want to give people the vision so that you're on similar pages, but then let them surprise you.

"There's an energy that you need," says Charlie Wheeller, co-founder of Barely Methodical Troupe. "I have to be excited by the stuff I'm working with, and you want to be with people you can tell that are incredibly excited by the stuff that is in front of them, the stuff that they're going to light or costume."

When we did our first version of *Sweat & Ink* we hired our director, JP Cloutier, who, for the first draft of the show, also doubled (tripled!) as lighting, set and costume designer. He designed our set (which was fabricated at an aluminum shop to save on weight for the cargo), which we painted together in the days before our first work-in-progress showing in Philadelphia. We used music that already existed, and then while in Philadelphia we bought off-the-shelf clothing for costumes, and Cloutier worked with the local light technician to design lights. Many props we bought in a local thrift store.

After this first round of creation, we got more funding and went back into creation at Cirk La Putyka in Prague. Cloutier came with us and again helped to design the set, staying up late at night with us re-painting everything, including our props so as to make their color scheme feel cohesive throughout the show. This time however, we also hired a lighting designer (Arnaud Belley-Ferris), a musical composer (Betty Bonifassi), and a costume designer who we met locally named Kristina Záveská who worked with Cirk la Putyka. We had never worked with Kristina, but we didn't have costumes and she had made amazing stuff for Cirk la Putyka, so we went for it.

Costuming Highlight: Tristan's Dong Shirt

While in rehearsals for *Sweat & Ink* in Prague we brought Záveská into the rehearsal studio to show her some of the scenes we were working on. We could immediately tell she was excited. We explained to her that in the show Tristan's character gets hit in the head and loses his memory. We wanted the costumes to show a contrast between the "before" and "after" versions of his character.

A few days later she came in with some fabric. "I want to use this for Tristan's shirt in the beginning," she said with an impish grin. The fabric was a canvas of brightly colored crayon drawings. We leaned in closer. "Kristina," we asked, "is this a... dong?" She smiled and laughed. Indeed one of the drawings, snuck in amongst the flowers and scribbles, was a flying penis. Záveská picked up the fabric, "I love it," she said.

It was not something we would have ever picked. It was edgy. It was different. We loved it too. Tristan's dong shirt, that he wears for only the first 3 minutes of the show, feels like our little secret. Find creators you like that vibe on your project and let them surprise you. Fun fact: it turned out the fabric for Tristan's shirt was made by Vivienne Westwood, a famous clothing designer. Who knew?

Musical Composition

Lydia Bouchard (La Résistance) says when she has original music made, her job is to create strong images that will relate. "If I'm talking to the musical director, and he's like, 'Ok what do you want to do, what do you want to hear?' I have to say something, it's not just, 'Do whatever you want.' I will say, 'I want this song to sound like Elvis has French kissed Marilyn Manson in Beautiful People. Can you do that?'"

If the musical director says he doesn't see it, she'll try to think of a stronger example, something that hopefully in one sentence will put him on the right track. She says she will sometimes research 10 different songs to bring in order to make one track, explaining why a certain downbeat is interesting from one, or a crescendo from another. A big part of her job as a director is to be able to paint the pictures that are in her head in the language other people speak so they can also see that picture then use their unique skill set to create something she couldn't have imagined... but that fits.

Rehearsals for Dessa *by Creative Sovereignty. Photo by Eric Bates. Artists: Gabe Laberge, Zander Howard-Scott.*

Zander Howard-Scott (Creative Sovereignty) says that in his experience as a musical composer he has seen many things that can help the musical creation align with the director's vision- the key to all of them is to convey to the composer the emotion and what you want the scene to evoke. This could take the form of a mood board, colors, a list of adjectives, the narrative behind the story, and of course any video or live performance of the act itself. Do whatever you can "to help define what part of the sandbox you're playing in, because it's an infinite box."

Sometimes (read: almost always) you'll run into the question of budget. If someone can't make you all new music or costumes or props, etc, for the budget you have (or within the time frame you have), before looking for someone else, see if there's something they *can* do. Maybe they have existing pieces they could modify or rework to fit your concept.

That said, the difference between musical *curation* (picking out tracks) and *creation* (making all new ones) can be huge. Think of how memorable the original soundtracks to many iconic movies are. Custom music can embody the essence of what you're trying to make.

Keep in mind that when in the brainstorming phase of creation it's easy to be swept up in the dream and run into trouble when it comes to bringing your ideas to life in the real world. As Mason Ames said when talking to the people who would eventually build them a new circus apparatus/ set, "They said yes to everything in the beginning, and [then later] hardly any of it was possible." Unless you have infinite time and money it's likely that there will be compromises on the road to constructing your show from the vague blueprint in your head. If possible, give yourself some padding in your timeline and budget for these surprises.

PSYCHOLOGY

Backstage at Sweat & Ink. *Photo: Eric Bates. Artists: Alexandra Royer, Mason Ames, Eve Bigel, Eric Bates, Stefanie Fournier.*

Keeping the Team Happy

> *That night we sat on top of the circus tent and talked about quitting. It wasn't fun anymore, we didn't feel respected or valued by each other. What was the point?*

> *We had won awards at circus festivals together, performed for presidents, been on television shows. We were living the dream, and yet, it was falling apart. Our foundations weren't solid. After over eight years together, the house of Barcode was crumbling.*

It was 30 minutes until showtime and it had started to rain, but we kept talking. We reminded ourselves of our strengths together, our shared passions and values and vision of how we wanted to do circus together in a new way. That night we agreed we wanted to figure it out. We wanted to keep the band together. By the time we had to go onstage we had hugged and decided as a team to see a therapist together.

Making a show is hard. There are deadlines, budgets, creative struggles, decisions, less time for significant others and friends and yourself; and on top of all this, there's a good chance that you're going to be doing more work for less money than when working for other companies as an artist. If it's not fun, what's the point? This chapter will address conflict resolution, division of tasks and general strategies creators have employed to keep the vibe positive so you can enjoy the positive sides of bringing your dream to life.

In a creation, morale is key. You need your team to be rowing in the same direction towards the invisible island. You will need a way to deal with and resolve tension. In any creative endeavor there will be conflicts of ideas, egos, energy, ways to proceed, urgency of schedule, personalities and more. Above all, there is rarely a correct answer in a creative process. Any idea can work if the team supports it.

It is easy to build resentment and frustration if the team doesn't actively work to diffuse problems and make sure the group morale remains high. As Tristan Nielsen, co-founder of Cirque Barcode says, "It's never a waste of time to sit down and address something that's going to eliminate conflict or clarify a situation. It makes more sense to take 10, 15 minutes, an hour, to stop and clarify something than to assume it will work itself out amidst all the other craziness."

It is important to provide an outlet to resolve problems in a productive way, as well as seeking out what other stressors people might have in their life– impending deadlines for something they're working on in the project itself, family issues, relationship issues, etc. All of these can act as wedges to drive a team apart; or as opportunities to support each other and grow stronger together. First we'll get into some general principles that go a long way towards keeping a positive environment for your creation. Hopefully that will keep you from needing to use Barcode's method for conflict resolution- but we'll get into that by the end of the chapter, just in case.

Research by Frederick Herzberg in the 1960s identified the top two motivators in the workplace as recognition and achievement. Recognition is nice and it is free to give. This is something you can start practicing from the beginning—a lot of frustrations go away if people feel they are being adequately rewarded with recognition of some sort, and making a general habit of positivity will also serve the double purpose of making your team feel more comfortable together. People that feel safe are more willing to try new things and dive deeper into more vulnerable spaces in a creation, making your show richer.

The second motivator, achievement (or a sense of progress), is best used or understood when made visible, i.e. when it is measured. If people don't know if they're succeeding or improving, how will they know if their efforts amount to anything? Figuring out a way to track your results can paint an honest picture of where your team is at, absent any rationalizations or excuses. This is easier to apply to many of the logistical steps involved in making a show such as space booked, phone calls made, or technical tricks achieved etc. It's harder to track creative progress. What to do?

Celebrate small successes, since you'll always have more obstacles to look forward to. Even if you spent an hour trying things that didn't work, that's an hour you would have had to go through sometime on your way to finding the things that do work. If you can say "Hey, in that hour we found that one little moment today," that's a success that you can build on.

Acknowledge Warning Signs

Take a break if you hear the rumblings start... don't wait for them to get loud. We have sat down in the middle of a Russian bar rehearsal to talk when needed, rather than try to push through while we're at each other's throats. Circus is a big mental game—a lot of it is about trust, both physically and mentally. The foundations have to be solid. Trust is what allows you to take the creative risks that will make your creation special. It's also one of the key ingredients in performances that audiences want to see!

When you can feel the group energy getting low and the frustrations starting it is better to acknowledge the tension and break early for a snack or lunch rather than to try to battle through it for the extra ten to twenty minutes. Sometimes all that is needed is an early lunch, other times you might need to address conflict head on, before it builds into resentment and retaliation.

Talk to Each Other

"We have so many good communication tools, but it's like we don't use them," says Claude Tremblay, project manager for Moment Factory and former project manager for Cirque Eloize. "Sometimes you need to make things happen. You need to hold people by the hand and tell them to talk to each other."

She says that as a project manager it's important for her to try to understand everyone's roles and their challenges on the team. Maybe the tech crew is always grumpy, but why are they grumpy? They're on all fours, crawling around in dusty places all day. They've got a hard job. Artists can be picky, but it's because they're often putting their lives at risk, and even if they're not, it's them onstage and they don't want to look like a fool in front of people. For those two reasons alone, and many more, it stands to reason that they might be picky about their costumes, the lights, the rig. The better you can try to understand everyone's concerns the better you can manage all of this. "If you understand the other you will respect the other," says Tremblay, "and you will try to find solutions to help them, and they will be more open to your position."

We were having a horrible time in the early days of *Sweat & Ink* because the light designer that had designed our show had made it on a light board often used in music or stadium shows, not a little circus show. Few of the light operators we worked with were familiar with the board. Just getting to a 'work light' cue could be five menus deep! This resulted in a lot of frustration on the part of the artists because the lights were inconsistent, and frustration from the techs because they were battling against the unfamiliar and often buggy technology with no time to do anything about it. We kept asking them what they needed, and eventually found a theater where we negotiated extra time before the premiere to rehearse and migrate the show to a more familiar light board. It took an extra week of rehearsals, but the consistency of the show and the mood on tour improved immensely. On top of that, we had a number of injuries on that tour which resulted in a lot of fast adaptations that the techs were able to handle gracefully—something that would have been impossible on the original board. **Keep asking to understand the challenges your team is facing and what they need so you can help them solve their problems and improve the situation for everyone.**

Unifying the Vision: Jan Rok's Questions

When The 7 Fingers were first starting they sat down with the late Jan Rok Achard, co-founder of En Piste, the Tohu and former director of ENC, and he asked them guiding questions to help clarify their vision and goals. They were not necessarily complicated, and in fact were often intentionally redundant:

Questions like "Where do you see yourself in five years?" or "If you could have another life…" can tap into desired goals and lifestyles from different angles.

What worked well for The 7 Fingers was when everyone took the time to write out their answers separately instead of talking it out in front of each other. "There's a certain freedom and honesty you have when you're at home writing an answer to a question," says Shana Carroll. "You don't necessarily feel that same freedom and honesty when you're face to face with someone."

Jan Rok would then pull out certain themes and write them on a white board. This allowed them to see themes they shared, but also conflicts in their interests, either between the members or within their own collectively stated goals. In one case, the amount of money they were interested in making in five years conflicted with their wanting to do volunteer work in South America. "You want to make this much money," Jan Rok pointed out, "but you want to do shows for free." The exercise helped reveal things that were contradictory in their vision and thinking.

Getting a team on the same page is not a one-time exercise, it is an ongoing work you will have to continue to do to ensure everyone is happy and motivated throughout your time working together. This might not be your favorite or easiest work, but it can allow you to do things you could never do alone. As

The Thing-In-Itself *by The Chita Project. Photo by Eric Bates. Artists: Anna Kichtchenko, Pablo Pramparo* the motto of the French circus company XY goes, "Alone you can go faster, but together we can go farther."

Emotions Meetings

The act of collectively deciding to work on a relationship is a big step. It's already a signal of openness, and of acknowledgement that the dynamic needs work.

After our episode on top of the tent, Barcode went to the therapist as a group, individually, in pairs and as a group again. It was expensive. It was difficult. But it was a start. Already after one meeting we could feel a difference in the vibe. We had a place to talk about the hard stuff, a lot of which we had ignored in order to get through whatever current gig we were on at the time. And the next one. And the next one. We also had a place to talk about the good things, the positive sides of our relationships that were getting suppressed under layers of resentment and frustration.

When we finished that contract a few weeks later, we left with a plan. We called them, self-consciously and for lack of a better term, "Emotions Meetings".

Emotions meetings. Temperature-taking. Check-ins. Shit talks. Different groups call them different things, but the principle is the same: you need to establish a consistent way for your team to talk about the hard stuff, the problems, the slights, the bullshit; those angry embers that will bloom into massive fires if left unaddressed.

Since that contract, we have held regular emotions meetings. These meetings are a chance to discuss uniquely interpersonal or emotional issues between team members, without getting bogged down in everything else we have to do as a company. Just team morale. The goal is to celebrate the good things the team is doing, and to address the small sparks before they grow into wildfires that will burn our team down.

"What makes those conflicts and interpersonal relationships way worse is if they're not talked about but everyone knows about them and they're all in the background. They're really a poison that then goes out in the group and can really damage relationships," says Lewie West (Gravity & Other Myths).

These meetings need to be regular (we do them weekly when we're on a contract together), and they need to take place in a constructive environment where you're committed to working through it as a team and where it's clear that while you might say some difficult stuff, you're on the same team, rowing in the same direction in order to work through it and make the team stronger.

It's not always easy. In fact, it's rarely easy. But we're there for that, to talk about each moment where we might have hurt or have been hurt by someone accidentally, in a space where we are working together to improve and move forwards.

Example: There was a terse interaction the previous week, enough for us to agree it was worth bringing up. I needed documents for a grant I was working on, and thought Alex might have them. I find her with headphones in, doing aerial hoop in the theater late at night. "Alex! Do you have that USB key?" She either ignores me or doesn't hear me, who knows? "Alex!" I'm frustrated, I think she's ignoring me. When I finally get her attention, she snaps at me! "What!?" Tense interaction ensues. I don't get the drive, Alex feels like she's out of her flow state. In the emotions meeting later, Alex or I bring up the interaction, and say we didn't like the tone of how that went. Both of us felt like the other person was being rude. Through talking about it, we learned that I was under due-date stress to finish a grant and felt like I was doing it alone (but hadn't asked anyone for help, so how would they know?). Alex felt like I was interrupting a delicate creative zone she had finally gotten into after a week of feeling creatively empty (but hadn't asked for private creation time in the theater that we were all living in, so I didn't think to not interrupt). In the end, I learned to ask for help with the grant, other people learned to check in with each other when someone seems tense to see if they can help, and Alex learned to ask for private space if she needs it to rehearse. I also learned to practice a little more patience and awareness when approaching others that look occupied.

The benefit of emotions meetings is twofold. One: the fires don't get bigger, they get dealt with. We get to "clear the slate" every week. Two: you learn to know your team better, and can be more respectful and attentive to how they interpret your words and actions in the future, and vice versa. This, hopefully, will lead to fewer conflicts and a stronger team.

Another benefit of emotions meetings for me was to see just how much everyone else was doing so I could better appreciate and help them. Appreciation is a valuable currency in the world of the new company, where everyone is hustling hard, and constantly feeling like they aren't doing everything that needs to be done. Congratulating people for the tough choices they are making in the face of uncertainty can be extremely validating and encouraging.

In conclusion, have emotions meetings regularly and try to make peace with everyone's various skills, strengths and weaknesses—it's a lot more enjoyable than trying to make everyone help in the way you think they should help.

The process: how to run an emotions meeting

The first principle of running an emotions meeting is that everyone has to come to the table hoping to make it work. This means not just coming with grievances, but being ready to acknowledge that there will likely be ways that you, yourself, can improve the team dynamic by changing your own behavior. In the beginning it might be worth seeing a professional (or at least a neutral third party) as a team to bring everyone to this point. We were certainly not ready before we saw a therapist together.

So, you sit down together with good intentions, then what?

Step one, you take turns talking about the past week. For Barcode this tends to start with a mix of acknowledging good things and occasionally apologizing for moments of hot temper throughout the week. Each person talks alone with everyone else listening. It's not a conversation, it's a moment to reflect on the week, say how you're feeling and what sort of emotional baggage you're bringing to the process that day. This helps the rest of the group be more patient, understanding and aware of other issues in your life that might be detracting from your performance as a team member, and instead of writing it off as you being "lazy" or "unmotivated" or "difficult", everyone can support each other when they need it.

It's also a nice chance to acknowledge the work other people have been doing, since often we're so busy with our own challenges we might be tempted to think we're the only ones working hard.

Nathan Biggs-Penton explains that in their "Check-ins" (Acting for Climate's version of an Emotions Meeting), it's about, "having safe spaces related to non-violent communication and awareness, and also the idea to be able listen to something that someone needs to share and not feeling like you have to fix it for them."

Step two of the emotions meeting is talking about problems. When we were with the therapist, he would often crack open the first two minutes of the conversation with, "So, what's the problem?" It's easy to beat around the bush, especially when you've spent years 'successfully' working together by avoiding direct confrontation in favor of passive aggression interactions, but eventually you're going to have to talk about what's going on, and listen. Usually after everyone has said their piece, if no one has brought up any conflicts, we will sit around awkwardly for a second, no one wanting to throw the first stone, until one of us gives a little prod. "So... any issues this week?" (Pregnant pause) "...Eric...?...Eve...?" Then we get into the tough stuff, or even tiny little annoyances, and begin to work through it.

One of our therapist's rules for a successful emotions meeting was that everyone needs to talk for the same amount of time. This is because some people will be more reluctant to talk, and some more eager, and the danger is that it will unbalance the conversation towards these natural tendencies and possibly exacerbate problems that might have come from these tendencies in the first place.

If you're doing these meetings weekly, these issues tend to (hopefully) get smaller as you go. By fighting the big, deep ground fires first, over the weeks (hopefully) you'll be left with just little flames to stomp out here and there that crop up in the ordinary tensions and uncertainties of creation. The goal is to be able to bring up "stupid little things" and resolve them before they grow into something bigger; this allows you to start the next week fresh without any feelings of bitterness or resentment.

Check-ins

As mentioned, Acting for Climate has a similar process to emotions meeting, what they call "check-ins." They are similar in that everyone takes turns around the circle talking (if they want) without interruption. When each person is done talking they will say so, because sometimes people need a minute to translate how they're feeling into words, and this doesn't mean they're finished.

"If ever something really touches you, or bothers you in something that someone has said, you can ask for permission to make a comment or ask a question about something they've said," Biggs-Penton explains. Maybe they will be happy to expand on it, but maybe they would prefer to talk about it later in private, or maybe they'd prefer not to expand on it. All of those are viable options. The practice is in taking the time to listen to each person without adding or commenting, giving respect, and restraining yourself from having parasitic comments or noises throughout the exercise.

When everyone is on the same page and feels at ease with the group, the work will be more fruitful. It takes time, but Biggs-Penton argues that that time is worth it if it means you can work in a more positive environment where people better understand each other. If a check-in takes two hours (without unnecessary comments that slow it down), that's because it needed to take two hours. Sometimes Acting for Climate will do a check-in with ten people and the whole thing only takes five minutes.

"That's part of the check in process," says Biggs-Penton. "To learn how to be concise with your own needs. What is the thing that I need to share with the group right now, what is important for them to know, what is important for me to say to feel at ease within myself?"

Using some sort of tool regularly such as a check-in or an emotions meeting allows your team to practice being able to auto-evaluate where they are in the day. It takes practice to be able to do well- to be able to articulate what's going on in your internal state so others can understand, to develop the confidence to say the things you want to say even if they're uncomfortable, and to develop the respect to be able to listen to others with the goal of understanding them.

Working With Your Life Partner

These tips and tools about appreciation and attitude are all the more important if you're working with your domestic partner, Brent McCoy (Vermont Vaudeville) says, because at the end of the show you're going to go home to be with that person without all the pressure of the creation. "But the decisions you made to be an asshole during the production, those haunt you."

In a creation you will end up spending so much time together working through problems and uncertainty, maybe even more so than you usually do at home when you are on separate projects. Creativity, finances, personal taste, work habits, time management, priorities—all of it will be called into question in a creation. Many of the same tools previously suggested for getting along with the rest of your team still apply in partnerships—regular check-ins, clear roles, respectful communication, etc—but perhaps even more so since you will have yet another level of relationship to balance on top of your working relationship.

Things to talk about with your partner before starting a creation together might include establishing boundaries, how you want to interact with each other during creation, and how to not play favorites (giving unfair preference to your partner's ideas or input) if there are other cast members involved. It's also worth discussing how you will protect your

The Thing-In-Itself *by The Chita Project. Photo by Eric Bates. Artists: Anna Kichtchenko, Pablo Pramparo*

romantic and non-work relationship, since it's easy to continue discussions from the creation studio when you get home at night and end up totally engulfed in your project for every waking moment of your day.

Working together can be made easier if you have complementary skills. If one person prefers to work on set design while the other enjoys rigging acrobatic equipment (for example), this can naturally reduce potential conflicts. These sorts of roles clarify who will naturally defer to who depending on what you're talking about. For example, in my own relationship my partner is a dancer, so between the two of us she will often edit music if we're collaborating since I know she has a better ear for it. On film projects she likes to do pre-production while I like to think about technical camera details, and we enjoy brainstorming together and testing each other's ideas in a positive, non-competitive way. Being able to clearly express what you *enjoy* doing and what you need from your partner (as opposed to what you think they should do) are some of the key tools listed in the book "Nonviolent Communication."

One of the main differences when working with your life partner is that you don't get a break from them. That person is always there, in the room, in the car, in the apartment. Ensuring *voluntary* time apart to enjoy your own hobbies, friends, etc can be a good way to preempt the need to push the other person away in order to get this space. Talking with other people about your project can also be a good way to get much needed outside perspectives on issues you're struggling with.

Just as you might need to schedule time for yourself apart from your partner, making sure you also have time during the day to enjoy your relationship together apart from your work is also important. Set aside part of your day to discuss other things than work. Digitally, my partner and I also try to keep work and projects confined to emails or other digital communication tools apart from the one we tend to have personal conversations on.

Gypsy Snider (The 7 Fingers) says a technique that helps her, regardless of who she is working with, is to understand that between yourself, your collaborator, and your work, you've created a triangle. The actual art itself is on a point that is independent from you or your other collaborators. This introduces the idea of multiple perspectives on the art, which may help take your ego out of it.

Fun Matters

All of the advice in this chapter is designed to help get your team to be in a good place together and to trust each other. The goal of this is twofold: to make the process more enjoyable, yes, but also because trust and comfort with your teammates is vital to finding better material. Fun is essential because if you're afraid to look stupid because you think your partners will judge you, you'll take less risks and miss out on all the beautiful opportunities 'looking stupid' can afford you. A lot of what's funny is stupid. Things that have never been done before often sound stupid at first. Stupid can be good.

To clarify, "fun" can also mean a lot of things to a lot of people. One person might think it's a blast to do backflips until you collapse, another might want to do contact improv for hours on end in silence. Another might love the rush of getting emotionally worked up and screaming at each other while hanging from a trapeze. We all have different things we enjoy, so do your best to humor your partners' tastes, even if they're different from yours. Mason Ames says, "Finding the pleasure in sucking is a useful skill to acquire. Be able to laugh at yourself and go, 'Oh boy, it's not going well today.'"

Shana Carroll describes their creation of The 7 Fingers' first show *Loft* as a painful creation process that resulted in a cool collage of their ideas that was generally heralded as a very successful show. "Fun, but difficult fun," she admitted. For their second show, *La Vie*, they knew each other better and were more on the same page artistically, which they felt allowed them to take risks with a really cohesive vision. This show however, she says was "rough in the beginning."

Carroll's conclusion was that there are no rules about how much fun one should be having. A fun creation process, or lack thereof, won't guarantee a successful show. I feel confident saying, however, that if your creations are consistently *not* fun you will be unlikely to stick with it for very long.

KEY TAKEAWAYS:

• It's worth taking time to resolve conflicts rather than trying to ignore them.

• A formal process such as an emotions meeting or check-in can be a helpful tool.

• Creating new material together can be vulnerable, and circus requires trust, both physical and emotional. Your creation will be stronger if people feel comfortable around each other.

SECTION 5:
TOURING

SUSTAINABLE TOURING

"Wait... everything here would have been thrown in the trash?"
I looked around Écoscéno's warehouse. All around me, stacked to the high ceilings
on beefy metal shelves were decorative chairs of every sort, bolts of fabric, wood,
paintings, masks, fake rocks, trunks, candlesticks...
"Look at this!" Dom said, gesturing to a massive platform. It was a full size
pneumatic stage that could raise up and down, used in the Just for Laughs festival.
"Forty thousand dollars! They used it for two weeks, then it would have gone in the
dumpster if we hadn't saved it."

Filming Branché. *Photo by Valentin Belleville. Artists: Agathe Bisserier, Heidi Blais, Adrien*
Malette-Chénier, Anna Soltys Morse, Anne-Marie Godin, Clara Scudder-Davis, Eric Bates,
Nathan Biggs-Penton, Samuelle McGowan-Richer, Sorrell Nielsen, Tristan Nielsen.

Barcode's second show *Branché* (made in collaboration with Acting for Climate, an acrobatic show that takes place in forests and parks), we were inspired by the question: "What would Sustainable Circus look like?"

Traditionally, touring a show takes a lot of resources, our first show *Sweat & Ink* included. Planes, shipping the cargo, hotels, costumes, set construction, lights, etc. A lot of the environmental impact your show will have over its lifetime will be baked into the process during its conception. If you consider this from the beginning, you might be able to significantly reduce your impact.

As we've seen, creating restrictions for yourself can also unlock a lot of creativity and may help you make something different from what's been seen before in the "traditional" model of touring.

If you are interested in making a more sustainable show, it's worth thinking about a few things. The first is what you're going to say and do onstage— while you could make a show about anything, it might be interesting to you to have at least a part of your show about the climate crisis: there are so many possible stories, angles, and perspectives on this topic, and it will only continue to get more relevant. It's a vast and varied subject that can lend itself to interpretation via the abstract language of circus. You could focus on the feelings of frustration and helplessness at being powerless within a big system rumbling towards its own destruction, or on the energy transition, or on how various social inequalities might be preventing us from tackling the big problem of climate change, or how it affects different people differently around the world.

But there are other things than climate change (important things!) you could also make a show about that you might be excited about, and have every right to. It's your show! So while there may be plenty of interesting stories to tell involving the climate crisis, there are also many interesting stories to tell about other subjects. The good news is if you're not interested in addressing sustainability in the content for your show, you can still focus on your behind-the-scenes decisions—where your props, costume and scenography come from, and how you plan on touring your show. Let's focus on these.

There are many factors to consider, but a good place to start would be talking to a place that recycles scenography and/or costumes during your conception phase, or looking in second-hand shops or vintage and thrift stores for costumes. You can then alter these props and costumes to suit your needs.

The next, and frankly, the more complicated issue, is figuring out how to tour a show with less impact. Here are some examples: Nowadays, when we play *Sweat & Ink* in Europe, we only take trains to travel (although we still take planes to get there from North America). Barcode has performed a show on a sailboat off the coast of France with Elemen'terre, which you would think would be inherently zero impact- but if the wind wasn't blowing it forced us to decide whether arriving for the scheduled performance time was worth using the diesel motor. The company Marguerite a Bicyclette created *Cirqu'Avélo*, a show that tours Quebec by electric bicycle. Our street show, *See You Down the Road*, traveled by van around Europe, which one day we hope to replace with an electric van. Our show *Branché* was designed to have no set, no lights and no props (and therefore no cargo); we used reused fabric for costumes, and traveled only by ground transportation. All of these things tend to be easier in Europe where arts and infrastructure are seen as priorities, the cities are close together, and there are lots of festivals and a good train system. "Not taking planes" hardly even counts as a gesture there, it's just the norm. Your effort might look different depending on where you live and the communities you plan to play in.

When creating *Branché*, one challenge we faced was figuring out how to sell the show. Shows are traditionally hired by a theater, which then in turn sells tickets to the public. The theater is responsible for advertising and promotion. Generally, theaters are the liaison between audiences and performance companies—they have access to local crowds to advertise and promote the show. But not all theaters have access to a private yet accessible outdoor space. This meant Barcode's agent at the time, who was used to selling the show to theaters around the world, wasn't the right person for the job—he wasn't interested in trying to rethink the model he knew well. There were also practical and legal issues such as insurance (trees on public land such as city parks tend to have a lot of red tape around them, even if it is for good reasons). We had lots of interest in Europe, but we had decided not to take airplanes to perform the show. If we wanted to make a second cast in Europe, how would that work to hire Europeans as a Montréal-based company? Would that effort be worth the trade-off compared to just flying our cast over for one season? Was it better to not take planes or to not perform the show (which could result in our performers taking other work, some of which might involve taking planes)? Also, how could theaters ticket outdoor shows? Many of the *Branché* performances have been free of charge, performed at festivals where the performance was open to the public—which is great, as the show was made with the support of public money—but a business model centered around free tickets is unappealing to many theaters for obvious reasons. There were few easy answers when dealing with such a complex problem as climate change, and we spent a lot of time in discussions about what our principles were, what we could compromise on to get the ball rolling, and how we could continue to improve our practices.

Slowly but surely we started to figure these things out—writing to lots of people, attending lots of pitch sessions, doing research to see who hosted outdoor shows within driving distance of Montréal, and trying however we could to make ourselves visible so that the places that *Branché* would be well suited for could find us. We also made adaptations—we performed the show in a hotel, and in downtown Montréal in a section of town where there were no trees. The show suffered in the short term for it, but it kept teaching us about the show and kept us working to improve it.

I've been told that when you play in the U.S. theaters and audiences are eager that the products and shows they support stand for something. Yes, you need an impressive and entertaining show, but people also want to know they're supporting a good cause by buying a ticket to your show. One producer mentioned that it was almost mandatory to have some sort of accompanying workshop when you tried to sell in the US. I don't know whether this is entirely true, but as a consumer myself I can relate—we have so many ways to spend our time and money these days, if I have to choose between similar products or experiences I prefer to choose the one that will make me feel the best about myself whether it's because it supports a good cause or because I've heard the best things about it and I like the story behind it. It's also possible that the workshop angle is a way for them to split the show's fee between multiple departments.

My last point is this: Audiences and theaters are always looking for something they haven't seen before. Think *Sleep No More* with the audience all wearing masks and wandering around the space as the performers surround them, or *Fuerza Bruta*, the energetic and immersive dance show in which the audience is standing and the performers play amongst them and above them. I saw a show made for an audience of 15 people in the back of a box truck once that I still think about to this day. Trying to do things in a new way in order to talk about new challenges and issues we face can lead to some really cool art.

On Working with New Team Members

Since Cirque Barcode often works with other companies on projects we noticed a few things that consistently made us feel comfortable, which we try to employ when we hire people for our own projects.

Make People Feel Welcome and Ask Them What They Need

A personalized version of, "Hey, so good to have you here, thanks for joining us on this project!" goes a long way. The next thing that helps is asking them what they need. Maybe they just got off a plane and want to sleep rather than go out to an elaborate dinner. Or maybe they're worried about getting fuel for their torches, or food for their dog. Maybe they're excited to start but need to know where to hang their coat. Taking a moment to ask what they need shows that you value their needs and clears the deck so you can start on the right foot.

Clarify Expectations and Ask if it Works/ is Realistic

If you have expectations for your project it's good to get those out in the open (Example: "We want to have a first draft ready in three weeks because we have media coming. We would love that it includes at least some Russian bar in it for the cameras."). When we were on board the Pen Duick VI sailboat with Elemen'terre we were given carte blanche to make a new short show on a different environmental theme every weekend. Were there any expectations, we wanted to know, for what we made in terms of duration, circus content, etc? Or was it truly carte blanche and they would be equally happy if we ran around naked for 5 hours or if we did a 5 minute Russian bar act?

Expectations might also include duties like cooking or cleaning up, or how timely the start of the day tends to be. "We'll all gather and drink coffee together at 9am" is quite different from "Be warm and ready to run at 9am."

Also, if there is a clear hierarchy it's good to know early: "This is our director," or "We're going to be working together to create this thing, and will make decisions by voting if we have disagreements."

Lay Out Long Term Plans, Set Short Term Goals/ Checkpoints

Language around checkpoints sounds something like, "Here's the big picture, here's what we're going to work on now."

A rough timeline or way of working gets people on the same page right away and can quickly address concerns you may not have predicted. Setting expectations for your own team can be helpful for the whole production. Here are a few examples: "We will need time to warm up before doing a full run of the show" or "We can't do circus right off of two days on a sailboat... our balance is all off." Yes, you might have sent this by email before the project started, but it's good to touch base in person on this sort of thing again anyways.

Establish a "check-in" or "emotions meeting" on day one, so it's easy to do check-ins regularly/ if needed. Set these up before any conflicts arise so you can get ahead of any potential sources of trouble.

Beyond that, for a successful long-term relationship, Emilie Fournier says at Machine de Cirque it's important for people to keep growing with the company. If artists get bored they tend to leave, so it's important to keep challenging people and giving them responsibility so they feel involved.

Finally, you might find yourself working with incredibly talented people that do nothing but paralyze the process. Just like in emotions meetings with your own team, you need to address it head on, but since they're not part of the core team and don't have the same level of decision-making power in the company or creation, sometimes other techniques can be called for (although a check-in or emotions meeting can also be good to get stuff on the table). Shana Carroll (The 7 Fingers) says she has taken artists out for coffee and basically explained that 'not every show you do has to represent every corner of your soul', and it can be a good challenge to try to help fulfill what the show needs (from the perspective of the director). "That's a way of seeing the plus sides of being an [actor], to maybe get out of your comfort zones and try new things."

LOGISTICAL CONCERNS

Sweat & Ink *Set up. Photo by Eric Bates. Sound Tech: Steve Marsh.*

There are many things you won't necessarily think about if you haven't been a technical director for a show. They're not the fun, sexy, creative decisions that probably drew you to making a show in the first place, but they are worth thinking about as you start your creation process, because they can affect how easy it is for you to tour down the line.

In general, the lighter and easier your show is to set up and transport, the easier it will be to book, but there's a compromise to be found in terms of production value (i.e., how good your stage looks once it's set up). Moving-head lights and a big set might open up some interesting opportunities for creativity, but the extra expense, weight and road cases might not make any sense at all. There are also creative solutions to be found. For example, the Australian company Circa contractually requires all of their artists to carry a certain weight of rigging in their personal touring suitcases in order to save on transportation costs. It might be inconvenient for the artists, but it might also allow more money to end up back in their pockets and the company's pockets instead of going to transportation companies.

Who can help you navigate all this when you're brainstorming your show? A producer will generally have experience with this sort of thing, or you can hire a technical director to consult during the creation of the set. Ideally, these people will work in collaboration with the people that will actually be touring to make sure everyone is on the same page once you're on the road.

While "logistical concerns" could include many things such as tour planning, specialized requirements for lights, marketing abroad, projectors, etc, this chapter will focus primarily on two of the main issues I encountered with *Sweat & Ink*: the use of spoken language in your show and cargo.

Language

Every theater, producer or agent you come across will ask you if there is spoken word in your show, and how you plan on dealing with it if you're not performing in your native language.

Options we have used include:

- Artists learn the whole show in another language. This will likely affect the quality of the show, plus it's a lot of work if you have a lot of text. This is what we did for *Sequence 8* with The 7 Fingers.

- Subtitles or supertitles with translations in the local language projected above or below stage. This will involve translating the whole show, and the audience will have to read during the talking scenes, but you can do it ahead of time based on the countries you're going to. *Undermän* from Cirkus Cirkor used this technique, and it has been a staple of opera shows for decades.

- Change the speaking scenes somehow in the new countries, for example, by figuring out a version without talking.

- Play in your original language and translate key words or phrases here and there. This might mean playing 90% of your show in English, and 10% in French/ German/ Spanish/ whatever the local language is. This can be fun if you throw in a fun local bit of trivia or slang, and if it's a country that generally speaks the onstage language as their second language proficiently they might be able to follow along well enough. When we use this method with Cirque Barcode we will ask people around the theater for local trivia or slang we can include as a joke- a local dish or well known celebrity that we could reference in the local language, for example. The plus side of playing mostly in your native tongue is that your acting, pacing and emotion will be able to shine. Sometimes this is more important than what is actually said, but beware: the drawback is that the audience might feel like they missed something if they don't understand your native language, whether or not what was said was actually important. Cirque le Roux used this method in their first show *The Elephant in the Room*, but worked hard to keep whatever was said to simple words or sentences, often repeated, that were more easily understood by international audiences. "Ridiculous!"

Language, speaking, and audio also bring their fair share of logistical concerns. How you will mic or amplify your artists if they need to be heard? The audience will feel frustrated if they can't hear what is being said, whether or not what is being said is important. Generally, this will be the job of your sound technician to help figure out... but because circus includes acrobatics, you might have to get creative.

Audio Solutions

- Hanging mics, shotgun mics and floor mics. They work, but can be medium effective and can interfere with aerial acrobatics. In our show *Sweat & Ink*, we use shotgun mics on the sides of the stage directed at two of the locations where we speak that are close to the wings.
- Pack/lav mics (hands free mics). These can be difficult to put on quickly and difficult to do circus safely with. In *Sweat & Ink*, we hide a lav mic in one of the props onstage (the cactus mic!) that a character is holding, and point the cactus mic at the person speaking. Broadway productions often employ a lav mic hidden in a wig.
- Handheld mics. These might be the easiest to use logistically and guarantee good audio, as they only require figuring out the traffic of where the mic goes if it is needed again. Most theaters have at least two stick mics. Their presence will feel more 'formal' than hidden mics, however. We use two handheld mics in *Sweat & Ink*, one handheld and the other sat in a mic stand placed on a desk where a character is speaking.

Cargo & Set

How elaborate should your set be? This is a tricky balance between what you want to accomplish with your show artistically vs. how difficult and expensive it is to tour it. This is where you'll need to have a serious think about artistic vision and the feasibility of touring your show. The good news is there is no "correct" size cargo—both minimalistic shows and elaborate sets can work.

"What makes your show different?" says Chris Lashua (Cirque Mechanics). "Our shows look different because we have this big honking thing on stage. Does that make life more difficult? Absolutely. But in some ways it's our hook now. What started off as being a real Achilles heel turned out to be our thing."

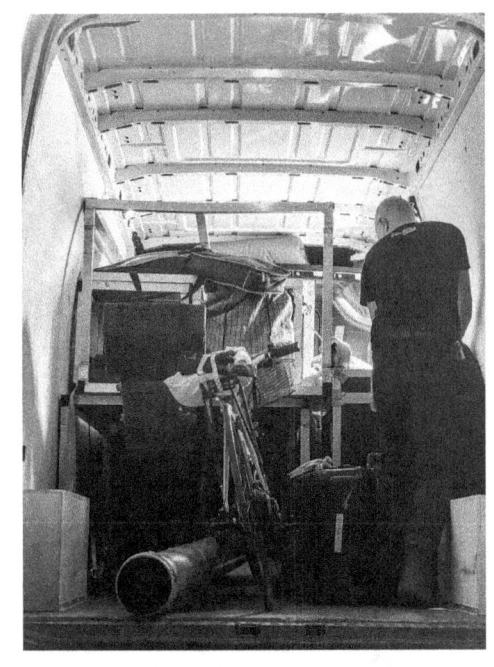

Sweat & Ink *Load Out. Photo by Eric Bates.*
Technical Director: Vladimir Cara

"It has to do with who you are. It's your identity. On one level I would say don't bring anything, because then you can fly everybody [without needing to drive the set]. But if you can fly everybody and if you can unpack and inflate your set, then you're likely going to be competing against a lot of companies that are trying to do the same thing."

Let's get further into some considerations to keep in mind when building your set.

Having a set means lots of logistics such as getting the set from place to place, storing it when not in use, making a Carnet ATA (a 'merchandise passport' used for temporary importation of goods into foreign countries that lists every single item being shipped), and negotiating with cargo companies, etc. All of this can be accomplished by someone on your team or someone you hire, but when you're designing the final version of your set, having a technical director be part of the conversation will save you trouble down the line.

(Left) Drawings in Sketchup by Cirque Mechanics. Machine designers: Sean Riley and Chris Lashua.

(Above) Hair hanging and wheel of death performed on the apparatus in Zephyr. *Photo credit: Paris Photographics. Wheel of death artist: Ossy Sanchez. Hair hang artist: Erika Radcliffe.*

Having a set also means you should consider the set up and takedown time of your show. Your chances of playing will be higher if you're able to load in the show in the morning and play in the evening, but that's also a lot of work between set up (when you install the set and lights onstage), light check (tech rehearsal in each new theater when the light technician walks through the light cues with one or more members of the cast to clarify positions and ensure safe lighting conditions for acrobatics), warming up and playing the show, and taking it down after. Some American fringe festivals even have policies that specify how much time you have to set up and take down your show since there are so many shows booked in the same theater on the same day.

We tried to get around the issues that come with a big set in *Sweat & Ink* by relying more heavily on lighting to shape the space rather than an enormous decor; by using a projector to make clean and varied images on the stage, but this led to its own set of headaches when we found out many theaters didn't have a projector strong enough to deliver on the original vision. Although our technical rider specified a certain strength projector, some of the theaters' bulbs were too old to deliver, and the quality of our show suffered. We could have bought our own projector, but that would have been more money that we didn't have in the beginning—and didn't know we would need until we discovered theaters weren't always meeting our specifications. Although our projector's requirements were specified in our contract, they weren't always met, which put us in the tough position of trying to make do with what they had—it wasn't like we would pursue legal action, or not play the show after all the effort to get there. Those options would have burnt too many bridges and didn't seem worth the trouble. Best practice: make it as easy as possible for theaters to meet your needs!

When sending a cargo shipment by boat, shipping containers are standardized sizes, with prices based on how much of them you fill, and weight. Since this transportation cost is usually covered by the theater, it can affect whether theaters are able to hire your show, or how much of their budget will go to transportation rather than to your company.

Where will you store your cargo if you're playing away from home? Ideally you will have a consolidated tour on the same continent, if not, you will have to balance the cost of storing your cargo somewhere and making a second cargo for the other continent against shipping it back and forth. Shipping it also requires its own Carnet ATA, which comes with its own set of logistics and costs.

It is likely that as you move from creation and discovering what your show is to thinking more about how to tour it that you will have to retool some of your original ideas to meet the restrictions of touring. This is normal! Redoing lighting, redesigning the first draft of your set, reworking scenes once they see an audience—a show is constantly evolving and will only grow from each new iteration. Think of these challenges as opportunities to continue improving the show.

See You Down the Road *by Cirque Barcode. Photographer: Nikola Milatovic.*
Artists: Tristan Nielsen, Mathilde Jimenez

SELLING AND PITCHING

As you begin to have a more concrete idea of what your show is, you're going to want to start the process of getting it booked. This has to happen ahead of time, as theaters can book as far as a year in advance (or more!). Let's break the process of promoting your show into two categories: *selling* (less formal, or on more of an individual basis) and *pitching* (making a presentation at some form of event with an audience).

Elevator Pitches

You'll get better at these the more times you do them as you see what elements people react to. In the beginning our *Branché* elevator pitch sounded like: "*Branché* is an acrobatic circus show that takes place in forests and doesn't use props and doesn't tour by airplane." That didn't hook people very well. They were still like, "So what is it? What does it look like? What happens? Climate crisis, is it going to be didactic and depressing?" As we came to understand our project better, we started to realize the parts that were more interesting to people, and dropped the parts that weren't- even though the project didn't change. Now we say something more like: "*Branché* is an acrobatic circus show that takes place in forest and parks and addresses the climate crisis in an uplifting way by getting the audience out into nature in a way that's tailor made for their own backyard. The audience walks into the woods, and you get that feeling of the lights coming down in the theater. We bring the audience to three different locations in the woods, with mini scenes popping up next to the trail along the way that continue the story. We have scenes like 'reeds in the wind' inspired by nature, but also scenes like 'shrinking space' where we pile more and more people onto a big boulder that reflects how we're running out of resources in the world as the population grows. At the end we see kids running around, imitating moments from the show, and it makes you think, if they're imitating the acrobatics—maybe they'll also imitate how the artists supported and took care of each other and nature."

Selling

The concept of selling your show might sound uncomfortable, but really it's just talking about your project with interested people, and giving them a way to take further steps if it aligns with their interests. Many people are uncomfortable selling themselves. It can feel egotistical. Who are you to think you're so great that you go around telling people about it? In order to sell yourself successfully, you need to change your perspective.

One advantage of having a show or a company is that it allows you detach yourself from the product, and talk about it as something separate from yourself. "*This show* is something that is great that I believe in," is a lot easier to say with genuine enthusiasm when it's not just *yourself* that you're talking about. In the book *Start With Why* by Simon Sinek, Sinek writes, "People

don't buy what you do. They buy WHY you do it." Why are you making this show? Why is it important to you? You can focus on these reasons when you tell people about your show. You probably made a show to address a concern or enthusiasm you have, and this is a great place to start the story of why your show is so important.

Interviews. Photo by Stefanie Fournier.
Artist: Eric Bates.

What you do serves as the proof of what you believe. Rather than telling everyone how great your show or company is, it might even be a better strategy not to, but instead to talk about why you decided to make that show in the first place. What were you trying to accomplish? What is so important to you that drove you to put all this effort in? Tell them why your show or your company reflects that.

"The company really helped us to be proud of our ideas," says Charlie Wheeller of Barely Methodical Troupe. "It's so wonderful to be able to talk about the company, and distance myself from it, but still feel really warm when I'm talking about it. That's useful as an artist, to be able to speak so complimentarily about something you're involved in, but you can also slightly step away."

Once you've found a way to feel comfortable selling your show, "You still gotta put in your hours," says Chris Lashua (Cirque Mechanics). "It's like with any skill, you gotta put in the time." That will mean a lot of banging on doors, sending out emails, attending conferences, continuing to check in with presenters, then banging on more doors.

Selling yourself as an introvert

If you're like me, you don't necessarily like talking to people all the time. Especially new people. Maybe for a bit, in inspired bursts, but then you need to recover. In Cirque Barcode Alexandra loves talking to new people. She lives for it. Name any person in the circus world and it's likely she knows them and has possibly had dinner with their mother. What do you do (besides assign the promotional stuff to the social butterfly in your company) if this is not your natural tendency?

Edgar Zendejas (Ezdanza) says he did a lot of meditation and it changed his perspective on things. He says now when he meets someone in a position of power, maybe a theater director or someone famous, he respects that person for where they are and that they must have done something to get to that position, but he recognizes also that they are equals in a way. There are many things that he himself is passionate about and good at that the other person does not do, and there will be an infinite number of things that he does not do that other people do very well. "It's not to put myself at the same level, but to put myself at a level where we can all relate and respect. This person may know more about some things and I know more about some things," he says.

The people that do like these interactions and feel genuinely charged by them are typically very curious people. They're excited to find out about all of these things that other people have done and know and are passionate about. Through their curiosity, they find ways that they can relate to them, ways that they are similar, and also things they can learn from the other person. This curiosity is (usually) extended back, at which point you can talk about the "why's" that you are passionate about, and by extension, your show.

Some people I talked to described selling as a seduction of sorts. Not in a sexual way, but in the way that people get interested in other people and ideas in general—through humor, through enthusiasm and passion, and through engaged conversation and shared interests.

After that, if they do contact you, you have to behave in a way that shows them you are on top of your business, says Héloïse Bourgeois (Cirque Entre-Nous). "If people give you their business contact and you write them the next morning with all your files that are professionally done, then they see, 'Ok, this person talked to me yesterday and today I have this email with everything.' You can be an amazing artist but if you're not able to deal with your emails, not able to contact anybody, people will be like, 'Yea, he's great onstage, but watch out to sign the contract.'" If this isn't your strength, maybe it makes sense to delegate that role to someone else with your sole responsibility being to send them a quick note with the email/ person to follow up with.

When talking to potential bookers, Bourgeois will also mention (tactfully) that she has multiple tools in her toolkit- she and her partner have a Chinese pole act, a hand-to-hand act, they love to teach workshops, and she's comfortable with directing. This way if they're interested in working with you but already have a Chinese pole act, you might still be able to get a gig, if those other skills are genuine interests and strengths of yours.

Barcode has used this technique successfully throughout our careers. "You're interested in our Russian bar act? You might also like our aerial hoop, hand-to-hand and cigar box juggling acts." In fact, we only offer one tech rider that includes all of the information for all of our acts, so potential clients could see all we have to offer. They might not know if you don't tell them. By telling them you might create a win-win situation: the artists make more money, get to do all their specialities they love, and the show gets more bang for their buck (multiple acts with fewer flights and hotels to pay for).

Spreadsheets/ CRM (for Selling)

When James Tanabe (51/49 Productions) was putting together some of his projects he would use excel spreadsheets to keep track of all the people he talked to. If you're someone like me who likes meeting people but has a memory like a goldfish, this can be a good way to not have to sacrifice the genuine connections you make with people because you're focused on present projects—a real problem when you meet so many people around the world that you don't have regular contact with. In Tanabe's spreadsheet, he would list the person, when and where he met them, what they talked about, the things he might be able to help them with one day, and the things they might be able to help him with one day. He would often also track the last time he wrote them an email so he would never go more than a few months without following up on what they were working on.

Customer Relations Management (CRM) software can be used to automate some of this, giving you reminders to write to people. Some people may feel this is disingenuous; that it's too systematic to foster genuine relationships. But I would argue that you will have stronger relationships with the people you have regular conversations with, regardless of how you remembered to write them. There's nothing that says you aren't genuinely interested in people when you do reach out to them, and I know I'm personally thankful whenever I see a reminder in my calendar or CRM to reach out to someone I haven't seen in a while.

Selling your show means connecting with people on a human level. This means telling them why you made your show, and learning about what motivates them to do the things they spend their days doing.

Pitching

Pitching is a more formal situation than just talking about your show with people. Maybe it happens at a designated time (at a festival for example), or in a meeting where people are there to hear your idea and you're trying to generate interest in your project and get people to join you in some capacity.

Like selling your idea in informal situations, pitching will be different depending on who you're talking to. Producers, theaters, artists... Many of them will be curious about different parts of the project, and you will likely need to talk to each of them differently. That said, the reason you're doing the project (your *why*) likely won't change, and the passion you have for it will be universally useful. So remember, when you adapt your presentation to fit who it is you're pitching to, don't forget to always include your why!

If you're a new company, one fear that presenters will likely have is not about the quality of your product, but rather whether your company will even be around at the time of your performance with them a year or two from now. Chris Lashua (Cirque Mechanics), says that "...the presenter gets a big question mark in the back of their head. They're afraid that if they like you, they're going to contract you, but then what happens six months or a year from now when your collective just falls apart? Recognize that your greatest challenge in the beginning is the fact that it's the chicken and the egg. You haven't been around very long, so the people that are looking at you are afraid that you're not going to *be* around. The only way to prove them wrong is to be around. Then the next year to get ahold of them and say, 'Hey, we're still here.'"

Pitching tools

Good tools will help you. These can be visuals, video, photos, and/or a nice PDF. In general, people will be interested in the video—it's the easiest way to communicate the thing you're trying to communicate, since circus is a visual (and auditory) medium, but sometimes it makes more sense while you're talking about your idea to also have simple images or even a mood board to look at that can help spark the imagination (ex. if you don't yet have your set built yet). Social proof in the form of good references can also go a long way, once you've played a few places. Before Barcode had made any shows under our own name we made sure to always mention the various companies we had performed for and done original creations with in the past, either when presenting the company in a grant application or in a promo video we made for the application. When pitching *Branché* in its second year of touring we often said something like, "One of the great things about this show is how adaptable it is. We were able to have up to 300 guests at the Tohu in Montréal, and as few as 50 at Jacob's Pillow to accommodate for restrictions due to Covid." This (ideally subtle) name dropping shows people that we have played in reputable places they might recognize while simultaneously illustrating a point that might be on their minds—namely, will the show fit their specific venue?

If you don't have any shows to point to yet, a similar thing can be done by mentioning some of your past experiences—maybe when you have worked with some of your team members before, or amazing things they have done. Basically anything that illustrates why people should trust you.

Promotional video

Want to get funding, creation space, or any sort of support? One great way to do this is to make a video saying who you are, what your idea for your project is, and film some clips of the type of stuff you're working on.

Want to get your show booked? Having a high quality video, both a trailer and full length, will allow producers that wouldn't be able to see your show live to book it with confidence. If you use an agent to sell your show, it will allow them to

Branché filming. Photo by Valentin Belleville. Artists: Kes Tagney, Anne-Marie Godin, Agathe Bisserier, Adrien Malette-Chénier, Tristan Nielsen, Sorrell Nielsen.

speak to the qualities of the show (and hence, sell it where they think it will fit best).

By its nature, a show is an ephemeral creation. This means that once the show stops playing, it ceases to exist. Therefore, anyone that wants to support the show (fund it, tell their friends about it, book it in their theater, give a residency to it, etc), has to be either in the room to see the show/work-in-progress, or you'll need another way to share the experience with them. Reviews are one way, but through the lens of someone else's taste. If you want to let people decide for themselves, one of the best tools you have is video. Video will also be useful as an archival reference to the show's existence. It gives your company a visible track record you can build on when you're making your next project.

Having high quality video is helpful at almost every step of the process. Each time you have a good video it will make it easier for you to advance to the next step of the project. Get good video early and often. Don't wait until the show is finished to start shooting. Below, I'll outline some of the instances that you can use video to promote your show before it's even finished.

When we were working with The 7 Fingers to create *Sequence 8*, about three months into our five month creation period they filmed a video of the acts in progress with no costumes, no lights, and in a rehearsal space. They cut it into a one minute trailer that was used by some of the early booking theaters to promote the show. A rehearsal video! I've even heard stories of Cirque Eloize filming promo videos with temporary lights and costumes in the first month of rehearsals, just to be able to start the marketing machine.

Full show video

Producers will always want to see either the live show (best case, but difficult in the beginning) or a tape of the full show. In this case, good quality video helps but the minimum is having a full-length version of the show. Even a house camera will help here. In the early days, whenever you do a run-through of your show, especially in front of an audience, you need to get a video.

Teasers & trailers: essential videos

Besides a house camera taping of the whole show, you can also shoot video specifically for promo material. This might include close ups or slow motion, or be set somewhere other than your actual set—the idea is to get people excited about seeing the live show. This will be useful everywhere: for your website and social media, for theaters' sites to sell tickets, to gain more support via private donors or grants, etc. Whatever stage your project is at, it is worth it to get quality video of the process.

How to get good video

Hiring a professional service is expensive, but the good news is that if you ask around you're likely to find someone that is comfortable working in the performing arts industry that could film for your budget, perhaps someone who is trying to make a demo reel and needs a project to add to their portfolio. Even if you have to shell out for a professional video, it will be worth it in the time saved as you try to book more shows. Just make sure the person shooting is familiar with your genre so they understand and get the type of shots that will work well in an edit to sell where you're trying to sell.

If at all possible, organize a day dedicated just to shooting video and nothing else. We learned this the hard way by bringing in someone to shoot the premiere of our show in Prague. Imagine trying to warm up all the tricks for the video and the show, adjusting the lights for filming when the camera needed more light and doing our presets for the first time, all with our director running around giving notes for the actual show. It's worth it to block a day, or at least half of a day, dedicated exclusively to filming.

Don't try to do anything else except film, and make a list of your top priority shots you want to get. If you'll need lights and costumes for specific scenes, plan this in advance as well. At the very least, wear clothing that might reflect what your eventual costumes might look like one day (all black, all earth tones, all fluorescent colors, etc), with no brands.

Is it hard to film things before you have a finished product? Yes. Is it tempting to say "We'll wait until it's perfect"? Yes. Do it anyway. I assure you this is how anyone that's been in the game for a while does it, and it's how you should do it too. Then you have the option whether or not to use it. If you don't make the video, you don't have the option.

The "no video" alternative: Let's say, by a stroke of luck, that someone books your show by coming to a preview, or without having seen it at all. That first booking will take place usually at least 6 months to a year from the time the person saw it. Until then, it will be hard to sell your show without video, so you invite more producers to come see this first performance the following year. In the meantime, since it's been a year, you're rusty, so you have to do rehearsals for the show, and possibly teach new technicians since your original techs aren't available a year from now for one date. At this first show, some of the producers you invited can come, but many aren't available or don't want to travel to see your first time creation, so there's only one or two bookers. Maybe one theater books it. Another year goes by, same story with the rehearsals and the techs. More producers come to this next showing, and a handful even book it for the following year. Now you're already in year three since your creation and you've only played in a handful of theaters. By the time the show takes off, you will likely be tired of trying to keep it going.

With video, you can start your presales before the show is even finished. Pique the curiosity of producers with a short work-in-progress teaser video of some early moments that show promise. Record a video of the whole show with no costumes, no lights, and let their imagination run wild about how much better it will be when it's finished and tightened up a little. Then, as the show comes to completion, do it again with a teaser and a full length video. Then the entire time you're waiting for your next performance you can be sending out those tapes (or having your agent do it for you), selling shows or garnering enough interest to get producers to come say, "I have to see it for myself before I decide, but this is worth taking a look at."

Top Tip: When you get photos or video, name each video file or photo with the photographer's name that took them (ex: Caroline_Thibault_Eric_Mill's_Mess.jpg), in a folder with the photographer's name. In the same folder where the pictures are, add a document with that photographer's info and any requirements they have for use (for example, their instagram handle or website). This way when people ask for the photo in two years, you won't have to run around trying to figure out where each photo came from. It'll be right there on the file name.

Lydia's Pitch Process

Director and choreographer Lydia Bouchard (La Résistance) has done a lot of special events with Cirque du Soleil, which means she has had a lot of experience working with people from publicity and visual design, and a lot of experience and feedback about actually pitching a concept. She says she will work on a pitch as much as any act—she's always open to taking advice and feedback about it to make it stronger. She says the pitch is one of the best tools in her toolkit as an artist, because it helps her clarify her idea and make sure everyone involved in the project, from the artists to the producers, all share the same vision.

"Making a pitch for your idea is like making a business plan for your idea," explains Bouchard. "You need to be really clear. As an artist that's the first thing that I'll do. I'll have an idea, I'll write the pitch. Because I'm pitching this in my head, I'm going to have to explain it so clearly in one sentence... What's your show about? If you can't explain it in less than ten seconds your idea isn't clear enough."

After the one sentence elevator pitch, she makes what she calls "the context slide." This is the why: How did she come up with this and what is the context of the world that she wants to put this art in? How does it connect to anyone outside her own mind? In her actual pitch she'll usually start with this, building context and creating curiosity, then follow it with the elevator pitch.

After that you can get into details, talking about the aesthetic, the cast, maybe show a mood board. Really consider which images you're using for your pitch, since people will pick up on any clues they can to understand the aesthetic and the flavor of your idea.

"Context, concept, aesthetic, big storyline," Bouchard says. "After that you can do casting, who you're planning to cast and why, what you want the set to look like... ideally once you're talking about this you're no longer in the mood board. You have plans that you will show."

Storytelling & Passion

Both Bouchard and Shana Carroll (The 7 Fingers) agree that a good pitch, more than any technical strategies, is about being a good storyteller. It's about passion and getting people excited for your project, however you do that best.

Carroll tells me the story of when she was hired to direct Cirque du Soleil's performance at the 2012 Oscars. She had thought it was a done deal, but it turned out the producers were still not convinced.

There was a meeting with the top Hollywood producers, and Carroll was supposed to talk with them on phone while the Cirque du Soleil higher-ups relayed the concept. In preparation for the meeting, Carroll was describing her concept to the people at Cirque du Soleil before they left, talking with her hands, when Yasmine Khalil, Chief Executive Producer of the Cirque du Soleil Entertainment Group said suddenly: "I need to send you to LA. I need them to see your passion."

"Scariest meeting of my life," Carroll said. She was pitching her idea to these top Hollywood producers, talking about the story, when one of them held up a hand and stopped her. "So, why circus?" he asked.

"I could see all these Cirque du Soleil executives around me, and they're like, 'The *wow!* factor,' and they had their company line," she says. But she realized that this moment was the real reason they'd brought her out there.

"Why circus?!" she said, pouring out everything she believed about circus, about pushing the limits of human possibility, about how it empowers people.

"Ok," the producer said. "You got me."

"I used to think that to be good at doing a pitch you have to sound super pro and business and confident, and then all of a sudden I was like, 'It doesn't matter if I stumble over my words.'"

Speaking with passion and enthusiasm, one human to another, will further your goal more than fancy graphs and spreadsheets.

274

When I was selling *Branché*, I managed to get on a video call with Pamela Tatge, the director of Jacob's Pillow, a prestigious school and dance festival in Massachusetts.

I told her about why we made the show, why it was important to us, then showed her the trailer. She said it was beautiful, then asked me to describe some of the scenes in the show. I could tell she wanted to take the show, but needed to hear more since we didn't have a full video yet. She was telling me how she wanted to be convinced- through images and the poetry of the piece, the issues it addressed.

I described to her the feeling of walking into the woods and the hush that comes over the audience like when a curtain opens before a theater show. I told her about the scene in which more and more artists try to fit onto a small rock, the mass writhing and fighting as two people stand on top of the mob, rocking slowly in a carefree waltz. The metaphor is clear—climate change is shrinking our livable spaces and resources and the wealth gap will only exacerbate who is affected by these issues.

I told her about a scene in the show in which an artist flips and flops, exhausted and barely able to stand, collapsing with the rest of the environment, and about how we would see kids in the audience flopping to the ground as well, imitating him. "If they are imitating this," I asked her, "do you think they might also imitate the other parts of the show? The parts in which we take care of each other, and take care of the nature around us?" She did, and we performed four sold out shows in the woods of their beautiful campus.

KEY TAKEAWAYS:

- Get your tools together: promotional video and full show video.
- Know your *Why*.
- Passion can be more powerful than a slick presentation!

AGENTS

Rehearsals for Dessa *by Creative Sovereignty. Photo by Eric Bates. Artist: Mason Ames*

Agents book your shows and help to create tours. This in itself is a very big job and its own specialization. Agents will already have relationships with different theaters and networks of programmers, and should have a decent idea of where your show might fit the best. Booking a tour is an enormous amount of work, and even more so if you don't already know these networks and theaters. While having an agent isn't required in order to tour a show, it might be a good idea depending on the stage you're in. Agents will take a cut, and you might give up a little autonomy by letting them decide your show's schedule, but you will free up a lot of time, and will possibly end up booking more shows than if you went at it alone.

While selling *Sweat & Ink*, Barcode worked with four different agents. For the first two years of our second show *Branché*, we sold and booked the tours ourselves. Even with an agent you will likely be involved in a lot of the selling and pitching process—making videos, presenting at events like the MICC (International Market of Contemporary Circus); as well as managing the logistics of transporting your set, artists, where they will stay in between dates, etc. So having an agent does not mean you will have zero work to do. **No one will work harder for your show than you will! But an agent, with their preexisting network and reputation, can help pave the way.**

A typical arrangement with a booking agent or agency is that you will tell them your "cout de plateau", your show fee, that includes everything—paying your artists, technicians, rights to music and creators, administration, contingency, insurance, profit for your company, paying back investors, etc. They will then take this price and mark it up 15-20% and sell that to theaters to book you a tour. They might also help to design marketing and promotional material such as posters (although many theaters have their own in-house designers as well and prefer that you just provide them with high quality photos).

How do you find an agent? This is the first question many people have. One place to start might be to look at the website of a similar sized show as yours. Sometimes the agency will be found in the "contact" section, other times you might have to reach out to the company and ask them directly. Caveat: In the US, where circus is still considered more of an "oddball" offering in many theaters (and as such, theaters might only program one circus show a year), you might want an agent that is only selling one circus company; whereas in Europe, an agency with multiple circus companies on their roster might not mean your agency would have conflicts of interest selling you. Events like the MICC are also places agencies gather to find shows and network. You can also search for agents on circus directories like En Piste or CircusTalk. The trick is to find an agency that works with your needs in a mutually beneficial relationship. You want them to be excited about your show! It will be difficult for them to sell it if they don't believe in it.

Like I said at the beginning of this section, Barcode has worked with four different agencies to sell *Sweat & Ink*. All of these people we got along with, at least initially, and all were nice people. Where the discrepancies arose was in the number of shows they were able to book us, the prices they could get, and the amount of work they would do relative to the work we had to do. This all comes down to clarity of expectations—something I wish we had been more clear with when talking to them in the first place. In retrospect, I wish I had spent more effort getting a realistic picture of what our relationship would look like- it's easy to imagine the amount of work and unknowns that an agency will remove from your plate and not want to examine it more closely.

Sometimes it felt like we were doing all the work (going to networking events, handing over leads that had come to us directly, dealing with touring logistics, budgets and contracts) and handing them 20%. One of the agencies was used to booking smaller, local shows and wasn't having much success booking our show at the prices we needed to make it worth it as an international company. This was frustrating, and ultimately led us to finding a new agency that we felt was providing a significant amount of value. As we learned more about booking shows, however, we also grew in our understanding of the process agents go through in order to book shows in the future, and how they are rewarded for all the work they do only when shows finally book, sometimes in the following year or two. This means agencies are often playing the long game: it is more advantageous to them to support a company that plans on touring their show as long as possible and making more shows that will leverage the company's name recognition.

What should you discuss with a potential agent? An important place to start the discussion is on the topic of territory. Agents usually have a market that they specialize in, such as France, or Europe, or North America. If their territory is France, even if someone from France contacts your company, the contract will go through the agency (unless it was a prior contact from before the agency got involved). We have had multiple agencies that each worked different territories, which we managed by blocking off booking periods so they wouldn't double book us.

The Importance of the Agent's Role

What will your agents do for you? Will they handle the contracts, promotion, etc? For example, whose job will it be to write the contracts with the theaters? Who will design promotional material, and who will have the final say over what it looks like? Will they also book special events for you, or just the show? One agency we worked with happened to have lawyers on their team, so that was a service they provided. We didn't use that service often, but when we did we were happy to have them in our corner!

According to Chris Lashua (Cirque Mechanics), one advantage of having an agency represent you is that, "[Presenters] need to know you're serious. And one way to be taken seriously is to use the tools that are the industry standard. One of those tools is agency representation."

Consider the Booking Time Period

It's likely in the beginning stages of your show you will take whatever sporadic dates come your way. A show in Prague here, a festival in France a few months later, etc. It takes time to get a show going, and you need to give your agency the benefit of the doubt. Theaters tend to book far in advance (usually at least a year so they can plan their season and print their programs), so you have to afford your agent the time to book you. A good agent will take their time, setting up shows for longevity on the tour circuit which can require a year or two of commitment on their part but will eventually pay off for all parties.

That said, it is hard to keep your schedule open for individual shows here and there. Yes, you will likely need to do these sorts of "one off" dates initially as an investment in getting your show rolling, but with Barcode we soon realized that it was unsustainable to tour like this. The tours were less profitable, it made it hard to book other work, and the logistics of transporting and storing cargo in between each date made it unlikely that we could continue long term like this. We told our agency after the first year of touring that we would block specific months of the calendar for them and they could book as many shows as possible during those months. This also helps you keep your technicians, knowing you can provide them solid blocks of work rather than individual dates here and there, which saves you time and money teaching new technicians the show.

Don't Forget Logistics in Booking

When working with other agencies, be sure to cover the logistics. With multiple agents covering different territories, you'll have to discuss how they will work together—you don't want them to book conflicting dates and be frustrated. It will be your responsibility to have good communication with them and clarify the types of tours and dates that can work for you.

How Do You See the Relationship Working?

Many relationships tend to overlap in the circus world- coaches give their artistic opinions, friends become outside eyes, acrobatic partners become romantic partners and so on. Maintaining so many relationships from both a business and social perspective can quickly eat up your time, and yet it's easy to feel a pressure to be best friends with everyone. It's more likely people will want to sell your show if they like you, right?

Something that worked well with both our current agency and also with our transportation company was that they both saw the interaction primarily as a business deal. We have gone out for drinks with them and are always amicable when we see each other, but for the most part we have been content to hire them to provide a service, and one they do well. Some people might like more of a personal relationship with their collaborators, and that's also great. Some producers like to be outside eyes and give their opinions on what makes the show "work". Like with most things, the clearer you can be upfront about how you'd like your working relationship to function, the less friction you'll have down the line.

...Or Be Your Own Agent

Then there is always the DIY approach of booking the show yourself. Barcode and Acting for Climate have sold *Branché* ourselves since its inception. This means sending out emails, doing zooms, going to pitches and markets...it's a lot of work! Some of this you will likely have to do even if you do hire an agent, but beware—booking and planning your own tour is a big undertaking. The reason the agents take 15-20% on a show (besides their knowledge of where your show might fit, when different theaters book, which theaters are parts of networks that will work together, etc,) is that it takes many *unsuccessful* attempts to sell the show to land the ones that do work. We learned this the hard way while selling *Branché*. Excited to keep that extra 15% in our pocket, we spent an entire season trying to book *Branché*, sending hundreds of emails, making spreadsheets of people we contacted, trying to coordinate grants to match potential budgets, all to end up with just a few shows sold. The reward did not feel worth the work. I say this to remind you that while in the beginning time and money will both likely feel in short supply, if you find the right people (and give up some of the money), the benefits that return to you will be worth it. If the end goal is to have a show that sells well and tours, you need to bring in experts on selling shows and scheduling tours. It's possible to do this 100% on your own, but you will quickly learn that the commitments of time and energy needed to do the job well represent its own full-time job.

KEY TAKEAWAYS:

- Finding an agent or agency that is a good fit can be hard, but can be a valuable tool.
- Selling shows is like sowing seeds: it can take a while to see results, and therefore is inherently a medium-long term partnership.
- Discuss upfront the relationship: booking time period, who will take care of what, what exactly the agency will be doing.
- Having an agency doesn't mean you won't still have to promote yourself!

SUCCESSFUL SHOWS

Warming up for CircOpera 2.0 *by Oopperabaletti. Photo by Eric Bates.*
Artist: Alexandra Royer.

When I interviewed James Tanabe (51/49 Productions), I learned that although he had a lot of interesting and useful things to say about producing a show and different ways to get funding, he had also dedicated a large part of his career to figuring out what made a show successful. While he was working for Cirque du Soleil they had commissioned him to do a study about what makes a show successful- they sent him on a mission to watch as many shows as he could and understand what contributed to audience satisfaction.

"The number one thing I want to tell people that are starting on this journey," he told me, **"is to remember that people go to these shows to see humans performing.** They want those humans to perform something that no other human can do. That doesn't mean that it has to be the most difficult, doesn't mean the most challenging, it just has to be something that only those people can do."

Both of us agreed there is no magic recipe for a show: what makes a show "good" is subjective, and everyone has different definitions of success. Putting these caveats aside, he said his study focused on the question, "What are the factors in a circus show that are correlated with audiences having a positive reaction to the show? Aka: They liked the show, they would recommend it, and they would see another by the same company?" Diving down this rabbit hole, he discovered a handful of universalities and insights worth sharing here.

It's also worth mentioning that while this study was commissioned internally by Cirque du Soleil, at the time Cirque du Soleil was re-evaluating the long-held intuition of some of the organization, namely the acrobatic experts and coaches. Tanabe's findings with this study showed that some of this intuition was actually supported by statistical data, not the other way around!

To do this study, Tanabe told me he went to 30 different circus shows in one year from 19 different companies, seeing 587 acts and taking detailed notes. This data was combined with 29 historical videos of Cirque du Soleil and 45 Degrees (a subsidiary special events branch of CDS), for another 350 acts. He also looked at another 51 past shows from 6 different companies for another 612 acts, as well as 486 different acts from circus school graduating classes, and more acts from three prestigious circus festivals. In total, he analyzed 2,857 acts and interviewed 20 experts from both within and outside of Cirque du Soleil.

What were the results? Tanabe said that he found two key elements which played a large role in audience satisfaction: the *human performance element* and *acrobatic propositions.*

The first good news is that the number one driver of audience satisfaction for the shows was the human performance elements (as opposed to technology or set or decor elements), and these are made up of "acrobatic propositions," defined by Tanabe as the moments a performer does something that gives an audience the opportunity to react. This is encouraging for creators smaller than Cirque du Soleil. It means the primary factor that determines whether a show is well liked—the human elements—can begin to be created right away, and probably without needing much money. You can start creating right now! A big budget can help enhance human performance elements, but know that one of the best things you can do to ensure the success of your show is to start working on the material the performers will be doing, as that will be the main determiner as to how well your show is received.

To measure his findings Tanabe broke down how many acrobatic propositions were made per act. This meant, "How many times was the audience given the opportunity to react (gasp, laugh, applaud, etc)?" Tanabe summarizes it by saying, "Basically, how many times did the performers hit the 'ball' into the audience and give the audience the opportunity to respond back? The other thing I measured was how many times did the audience [then] hit that tennis ball back? How many times did the acrobatic proposition elicit a response from the audience?"

In terms of acrobatic propositions, Tanabe said what was most important was that the propositions were clear: every proposition they made, the audience responded to. This was due to years of sharpening and clarifying both the acrobatic and human, emotional elements that gave the audience the clarity to know that it was the right time to clap, or be afraid, or laugh. This stood true for both traditional and contemporary acts. What worked for both was that the audience always felt comfortable in their role.

It will come as no surprise that if you plotted the number of (clear) acrobatic propositions on a graph, along with the difficulty, you saw a strong correlation to how much audiences have traditionally liked Cirque du Soleil shows. The next strongest element was the "artistic elements" (choreography, level of artistic direction, level of narrative perceived by the audience). Finally, the level of technology didn't have a huge impact as to whether audiences enjoyed the show, unless it enhanced the human performance element. Maybe this meant nice lights, or something else that would highlight a performers' amazing abilities. Technology for technology's sake, however, did nothing to enhance an audience's enjoyment of the show. Furthermore, if technology (and this includes costumes, lights, props, the stage... everything) ever *prevented* a performer from doing things to the best of their ability, it would hurt the audience's perception of the show.

If you're anything like me, these results should not be terribly surprising to you. But it's worth asking why. The owner of one successful show in Switzerland that Tanabe talked to articulated it well: "The second I bring out a screen or a projector onstage, all 2,000 people in the big top know exactly what's going to happen, but if I bring out a performer onto an empty stage with a spotlight, none of those 2,000 people know what's going to happen." The man pointed up to a big 360 degree screen they had at the top of their big top. "I haven't used that in ten years because I want to make a show that makes the audience wonder what's going to happen, not reproduce for them what their phone in their pocket can already do."

The Whole Experience

If you're producing your own show, such as presenting at a theater in your hometown, you might have the ability to shape the audience's experience from the moment they walk in the theater. Maya McCoy (Vermont Vaudeville) describes the first time they put up their cabaret: "We were performing in it but also producing it, and we cared a lot about the atmosphere we were creating, so we made popcorn at home. We made brownies and brought them in. We sold the tickets at the door, we did everything to give it the feel that we wanted it to have."

I think in doing this, Brent and Maya tapped into an often overlooked element that can influence the success of a show. James Tanabe agrees: When interviewing the owner of the same Swiss circus mentioned above, one piece of advice the owner brought to Tanabe's attention was a question Tanabe hadn't even thought to ask yet: What happens before the show starts that contributes to the audience's enjoyment of the show? The owner said, "90% of my audience's reaction to the show is determined before the house lights come down."

This comes from the feeling of anticipation while you're packed in the entry with the rest of the audience waiting to go in, the smell of popcorn, people chattering excitedly around you, a beautiful red carpet. These are things not to be lost for the sake of "efficiency." Indeed, "inefficient" but personal touches can determine how much an audience enjoys a show before the lights have even gone down. Tanabe cites Circus Conelli as an example: they have ushers put a star sticker on the face of every guest that enters. He calls this the "mint on the pillow moment." He stresses that it doesn't have to be a big thing, but if you can integrate it into your creation process to come up with a way to have every single audience member feel that they've received a personal welcome, you will set yourself up for success. These touches are not limited to a tented circus setting where there are certain expectations of what audiences will experience once inside. The same applies to theatrical audiences—take the examples of *Loft* and *Traces* by The 7 Fingers.

In The 7 Fingers' show *Loft*, the audience was brought in through the back of the theater, emerging through a refrigerator onto the stage itself where they were welcomed by the cast members. It was a fun, personalized moment that most people had never experienced before at the theater, and made the show memorable before it had even begun. They did it again with their second show, *Traces*, by installing a camera in the lobby that people would make faces into, only to discover when they entered the theater that their image was projected to everyone in the audience! It made it a fun way to enter the space, laugh at yourself, and then feel a sense of unity with the rest of the audience as you watched the next people behind you pick a booger on camera.

What this does is help everyone in the audience make up their minds before the house lights have even come down that this is the best show they've seen all year, "Simply because of that anticipation, simply because they're treated like a VIP," says Tanabe.

This is all important to do before the show, but touches such as these can be added everywhere in order to make the night out to see your group's show memorable. When I saw Compagnie Rasposo perform, I was delighted at intermission to see the Italian acrobat I saw onstage just moments ago making espresso for audience members in a little booth under the bleachers. At Akoreakro at the end of their show the acrobats play live music while the audience lingers at the bar in their tent. **Start thinking of your whole show as the experience you're creating for your audience, not just the time the performers are onstage.**

Tanabe cites an example of how one company got this wrong when they were acquired by new owners. This company wanted to optimize the sales of concessions, so they cleared out the front of house. More cash registers, less lines, less obstructed sight lines so you could see the food and concessions from anywhere. This, the logic went, would make people more likely to buy something. The unfortunate effect of this, Tanabe says, was that, "You were basically walking into a giant warehouse under a tent." This actually had the perverse effect of making the experience less interesting for the audience.

How to Create An Ideal Environment if It's Not Your Own Tent

So you want to set yourself up for success like the examples mentioned in the previous section, but how do you control the environment if it's not your tent? There are always opportunities you can find to control part of the experience, like The 7 Fingers did with *Loft* in theaters around the world. Tanabe says if you examine the elements that go into an audience's experience of seeing a show, you can craft the experience of your show into something unique. "So much that you think is a problem that should be fixed," he says, "(for example—it's taking a lot of time for people to get to their seats) actually has the opposite impact, it makes people feel excited to be able to get in there to get to the seat, and when they come into the space to say, 'I finally arrived.'"

These don't have to be big changes, Tanabe reiterates: a star on the face might be enough to make people feel special and welcomed. Get creative! At one point in *Branché*, the audience is taken between two different sites in the woods with small scenes playing out along the way. At one site the path narrowed and traffic slowed down, causing some audience members to have to wait in line. This could feel frustrating, but we turned it into an opportunity. One of our artists gathered up a handful of fallen leaves and gave them out like "tickets" to enter the forest behind her. Many of the audience members kept their leaf after the show like a precious souvenir, coming up to show us after the performance that they were taking the leaf home with them! We incorporated the moment into further performances, whether or not we had a traffic jam.

Challenges in the Ensemble Approach (Non-acrobatic Aspects of a Circus Show)

One challenge of the ensemble, small-cast approach to making a show, is that you're never going to have the acrobatic density with a 3-5 person show that you can with a 60 person show. This isn't bad in and of itself, Tanabe says, but it means in order to not exhaust your cast you're going to need non-acrobatic acts as fillers, and these can often be underwhelming, especially to an audience that is expecting an "acrobatic circus show". You want them to be pleasantly surprised by the non-acrobatic moments, not disappointed.

Tanabe notes that many small-ensemble circus shows are comprised of upwards of 50% of non-circus material, and that this material likely wouldn't stand alone as dance or music or theater shows. Because the audience has already fallen in love with the show and the artists from their experience before the show and the acrobatic elements, they might find these moments fun and charming, but in general he foresees this as the biggest potential weakness with the next generation of circus shows that we create.

As a way to combat this, one suggestion Tanabe makes is to team up with people from another performance art, such as music or theater, that have a high level of circus *appreciation* (to limit the amount of misunderstandings and frustrations), but a different skill set that complements the circus artists' abilities. "It's maybe counter-intuitive to say if you're making a circus show to bring in non-circus people, but I think from the point of view of show composition it could actually take a lot of pressure off and increase the quality," says Tanabe.

Personally, I hear where Tanabe is coming from, but I often enjoy smaller shows with multidisciplinary circus artists. And as I'm sure we've all seen, a blend of artists from different backgrounds is no guarantee of success if they are not able to work together to make the show into something cohesive. My advice would be to examine your team's skill set and look at their strengths, then to be cautious about putting in too many elements that might be new and exciting for them but that they haven't refined as much as their other skills. A successful show like *Traces* by The 7 Fingers, in which the artists skateboarded, played piano, guitar, and basketball, was built on the strengths of those artists actually being incredibly talented at all of those non-circus skills- they weren't new hobbies the artists were just starting to develop. If your secondary talents pale too much in comparison to your main disciplines, really reflect on whether it will best serve the show to include them.

Lydia Bouchard puts it this way. "Know your people and put them to their best advantage."

Full Houses

Tanabe says another factor that can influence the success of a show is how full your audience feels. In some cabarets they will remove chairs on a slow night. Many theaters cover seats or will close a balcony to make it feel more packed. There's an advantage to your audience feeling like an audience and not a group of individuals—they will feel more comfortable to relax their defenses and act how everyone else is acting, which hopefully means laughing, applauding and gasping at the right moments that reinforce the emotions you're trying to convey with your show.

Another way of generating this feeling is being clever about how you schedule your performances, and possibly even limiting your number of performances if it will increase the number of full houses you have. Selling less shows does mean less money in the short term, but according to Tanabe it may prove beneficial in the long term for a few reasons. The first is the full house effect, which will increase audience enjoyment and want them to come back. The promoter might think to themselves, "I told them it was too few dates and I wish they'd listened to me because we sold out. Next time I'm going to book them for two weeks!" In their mind this makes your company a money-maker. They're going to want to invest more to promote you and bring you back. On top of that, selling out makes you a rare commodity. According to the book "Influence" by Robert Cialdini, this will make you appear more valuable to potential theater goers, if only for that reason. People that couldn't get tickets are going to act quickly next time to get tickets before they sell out again. "No one is going to bring you back if you have five shows at 40%," Tanabe says. "But if you have three shows sold out, you're hot property."

Choosing the number of shows you do must be a luxury reserved for already successful companies, right? Tanabe thinks there may be an opportunity here for first-time companies. You're convincing them to take a lower risk on you, which may enable you to fit into more holes in their schedule. "You say, 'Listen, do you have any space, is there anyone that dropped out of your schedule? All we need is for it to be a Friday and a Saturday night." Don't do this a week ahead of time, since that would likely also lead to a lot of empty seats, but six months in advance, that's far enough ahead that you might be able to fill those seats and make an impact.

KEY TAKEAWAY:

- Regardless of the size of the show you're making, it's good to remember that people come to shows to see humans do amazing things, and to be touched on a personal level. Any details that you can integrate that provide these personal moments will help the audience feel more connected and care about what they're seeing onstage. Use everything at your disposal- before, during and after the performance, to set your show up for success.

Circus in the Parks *by Midnight Circus: Photo by David Arredondo. Artist: Eric Bates.*

SECTION SIX: FINAL THOUGHTS

IN CLOSING

I'm hoping throughout this book you've learned a few things that will help your creation process go smoother. There are no magic bullets, but hopefully you've gained a clearer understanding of the challenges you're undertaking, and what tools you can use to deal with them so that each new obstacle you encounter won't seem insurmountable.

In parting, here are a few final words of advice from the creators referenced throughout these pages, as well as my own reflections.

Ask for Help

While I was writing this book, just before I started my first interviews, a fledgling group of artists reached out to me asking for help. They had just made a cabaret show and successfully performed it in a venue that they had hired themselves, and were wondering what to do next. Should they start a company?

Now I imagine they might have been nervous to reach out since we didn't know each other very well. Maybe they worried they might be wasting my time. In fact, unbeknownst to them, I was in the process of looking for people exactly like them to talk to! I wanted to know what sort of questions people had about making a show so that I could address them in my book. Their reaching out actually helped me! We spoke on the phone for an hour and I'd like to believe that both sides gained a lot of useful insights.

Circus, like any business, is built on people and their skills and relationships. You will realize quickly that there are so many things that other people are good at that you are less good at, and vice versa. Instead of trying to do everything yourself, see how you can leverage other people's experience and skills and all grow richer from the exchange.

You just put 20 hours into trying to make a website and yet it still looks terrible? Your friend that went to school for web design and worked professionally for seven years could probably fix it up for you in less than an hour. You just spent the afternoon scouring the internet for places that could host a residency? One social media post or phone call could bring you tons of answers while simultaneously making connections and starting a buzz about your project. **It's easier to help people that are clear with what they need help with!**

This is the power of sharing the thing you're working on—it helps you switch from the "how" mindset (*"How* will I do all of this?") to the "who" mindset. (*"Who* can help me do this?"). You are going to have more to do than you will be able to do, and it would take a lifetime to learn to do all of it proficiently. So stop trying to do everything yourself! Focus on what you're good at, and start to tell people about your vision so you can harness the power of *who*. Trust that your dream and hard work will inspire others to want to contribute, and allow yourself to be humble enough to admit that some people might do things better than you. Keep your hand on the rudder so you can keep guiding your dream, but don't be afraid to bring in other deck hands that can help bring it home.

Sharing your vision with other creators is an art in itself. As you start to bring your dream to life, continue working to clarify your vision as much as you can. Ask yourself why you're making it, what your inspirations are, what you have in your head so far so you can share it with other creatives with different expertise to you. They might be able to help take it beyond what you are capable of imagining on your own.

Multiple creators that I interviewed for this book mentioned the importance of asking for help. It might take a lot of asking before you find the right people, but when you do, competent people can vault you over seemingly insurmountable obstacles, and many in your network will be happy to contribute to your success in some capacity. Whether it's introducing you to someone, coming in as an outside eye, or helping with a specific trick, if people see you putting in the work they might be inspired to lend a hand along the way.

Who do you ask?

Start with friends

When he was making his first show *Filament*, Joseph Pinzon (Short Round Productions) reached out to friends. "Wherever you are, you always have friends that have what you're looking for or [they] know someone who has what you're looking for. You just have to ask. If you're too afraid to ask, you might not be ready."

Reaching out isn't as scary as it might feel at first, says Lewie West (Gravity & Other Myths). When he and his partner were starting their own small creation he said that, "Everyone we asked for help, we were overwhelmed and surprised by how generous they were with their time, with their knowledge. Everyone remembers how difficult it was to be in the starting-out position and will be eager to do what they can to help friends or circus acquaintances avoid the pitfalls they encountered themselves."

Do you remember the last time someone asked you for help with something that you felt competent in? When done in a way that's respectful of the person's time, it can be flattering and exciting. It's thrilling to realize you can put someone on the fast track to learning a trick, applying for the right grant, or can introduce them to a director who would be interested in their project, all with so little effort thanks to your years of experience. Remember this feeling when you're nervous to call someone up.

When there's a lot you don't know, it's also likely there's also a lot of people you don't yet know that will have the answers for you. Start with friends, and ask them to put you in touch with people that might be able to answer your questions, or that they would recommend working with.

Stop Apologizing for Yourself

A lot of times when we ask for help we do it in a way that is apologetic. We feel bad for bothering other people, for taking up their time for a project that we ourselves might still have doubts about. It can sometimes feel like you have to be a pure extrovert to get anywhere in this business, when in fact there are a ton of self-described introverted people that are amazing artists, and can almost certainly relate to the unease you might feel when approaching people to ask for help. Learning to push back on the tendency to apologize for trying to make your project happen, or talking yourself out of even asking, is a skill you need to develop in order to grow and succeed as an artist. If you don't apologize for what you do onstage, you shouldn't apologize for wanting to do it in the first place!

Be Specific

Asking for general help can lead to people helping you, but it is much easier for people to help you if you can specify what you need. Think about it. If you say, "I need help with my project," what's the first question they're going to ask?

"So...What do you need help with, exactly?"

Whether it's creation space or help reviewing a grant you wrote, asking for something specific cuts right to the chase. It allows them to quickly understand what you're looking for and decide if they are the right person for the job, or if they know just the right person to recommend.

Backstage at Midnight Circus: Photo by Eric Bates: Artist: Junebug.

See You Down the Road *by Cirque Barcode. Photographer: Nikola Milatovic. Artist:*
Alexandra Royer

CONTRIBUTORS' PARTING WORDS

Do It for Its Own Sake

Brent McCoy (Vermont Vaudeville) says to do it for its own sake, and because you want to do it. Don't do it because you need the feedback from the audience or because you're searching for stardom. "Make something that the world wants and they'll let you know," he says. Brent and Maya found something with Vermont Vaudeville that their community and their culture wanted, and that they themselves also wanted. Keep working to find the overlaps between what you want to do and what the world wants, or needs. With *Branché* we wanted to do something about the climate crisis, which turned out to be an issue on a lot of people's minds. It needed to be explored not only with facts and science, but also with the abstract tools of art.

Ask Questions

Charlie Wheeller (Barely Methodical Troupe) reminds us to ask people if you have a problem or concern or question. "We're so wary of looking dumb," he says. Surround yourself with people with whom you're not afraid to look dumb, or to appear vulnerable with, so you can continue to grow to your full potential. Ask for help when you need it. Héloïse Bourgeois (Cirque Entre-Nous) echoes this, saying not to feel shy to ask as many questions as you can to people that have already done a show or made a company. Ask these questions, she says, but not just at a bar, or after a show. See if you can take them out to coffee and really sit down to talk with them. "All the information you will get will save you so much time after," she says. **"I think when people start making a company they want to feel like they're on top of their stuff, but no**

one is on top of their stuff if they've never done it. You will make mistakes. Learn from other people's mistakes so you don't make the same mistakes."

There is a fear that you don't want to look stupid, or get taken advantage of if you ask naive questions. We've always heard "fake it till you make it', but there is a power in admitting your ignorance. Being honest about your experience and where you are in your journey will help people help you.

The Soup

James Tanabe says to be very selective as to what you put into your show. "Making a show is a lot like cooking, it's like making a big soup. Which means it's very easy to start throwing stuff in, but once you've thrown stuff in it's almost impossible to take it out, because everything you've put in has affected everything else." Be extremely thoughtful about every element you add in, and ask yourself if it's enhancing your ability to perform something no one else can perform (Tanabe's number one key to audience enjoyment!) Put everything through that filter before it goes into the pot: "Is this detracting, and have I done everything possible to enhance the human performance element?" Nine times out of ten, he says, the difference between an experienced performer or creator and an inexperienced one is that the inexperienced creator will put a lot of things that they *want* to be able to do, whereas the experienced performer puts mostly the things they know they do well, and maybe an element or two to challenge themselves so they can keep growing.

Creating Opportunity

Gypsy Snider (The 7 Fingers) says the biggest way she created opportunity both before and after The 7 Fingers was by leaving a place better than she found it. When you're on a contract, Snider says, try to really be an asset to the work and to the company so you know you could come back anytime, even in another role, because of your work ethic and your attitude.

Snider says to try to create in every place you go a network that extends beyond the thing you do onstage. This can mean finding something that's interesting to you and trying to figure out how you can connect the dots to make it happen, regardless of whether it's profitable or it's your name on it. People will remember who was hustling. Put your 100% into it and it will bring something to you as an individual or your company, but also to the world.

Failure

"You are allowed to fail, and you will fail, and it's ok," Claude Tremblay, (Cirque Eloize, Moment Factory), says. "You need to fail and be able to learn from it. A failure, if you learn from it, is never a failure."

While I was still at l'Ecole Nationale de Cirque in Montréal I got asked to juggle for a fundraiser show that benefited a foundation that provided seeing-eye dogs to the blind. The show took place on a tiny stage in a gymnasium. I checked my lights in the morning the same day as the show, not realizing that the light streaming in through the gym's windows from all sides would no longer be there come nightfall. When it was finally time for my act I had the horrible discovery that I couldn't see *anything*. Every cigar box I threw in the air became a dark silhouette. I had no lights coming from behind me at all. I also had no backup plan for this situation. The act was a disaster. But I learned a lot about light checks that day! Had I not done that gig I would have still had to learn that lesson, possibly in a situation with more pressure or bigger consequences for my career.

As humans we don't like to lose or to fail. We want to be good from the start, especially when as artists we are often already so good at what we do. But I'll let you in on a secret: This is not my first book. It's my third. I showed the first one (a novel) to a few early readers and was so discouraged by the feedback (and how much I still needed to grow as a writer and as a human) that I gave up on it entirely. The second one didn't even make it that far. Regardless of the outcome, I enjoyed the process and learned from my mistakes. I continued to submit articles to magazines. Many got rejected, but a few got accepted, and on those I learned to work with editors and continued to learn the craft of writing, and the importance of collaboration.

It's intimidating to start something new and to admit that we might be bad at it. Get all the advice you can, but strive to fail as quickly and as often as possible. Expose yourself to opportunities where there is a potential to fail, because those situations will also be opportunities to learn. Treat each new failure as a successful lesson learned on the road to improving your craft and knowledge.

Optimism

Gypsy Snider says there are always people that will see everything that can go wrong. She looks at these risks instead like a list of things she has to do well in order to achieve her project. "So let's do it!" she says, laughing. "Let's stop talking about it and do it! I don't want to focus on what we *can't* do, I want to focus on what we *can* do and make that cool."

The only way she has ever generated work, she says, is by working. Not by making money, but by producing the next thing. "I think there's a false feeling that in the arts that 'I'll do a show, I'll make money, and that money will produce the next show." For her it has never been like this. "If you don't have money to produce, produce anyway, just find a way." In other words, start where you are, with what you have. **You can't build momentum without taking action.**

As Charlie Wheeller (Barely Methodical Troupe) says, you just need to start. "There's lots of people that are talking a lot and they don't have a product... Get a product because people want to get behind stuff."

Live Theater

We live in a time of digital ease. While being able to talk to people across the internet has made our lives better in a lot of ways, it's a distant second to actually being in the room together. Live theater, Brent McCoy (Vermont Vaudeville) says, does the same thing for entertainment. "The ability to be in a room together, breathing and laughing, is cathartic in a way that is just good for us. And I'm sure there are empirical ways that this could be tested, but when you walk out of a room after experiencing some really good, funny live theater and your jaw hurts from laughing and you get to talk to your family or your kids and share your favorite memories, that doesn't happen even after a really good movie. With live theater you live it. That's why finding the thing that we found: a team, a place, a willingness to stick with it over time, it's so rewarding."

DOWN THE ROAD

Barcode: Photographer unknown. Artists: Eric Bates, Alexandru Ruyer, Eve Bigel, Tristan Nielsen.

I thought as a circus artist I had seen what there was to see across the contemporary circus landscape. I had done street shows, festivals, television, tented shows and theater shows. Making a show broadened my view of the possibilities of our art form, and humbled me by revealing how much there was still to learn, how much more nuance there is in every aspect of what makes up a show beyond just what the artists do onstage.

I still enjoy performing in shows. I'm so thankful I just get to play without having to also produce! But now when I see shows I appreciate them differently.

I look at the lights and the costumes, at the narrative arc, at the why behind the show and whether it came across to me as a member of the audience. I think of all the tools at one's disposal when making a show, all the different stories out there and all the different ways there are to tell them. I think of all the people that it takes to make a show—the granting boards and the grant writers, the administrators, the cargo delivery services, the prop and set makers, the costume designers, the musical composition, the outside eyes and directors, the coaches, the light designer, the light operator and sound operator, the technical director, the agents, the theaters themselves, the marketing team, the audiences that come to support live theater and, last but not least, the artists onstage. I think of how beautiful it is that all this energy came together to make something so ephemeral- just for a night, or a season, or a handful of years. Some of the shows and companies discussed in this book will have closed by the time you read this, and others will have opened, carrying on the tradition of live performance.

I've always been someone to do things myself, maybe because I'm stubborn, or curious, or just not the best at collaborating. Yet, one thing I've learned through my journey of making shows is that no show (even solos!) exist in a vacuum. They are *always* a collaborative effort. The good news is, we are a collaborative species. We are born to come together and share our stories, to struggle together, to create new dreams and make art that reflects the times. What does the world need now? How can art reflect that back to those that watch it? Hopefully, this book is but the beginning of that journey for you. Whatever show you make will evolve and grow like any living thing, and you in turn will grow as a person with it. I hope you continue to learn and strive to make new things, try different approaches, and evolve your practices to best serve your message and your audience.

Good luck!

ACKNOWLEDGEMENTS

Like making a show, this book has been a collaborative effort. I'm so grateful to everyone that has contributed to the body of knowledge in this book, helping pave the way for future generations of circus creators.

First and foremost, thank you to my partner, Stefanie Fournier, for supporting me on this and every other project I've taken on so far. She was there for the creation and choreography of Barcode's first show, *Sweat & Ink*, performed in *Branché*, and has supported me throughout the writing of this book and at every twist and turn in between. Ambitions of this scale can result in lonely moments of uncertainty, dark nights of the soul with no dawn in sight. Having an unrelenting cheerleader in my corner has been a blessing, always motivating me to pick up the pen and write until the path reveals itself once more. Throughout the years of writing and editing she has acted as my sounding board, first reader and research assistant, helping me question and interrogate further my assumptions about the creative process. I couldn't have done it without you darlin'.

Next up on this adventure was my magnificent editor, Kim Campbell. I'm grateful to Kim for their patience, attitude and work ethic throughout the time it has taken for this book to come together. Without their follow-through and organization this project would have long ago been abandoned to my tendency to pursue newer, shinier challenges. Their own plethora of experience and background in the circus industry and skill as an editor has taught me much throughout this process. Without them I would have lost interest and faith in this project long ago.

Thank you to Thom Wall of Modern Vaudeville Press, my publisher, for his enthusiasm for bringing humble books like mine into the world, and for having taken the time to learn to navigate the complex world of publishing so that folks like me don't have to. Thanks also to Benjamin Domask-Ruh for additional input on the layout, structure and edit of this book. No project exists in a vacuum, and Thom, Kim and Benjamin have shown me how much momentum a good team can generate together. Many of their insights worked their way into the text directly as well, and the book is richer for it.

Thank you to Sophie Picard for providing the sample budgets in this book, as well as for having held Barcode's administrative end together over five years. We wouldn't have lasted nearly as long without her decades of experience and vision. During that time I watched her quietly help countless small companies in Montréal get off the ground—she is a shining member of the legion of unsung heroes that make performance art possible from behind the scenes around the world.

Thank you to the rest of Barcode. Tristan, Alex, Eve: We learned it the hard way together, and grew as humans along the way. What a crazy ride to have taken together. I've learned a lot from each of you, and I'm excited to see where our paths lead from here.

Thanks to the rest of the people that were involved on the journey of bringing *Sweat & Ink* to life: Mathilde, Mason, Raf, Steve, Vladimir, JP, Arnaud, Gab, Rudolf, Dom, Betty, Kristina, Sophie, Jerome, André, Betka, Swift, Charlotte, Emilie, Greg and more.

Thanks to my parents for having supported my artistic career from the very start, whether it was circus, writing or otherwise. Their integrity and commitment to helping others has been an inspiration throughout my life.

Having such a reliable and supportive family at home has allowed me to take risks in my life, to venture out unafraid. Onward.

I'm extremely grateful to all of the artists that allowed me to interview them for this book, as well as answering follow up questions by email over the years it took to piece this all together. They have taught me so much, sharing knowledge and advice that I have brought forward into my own projects since. Their generosity in the form of the advice found in this book will hopefully pave the way for generations of artists to come.

Thank you to Zinzi Oegema for her book *GRIP*, a similar investigation into the creation of contemporary circus shows. I've cited many of her interviews throughout this book, and am thankful for the perspective they have provided.

Mason, Tristan, Brent, Maya—you have been my rocks growing up, you're all role models for me of how to be a better human. Thanks for letting me interview you for this book and sharing your lives with me.

See You Down the Road *by Cirque Barcode. Photographer: Nikola Milatovic. Artists: Eric Bates, Tristan Nielsen, Alexandra Royer.*

SECTION SEVEN: APPENDICES

APPENDIX A: FULL CREATION TIMELINE

This section will try to summarize broad strokes of what your creation timeline might look like. Obviously, it will adapt based on your needs and what resources you're able to access throughout the process, but the basic idea is the same. At every phase of the project you will already be "leapfrogging ahead", working on another phase one or two stages down the line. While you will have to fight to stay present while still thinking a few steps ahead, leapfrogging like this beats the alternative, which is often an inconveniently long wait between phases.

> *A note on cabarets: Cabarets tend to be quicker to put together since most of the material for the show is already 'written', usually being made up of individual acts that are, in the cabaret tradition, expected to stand alone. There's still plenty of organization to do, but cabarets tend to require less group rehearsal time.*

First Sparks (Creation Not Yet Begun)

- You're still figuring out what your idea is. It is time to write, draw, and clarify.

- See many shows, do Tanabe's research exercise ("Active Spectating" on page 41).

- Talk to other circus companies to get an idea what making a show is like for them. This can help you learn strategies specific to your goal and location that you plan on creating it in, as well as turn you on to more helpful tips, creation strategies and resources.

- Keep your eyes open for jobs and roles in the performing world that you don't know much about. This will help you understand the challenges those roles face, but also possibilities for your show you might not have imagined. Outside eyes, directors, project managers, light designers, sound techs, producers, agents, accountants. Start to make yourself familiar with all of this world, not just other performers.

- Work as an assistant director on another show, or volunteer to help on a project to get a feel for the sort of work it involves. Try to find opportunities (make opportunities!) to take on responsibilities outside of just performing. This will help you better understand all of the roles that have to work together to make a show happen beyond just that of a performer, and the challenges your team will face along the way.

- Find your team. If you don't know who they are yet, start putting out feelers to find them. See who seems excited about similar ideas to yours. Who shares similar values?

- Start playing around with organizational software or systems. It's likely you will have to try out a few systems or a combination of tools before you are able to settle on one that you continue to use. Having this in place already before your creation begins will help you stay organized as your project grows.

You're Doing It

For Barcode's first show, Sweat & Ink, *these first creation steps were about a year to a year-and-a-half before our official show premiere.*

• Jump in- Start telling everyone it's happening (ongoing!). This can be by word of mouth or through social media posts as you start to create in the room.

• Gather your team- Make sure everyone's onboard and can reserve the dates for creation. Whenever possible try to brainstorm and plan the creation, and try out whatever ideas you can in a less formal creation situation. It will all help down the line!

• Make a bunch of material- The idea is just to get in the room and see what it's like working with your team, trying out first ideas, seeing what immediately works and what doesn't, (and this applies to both product and process—what works artistically, but also explore how you plan on creating together) so when you get to the bigger block of creation time, you've got a slightly clearer picture of what to expect.

• Video (ongoing)- Film research video and keep it organized.

Likely 6+ months before your first creation residency

• Book space for a bigger, formal block of creation time in the future. Many places that host artist residencies book up to a year ahead of time. Finding private space that meets circus needs (rigging, etc), especially for free or for cheap, is hard to do on a short timeline.

- Identify and apply for grants for the first phase of the project. "Research & creation" type grants. Securing small funding/support before you apply for these grants is very good. See the note on "in kind donations" in the Success Breeds Success section of Grant writing earlier in this book to learn what kinds of support can be converted, alchemy-like, into dollar amounts to help with these applications. If you can have donated space worth a certain value, or someone's time, or a sponsor, these will all help a lot in your grant application.

- Ask around to find someone who can help with the writing or revision process of the grants.

- Start weekly meetings with your team. Assign jobs/ tasks for the week, begin experimenting with organizational tools.

- Start emotions meetings/check-ins before you need them.

- Put potentially useful/ important dates into the team calendar: grant deadlines, deadlines to apply for residencies, deadlines to apply for opportunities to present your project.

Your First Big Residency/ies

This is your first formal creation block, ideally at least a week of time dedicated solely to working on your show. For Barcode we did this block at Cirque Eloize and at the Creation Studio in the National Circus School of Montréal, about 3 months before our first public preview in Philadelphia, and ~14 months before our show officially premiered in Prague. This could be an early "test phase" block of creation, followed by the "main creation"

- Make a plan for food and cooking if living together.

- Make a ton of material. Some will naturally combine into acts or scenes or blocks, some won't. Don't throw anything out yet, and don't worry too much about the big picture. Follow the fun. The editor isn't in the room yet—we're just creating stuff to sift through later.

- Film research video (ongoing).

- Continue weekly meetings and emotions meetings (ongoing).

- Continue to check in on deadlines for upcoming opportunities (ongoing).

- Start looking into next phase grants for production and travel. Use video of your research so far to help apply for these.

- Start looking into another big block of creation space for the push to a full show. This one might not be close to home. If you plan to have lights and sound in your show, it will likely have to be in a theater.

Present 30 Minutes

- When you're starting to have material to work with, start to form it into 30 minutes to present (this might be a few residencies/workshops in). This often comes naturally at a sortie de residence, a required presentation at the end of certain residencies. Ideally, schedule it so you've had time to explore, and time to get your act together. This could be a short show or it could be a series of improvs based on things you've worked on. It's an opportunity to try out material however you want to get feedback on it without having to be attached to anything.

- Get a good video. Don't save planning this until the last minute, this will be your main selling tool from this point on. At the very least get a full length video, at the best, use the opportunity to get two angles of the run plus slow motion and close ups beforehand that you could cut into a more 'cinematic' trailer. Video is the most important thing that your nascent "marketing department" needs in order to do their job. Though this might feel like the 'finish line' for some departments, having a good video is the 'starting gun' for others!

- If you're happy with your 30 minute presentation, send this video to people (producers, agents, grants, potential presenters—they'll likely want to see a full show, and will book a long time in the future anyway but you may as well start conversations early if you feel ready). Often you have to sell the show long before it's finished, which makes no sense, but otherwise you'll end up making your show and not performing it for another two years. Thus, the importance of a good video. Get it early so you can start those conversations early about booking it, and hopefully get some interest.

- If you haven't booked your next block of space for creation, lock it in.

- Start more serious discussions about directors, outside eyes, light, costume, and sound designers if you plan to work with any of those people and aren't already collaborating with them.

Steps to a Full Show

Hopefully things will start moving after the 30 minute presentation, but the hustle isn't over! Depending on where you're at in your creation, you can continue to do creation residencies, and/or start to move towards producing the show. At the end of our first creation block of Sweat & Ink we had one week in the Fringearts theater in Philadelphia, where we were paid to play a work-in-progress of our show to a real audience. Maybe this could have been the final product show, but we weren't happy with it yet so we went back into creation one year later in Prague, where we redesigned the dramaturgy, lights, costumes, then performed in their theater for our official premiere.

- Search for more grants/funding. This time you're looking for more production type grants, or travel grants if you plan on doing the next phase of your creation far from home.

- By now you should have a clearer idea of what your show is, which will help when talking to potential funders, or crowdfunding, or co-commissions, etc, and you'll have a good video that you can use for these purposes.

- As you get a clearer idea of what your show is, you can revisit some of the earlier research material you filmed and see if any of it fits better now, or can be seen in a new light.

- How is the plan for costumes, set, and props developing?

- Did you have a director/outside eye in the beginning? Maybe you want one once again to help take it to that next level.

• Have you identified who will design lights and sound?

• Where will you store your set/ props, if/once you have them?

• Start looking for opportunities to book your show. This may be difficult, although the 30 minutes might have helped if you played it somewhere with visibility (and got a good video). This might come in the form of shopping it at a circus market like MICC (Marché International de Cirque Contemporain) or performing at a major fringe festival to meet producers. These aren't the only ways to find opportunities, though. You can also get started by asking around through your local connections—you're going to be thankful for both high and low profile opportunities to run and work the show. It can be a blessing to try out ideas in a lower pressure circumstance, maybe at a rural theater where you grew up, so you can fail quietly before inviting people you hope will book your show. There's a reason companies like Cirque du Soleil do soft premieres and works-in-progress!

• Continue emotions meetings. At this point they will likely be very helpful. Protect this time, don't let all the other stuff that needs to be talked about invade here. This is your time to work through the hard stuff together as a team, so that the rest of it feels lighter.

APPENDIX B: SHANA'S EXCAVATION QUESTIONS

- In what context do you feel the most in your elements and the "best version of yourself"?

- If you could "be" any other company (in the whole world!), which company would you choose to be?

- If you were the only director of the company, what is the first thing you would change?

- If you didn't have to wait for the approval of the collective, what project etc would you already be doing?

- What goals does the company have that intersect with your personal life goals? Make a Venn diagram of this to reflect on it.

- What's your group's biggest obstacle? What's your group's greatest strength?

- How does your collectivity make you stronger?

- How does your collectivity make you weaker?

- If your group was a superhero, what would be its superpower? What quality do you have that no other company has?

- If a super villain was trying to attack your company, where would they attack?

- What is your group's achilles heel?

- What do we not want anyone to know about us?

- What do we want everyone to know about us that we don't think they know?

- If you were the government/ a granting organization, what would most make you want to give our group money?

- If you owned a theater, what would make you most want to book us?

- If you were an office employee, what would make your job more pleasant/ rewarding?

- If you were on tour (artist, tech, tour manager, etc), what would make your job more pleasant/ rewarding?

- If you were a high end designer or artist or senior executive, what would make it more attractive to come work with us?

- If you were *not* a member of the group, and were at a festival with lots of choices of shows, would you buy a ticket to see one of ours? If so, why? If not, why not?

The Company:

- 3 things you love most

- 3 things you hate most

The Founding Members:

- 3 things you love most

- 3 things you hate most

Founding Members vs. the Company:

- Which 3 ways do we most help the company?

- Which 3 ways do we most hurt the company?

APPENDIX C: ORGANIZATIONAL CHART EXAMPLES

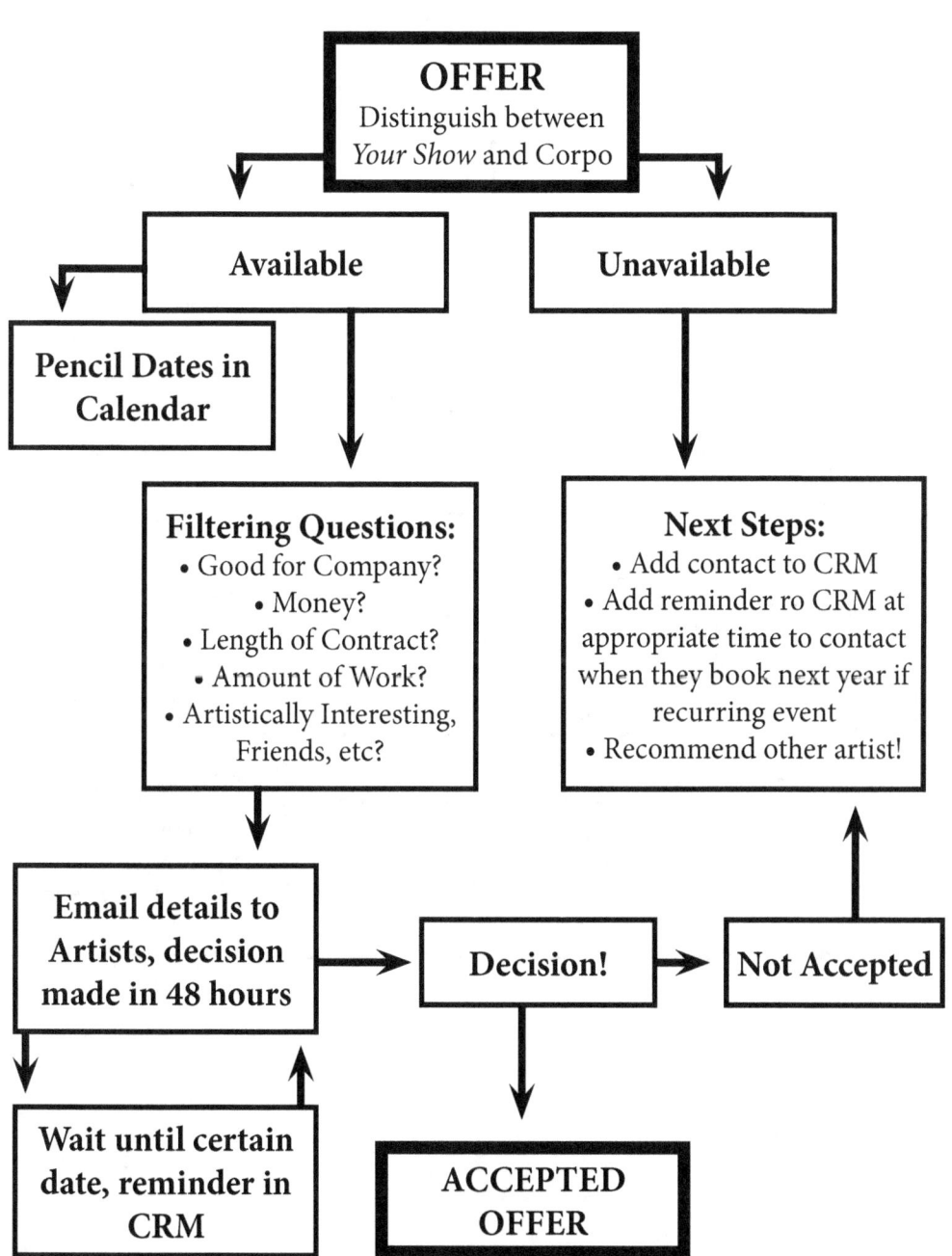

OFFER
Distinguish between
Your Show and Corpo

Available

Unavailable

Pencil Dates in Calendar

Filtering Questions:
- Good for Company?
- Money?
- Length of Contract?
- Amount of Work?
- Artistically Interesting, Friends, etc?

Next Steps:
- Add contact to CRM
- Add reminder ro CRM at appropriate time to contact when they book next year if recurring event
- Recommend other artist!

Email details to Artists, decision made in 48 hours

Decision!

Not Accepted

Wait until certain date, reminder in CRM

ACCEPTED OFFER

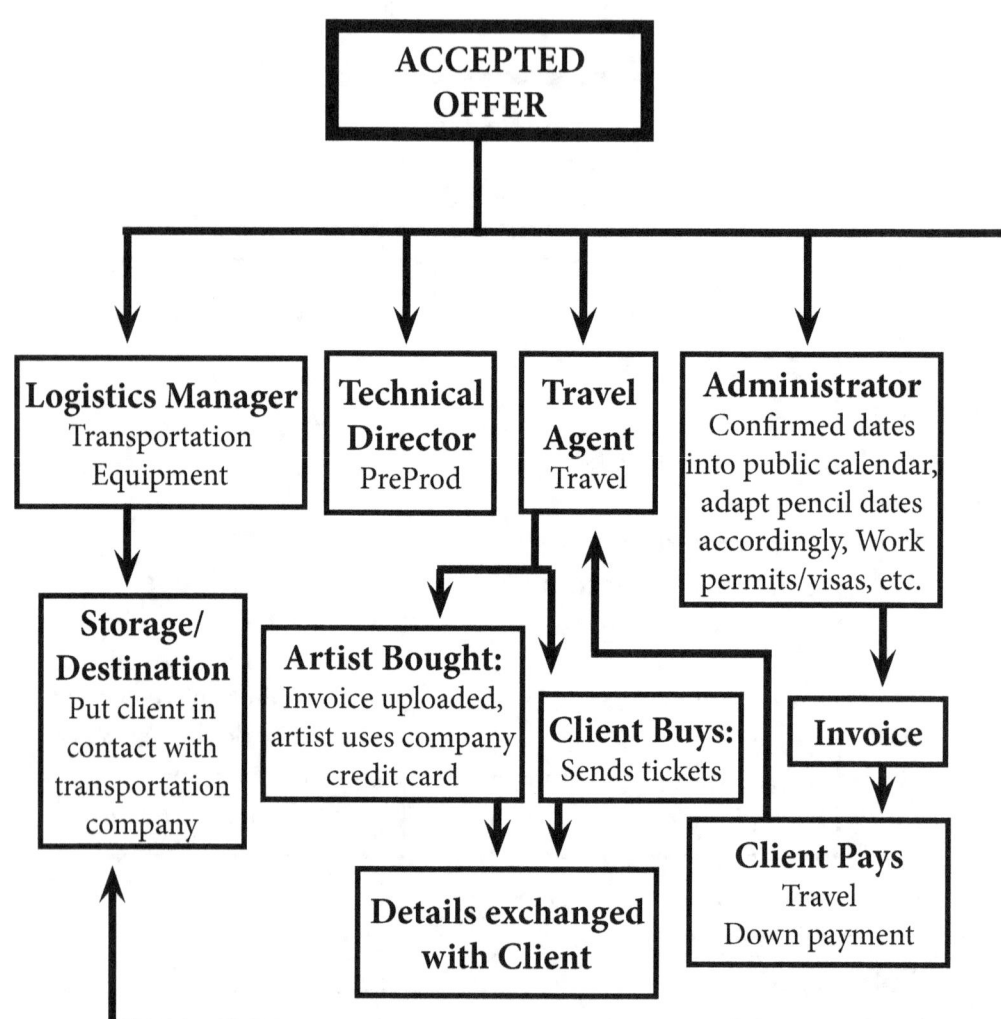

There's no one-size-fits-all solution for a company's division of tasks, but this is how Barcode works once we've accepted an offer. Depending on your team, a different workflow might be best.

For us, our skillsets allowed us to divide tasks into the following sections: transportation, travel logistics, accounting, pre-production, PR, and social media.

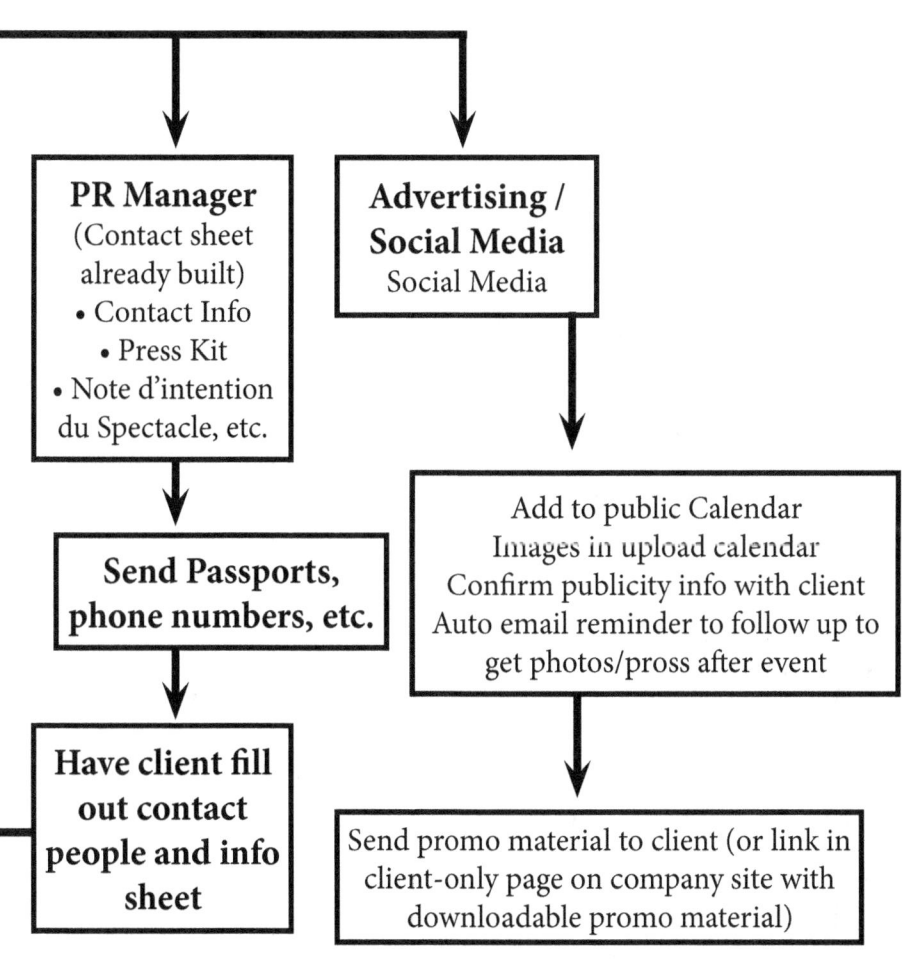

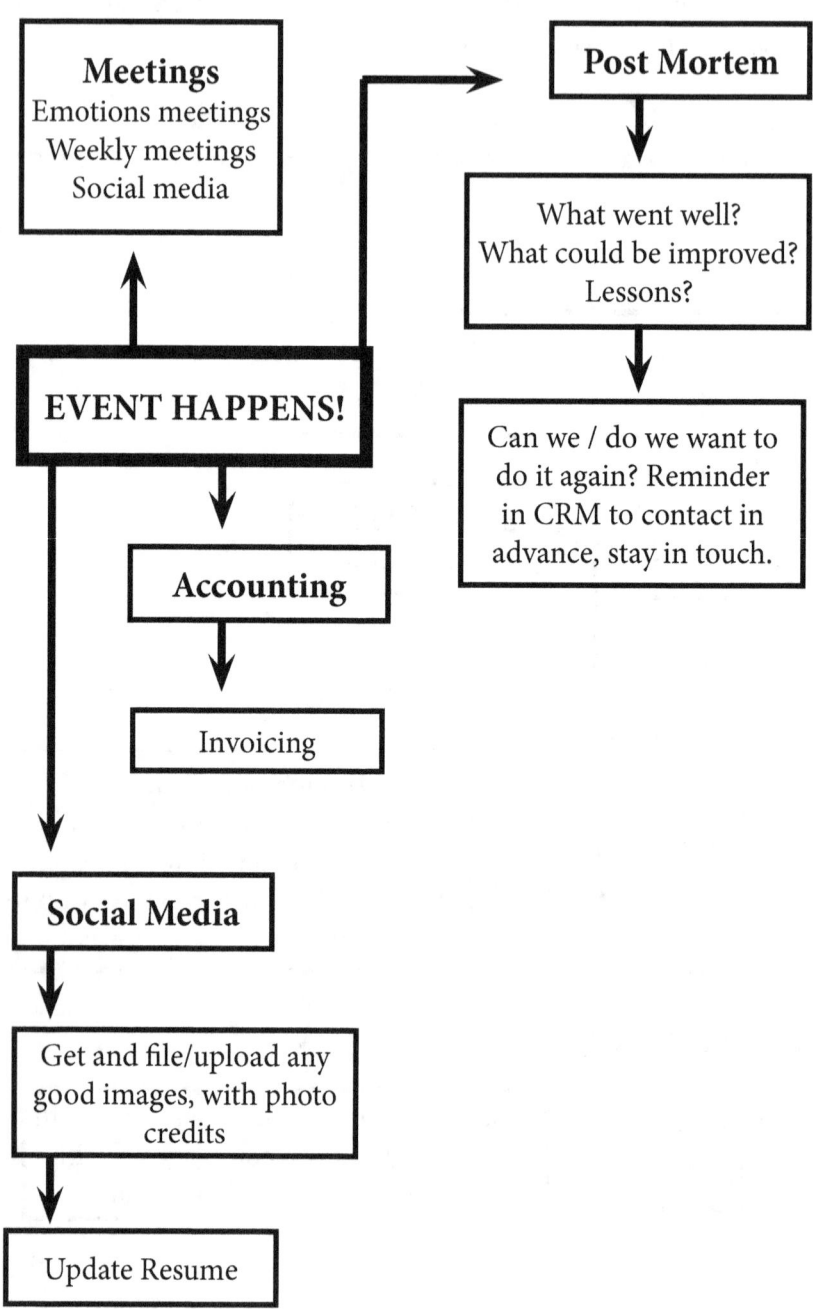

Meetings
Emotions meetings
Weekly meetings
Social media

EVENT HAPPENS!

Accounting

Invoicing

Social Media

Get and file/upload any
good images, with photo
credits

Update Resume

Post Mortem

What went well?
What could be improved?
Lessons?

Can we / do we want to
do it again? Reminder
in CRM to contact in
advance, stay in touch.

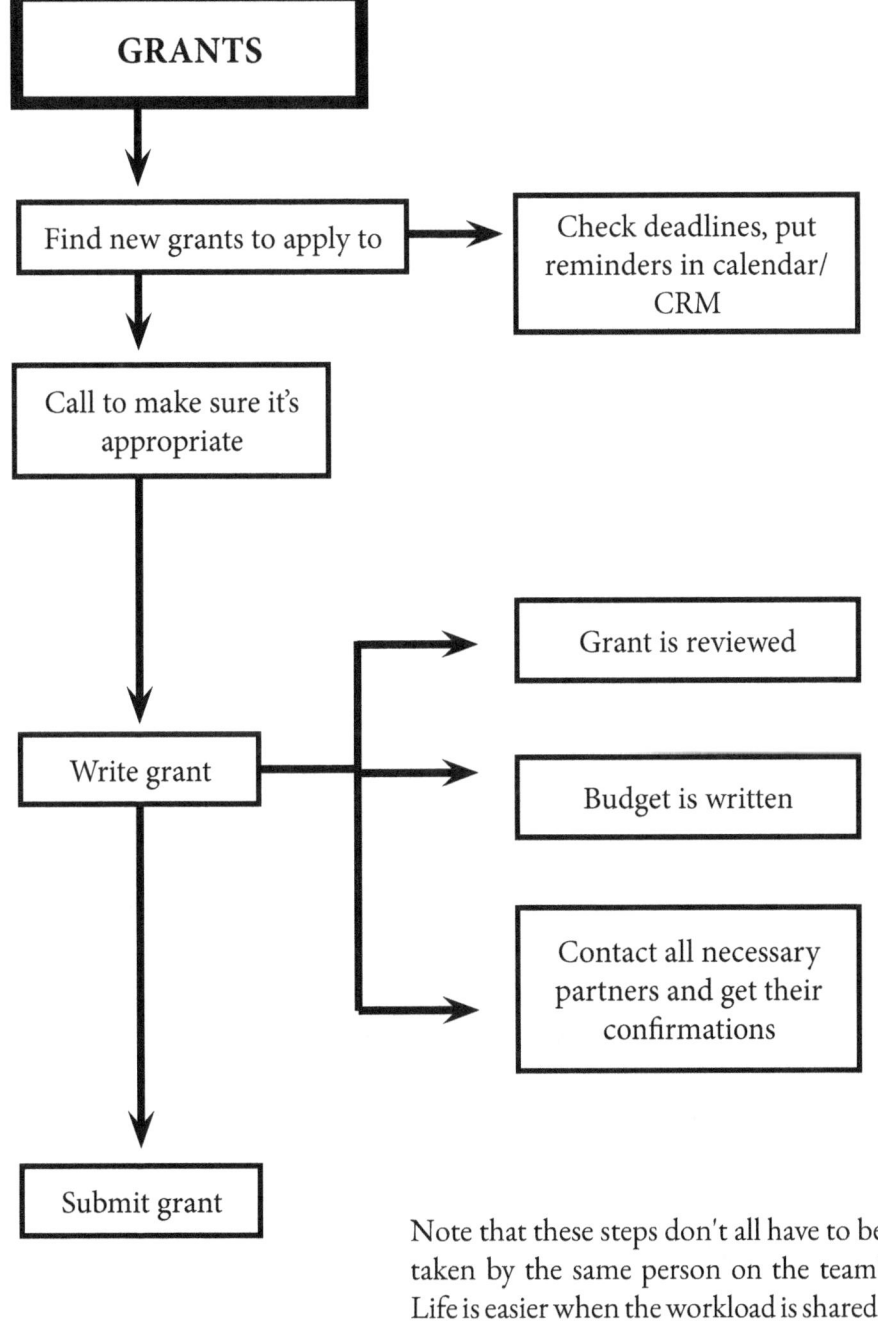

GRANTS

Find new grants to apply to → Check deadlines, put reminders in calendar/ CRM

Call to make sure it's appropriate

Write grant

Grant is reviewed

Budget is written

Contact all necessary partners and get their confirmations

Submit grant

Note that these steps don't all have to be taken by the same person on the team! Life is easier when the workload is shared.

APPENDIX D: ORGANIZATIONAL TOOLS

Organizational Tools

I can't list all of the available tools that are out there, but this chapter will cover some of the ones that Barcode or other creators I've talked to have used. In the beginning your team will likely take on many administrative tasks yourself, and therefore will have to familiarize yourself with at least some of these tools. The most important part of any of these resources is going to be successful implementation, and it can take some time to find what works for your team. This chapter will cover tool implementation, Claude Tremblay's communication strategy, a note on efficient meetings, and a brief description of useful tools.

Implementation of a Tool

Eve pulled her computer out of her backpack.

"What is that, a television?" Eric asked. The thing was massive.

"I have to bring it, my phone is broken."

She held up a spiderweb of cracked glass.

"Do you have the calendar on your computer?"

"What calendar?"

"The Barcode calendar we've been using for 6 months."

"Oh I never figured that out so I forgot about it."

"What?!"

"Me too," Alex chimed in. "Can you show us again?"

"Les amis," Sophie said, "I think we should move to dropbox, no one uses Google Drive."

"I just finished organizing the Drive!" Tristan said.
"It's not professional." Sophie said. "People won't take us seriously."
"How do I get to the drive?" Eve asked, face and most of her torso hidden
behind her gargantuan laptop. "I can't find it."

Implementing a new tool involves building a new habit for everyone on your team. It's not as easy as just reading up on it online. You have to make sure it works for everyone, and continue to work at it until it becomes ingrained in the way you get things done as a group.

Emilie Fournier (Machine de Cirque) struggled with the same conundrum. "We tried a lot of stuff and it didn't work out. We put a lot of information in certain tools and realized it wasn't complete, there was trial and error. That was a little bit the poopy part. I hate doing that. I want to sell shows. I don't want to take my time to enter information over and over... But I think it's a pain you need to go through to find the right tool."

With a digital tool this means you have to take into consideration that with everyone's different access privileges, operating systems, browsers, etc, they might not be seeing what you're seeing. We went literally months with some of our team members not being able to see the shared calendar because it didn't work on their phone, or they couldn't log in, so they just ignored it. Because they couldn't access it, they didn't know they were missing something, so they didn't think to fix it and they forgot it was even an issue. You need to set up the tool together and make sure everyone is seeing the same thing. If everyone's not using the tool, it will break down for everyone.

It's worth it, if at all possible, to do one meeting face to face where you use the new technology together and look at each other's screens to make sure that everyone is seeing the same thing when they log in.

It can also take a few weeks to get everyone in the habit of using a new system, and when in a rush people will tend to fall back into the old ways. Patience! Help yourselves by reminding each other to use the new tool when people forget.

Meetings

When in a planning phase (as opposed to a creation phase where you'll presumably see each other every day, although even then regular, formal meetings are also a good idea), try to meet with your team a minimum of once every week. At Barcode, we put these meetings on the calendar as a recurring event so unless stated otherwise it's the same time every week, and everyone is expected to be there. Of course we are also constantly talking on different messaging apps, but a regular meeting with the entire team is beneficial for many reasons. Regular meetings help keep everyone on the same page, and make sure no one is overloaded or without something helpful to do to contribute to the team.

To have an efficient meeting, it's helpful to have everyone think ahead of time what they want to talk about, and list those things at the start of the meeting in an "ordre du jour". This will help keep it moving and make sure you don't forget anything. We keep these meeting notes in a Google Doc that everyone can see and edit during the meeting, and check back on if they've forgotten something important during the week when they're working on their individual tasks.

A good meeting should feel efficient and invigorating, not like a chore every week. Keeping it tight and focused helps this feeling. Claude Tremblay (Cirque Eloize, Moment Factory) recommends having more and more frequent meetings as you approach your deadline.

"For this to be efficient, you need someone that leads the meeting. Because if you put a bunch of creatives together and don't have an agenda, it's going to [dissolve] and people will say, 'What a *!@ waste of time this was.' And when you're in creation for a show, people don't have the time. Thirty minutes, you go through all the departments. People need to take five minutes before the meeting to think about their major issues, then we address them. We come together to fix the issue."

Tightly run meetings like this work well to keep everyone on the same page and find efficient solutions together. When time is of the essence it's good to know that the prop you were going to stay up until 4am to finish in time is no longer needed. One last thing- at the end of every meeting, have everyone state their action items that they need to get done before the next meeting. And make sure to schedule the next one!

Next Actionable Steps

In his book titled *Getting Things Done*, author David Allen says one of the best things you can do is to make sure, by the end of the meeting, that everyone has their next action step. What, specifically, are they going to accomplish this week? The clearer you can be the better.

Instead of, "Let's write the grant," maybe it's "Eric will finish the written portions of the grant and send them to Tristan to read over for feedback by Friday. Eve will call the local aluminum welders to get prices and give them to Sophie so she can make the budget. Alex will collect the promotional materials and upload them to the grant site."

Or, instead of "Everyone research grants so we can find one that works for the team," go on the site together and look at the list of potential grants, assigning one or two to each team member to read and see if you're eligible. If, upon reading, anyone quickly discovers they're not eligible, they can reassign themselves to one of the other grants. The task could also include each person calling the governing organization that awards the grants to make sure the team qualifies, and if so, put the applicable deadlines into the group calendar with a reminder significantly far ahead of time that the team will have time to accomplish it.

More examples of concrete action steps:

• I will write or call 10 people that I know that have done creations to ask where they did their creations, then follow up on those leads by calling the places they suggested to find out and write down each space's availability and requirements.

• I will gather each team member's availability for the coming week by the end of the weekend, and will book studio space for the week Monday morning.

Lead and Lag Measures

When you're deciding tasks for the week, thinking in terms of lead and lag measures can be helpful. The book "The Four Disciplines of Execution" talks about "lead and lag" measures and describes how lag measures are an outcome that measures the result. Shows sold, grants received, money made, weight lost, etc. Lead measures are the input. They are the things you can concretely do to work towards affecting the lag measures. These might be the number of grants submitted, the number of people called to try to sell your show, the number of social media posts made for your business, number of miles jogged, etc.

You want to work on the lead measures. They're the things you can concretely do to advance towards your lag-measure goals. When you're brainstorming with your team, it's good to figure out your lag measures so you know what you're aiming for, but your next action steps need to be lead measures—they need to be things you can directly influence. Write down what you plan to do this week at the end of the meeting, so at the start of next week's meeting you can see what went well and if anyone needs help in an area.

Claude's Communication Strategy

I have an admission. I'm scared of the phone. I have been for a long time. When you write an email, you have time to craft the perfect sentence, and there's no risk of the other person asking an unexpected question you don't have the answer to. You have time to look it up so you don't feel stupid.

Claude Tremblay, project manager for Moment Factory, says that's a fear you need to get over. "The best way to communicate is always the phone. The most efficient way is to talk, and then send an email like, "As discussed, here is the next step to the project." Take notes while you're talking and send it immediately after you're done. This lets your email stand as a record of the conversation you had.

What I've learned throughout the process of making and selling our shows, and am still learning, is how much this is a relationship business. Why this matters is because the unexpected bits of information that are exchanged in a phone call can be extremely valuable, and are less likely to happen in the 'efficient' world of email.

I'm also learning that it's ok to not have all the answers, and the more you talk to people the more you'll start to understand people's different perspectives so you can anticipate their questions and constraints. In an email, you always have to "ask the right questions" to get answers, whereas on the phone it might be much quicker for someone to get an overview of your project and know how to help you, or to raise a point that they might not think worth mentioning in an email but that is key to understanding each other.

Talking to someone on the phone you might realize they hadn't replied to your email for a week because their grandmother died and they are at the funeral. Here you have a chance for real empathy and connection with them, whereas if you're just interacting by email this might not come up and you might just think them slow and inconsiderate when they finally do write you back.

Like Tremblay said at the beginning of this section, a phone call plus a follow-up message can be the best way to make sure everyone is on the same page. Do the scary thing. Get on the phone (then follow up with an email!).

Bonus tip: While you've got your phone out, fill out the "emergency contact" and "medical info" section that shows up when the screen is locked, and get everyone on your team to do the same. If any of you ever ends up unconscious, your team will be able to get the critical information immediately.

Show Organization Tools

When it comes to talking about the show itself (not the organization around the show, but the actual show), most of the creators I talked to tended to prefer basic physical tools—a big sheet of paper, sticky notes, notebooks. There's something visual, tactile, democratic and satisfying about them, and also you're less at risk of getting distracted by all of the other things a computer or phone can do.

Physical Tools (vs. Digital)

A physical solution like a notebook and/or sticky notes often works well for people, as long as you have an idea of where to find things if you need them. This is similar for both digital and analog tools—both can be helpful as long as you can retrieve the information you're putting into them. Digital tools, however, can be useful because the whole team can access the same information from anywhere without one person being the "knowledge holder".

Whatever the nuances of your process, rest assured that the creation process is often messy and involves a lot of head scratching no matter the method. In *GRIP*, Bram Dobbeleare of Cie Ae Ao describes it like this: "We often sat in a circle together, staring at those notes, talking. It isn't sexy at times. Then it goes like, 'We just finished the clubs act. If we stick another clubs act after it, that's a bit much.' So sometimes it really isn't artistically motivated, but solely practical."

Lewie West says that a lot of times you don't know why something doesn't work, and it takes a lot of moving stuff around and beating your head against the wall to get there. Once it's in the right order though, it seems obvious. That's just how it goes.

Digital Tools: Staying on the Same Page

There's a lot of digital tools out there these days: tools for scheduling, meeting planners, editing tools, communication tools, cloud storage and more.

General recommendations:

- Email: If you have one email for your whole group/ project, clarify who will respond to emails or how they will delegate from there. Remember that the person on the other end might get confused/ frustrated if there are multiple people responding to them from the same email. They don't know how much you all talk to each other.

344

- Keep work communications separate from more general conversations either by platform or by message thread.

- Have a group calendar that everyone is connected to, and use the alerts feature to remind yourself about upcoming events (so you can check in to make sure they're still current).

- There are a lot of great paid platforms, and usually there are free alternatives.

- Cloud storage is a helpful way to keep everything you use frequently in the same place: promo material, tech sheets, important documents for travel reservations, etc. Keep it organized in order to be useful!

- Regardless of what sort of project management software or system you use, make sure you assign who is responsible for each task and a due date.

APPENDIX E: BOOKS

Management

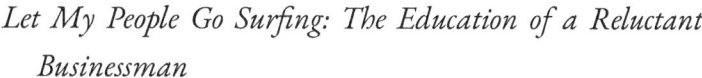

Let My People Go Surfing: The Education of a Reluctant Businessman
Yvon Chouinard
ISBN: 978-0143109679

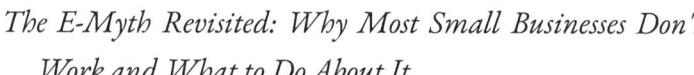

The E-Myth Revisited: Why Most Small Businesses Don't Work and What to Do About It
Michael Gerber
ISBN: 978-0887307287

Creativity

The Creative Habit
Twyla Tharp
ISBN: 978-0743235273

The Artist's Way: A Spiritual Path to Higher Creativity
Julia Cameron
ISBN: 978-1585421473

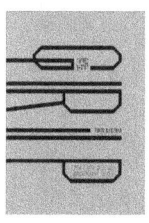

GRIP
Zinzi Oegema
Available at tent.eu

Theater Life

Technical Theater for Nontechnical People
Drew Campbell
ISBN: 978-1621535423

Grants

Winning Grants Step-by-Step
O'Neal-McElrath, Kanter & English
ISBN: 978-1119547341

Creation

Impro for Storytellers
Keith Johnstone
ISBN: 978-0878301058

A Practical Guide to Ensemble Devising
Davis Robinson
ISBN: 978-1137461551

Mime Spoken Here
Tony Montanaro & Karen Hurll Montanaro
ISBN: 978-0884481775

*Maximum Entertainment: Director's Notes for Magicians
   and Mentalists*
Ken Weber
ISBN: 978-0974638010

APPENDIX F: ABOUT THE CONTRIBUTORS

Brent & Maya McCoy - Her Majesty's Secret Circus, Co-Founders of Vermont Vaudeville

Brent and Maya McCoy are variety entertainers, producers, teachers, and partners in life. Since 2011, they have appeared as Her Majesty's Secret Circus on stages and street pitches all over the planet. They both have roots in comedy and circus, studying at the Celebration Barn and growing up with Circus Smirkus. They live in Northeastern Vermont.

"Authenticity is everything."

Shana Carroll - Co-Founder of The 7 Fingers

Director, writer and choreographer of their shows *Traces, Psy, Sequence 8, Feriamuse, Le Murmure du Coquelicot, Cuisine & Confessions, Passengers, Duel Reality, Dear San Francisco,* and *Mon Ile Mon Cœur.* She also directed Cirque du Soleil's *Crystal,* their performance at the Academy Awards in 2012 and worked as acrobatic designer and choreographer for their shows Iris & Paramour. Other collaborations include: *Queen of the Night* (World Wide Variety); *Soul of the Ocean* (Moment Factory); *Temporel & Cité Mémoire* (Lemieux-Pilon); the Sochi Winter Olympics Opening Ceremonies, and *Water For Elephants: the Musical* with Pigpen Theatre Co. Acts she has directed have received 6 gold medals at international circus festivals, and in 2023, Shana became a member of the Ordre des arts et des lettres du Québec in tribute to her remarkable contribution to development and reputation for excellence of Quebec's arts and letters.

Gypsy Snider - Co-Founder/Artistic Director of The 7 Fingers

Gypsy Snider is writer and director of *Dear San Francisco, SisterS, Réversible, Intersection, Amuse, Un Dia, Traces*, and *Loft*. She co-choreographed the revival of the Broadway musical *Pippin* which earned her a Drama Desk Award and an Outer Critics Circle Award. Gypsy began her circus career at the age of 4 when her parents founded The Pickle Family Circus. Gypsy has now come full circle back to her home town of San Francisco and taken on producing a new branch of The 7 Fingers at Club Fugazi. Gypsy is co-writer/director/choreographer of the resident show, *Dear San Francisco*.

Joseph Pinzon - Short Round Productions & Arena Stage

Joseph Pinzon is the founder and creative producer of the circus company Short Round Productions and its show Filament. With over 25 years of performing experience, he holds a degree in aerial techniques from ENC in Montréal, a BA in Psychology from UCLA, and an MS in Arts Leadership from USC. He currently serves as the artistic associate and casting director at Arena Stage in Washington, D.C.

"Don't feel obligated to define yourself by what you do."

Nathan Biggs-Penton - Acting for Climate Montréal

Nathan is an artist, creator and co-founder of Acting for Climate. Raised in the Appalachian Mountains of Virginia he found his home in Montréal. Nature inspires a desire for imitation; its beauty, adaptability and ephemerality. His process of self betterment seeps into his art. His work offers a state of calm that yearns for kindness, acceptance, consciousness and is presented with tenderness.

"Showing up, going to the studio is doing the work. Whether it's a good day or not, showing up is doing the work. Equally important, if not more, is showing up for yourself and for your close friends. A nourished life leads to nourished art."

Lewie West - Rooke

Lewie has worked mainly with Australian companies Gravity & Other Myths and Circa and is now mostly retired from acrobat-ing. He still maintains his love of circus through performing with Rooke, balancing brooms on his stomach, climbing trees and throwing his daughter around.

Mason Ames - Circus artist, Street Performer

Mason Ames is a New Hampshire born fella with a passion for the circus arts. Circus Smirkus, National Circus School of Montréal, The 7 Fingers, Cirque Eloize, Cirque du Soleil, Cirque le Roux and street performing. Cooking and playing outside are important ingredients in his life.

"Your tummy usually knows best."

Claude Tremblay - Project Manager

Curious about all forms of art, Claude is a project manager - or a chaos coordinator, as she to describe herself. Her management approach is based on empathy, transparent communication and kindness. "We rise by lifting others" may sound cliché, but she's a firm believer in this vision of leadership. Claude's purpose is to bring a little sparkle of magic in everything she does.

"Breathe, it's important."

Charlie Wheeller - Barely Methodical Troupe

Charlie is an acrobat, enjoying exploring the disciplines of Cyr Wheel, Teeterboard and group acrobatics. He co-founded the experimental acrobatic company BMT in London with Beren D'Amico and Louis Gift and their full length works focused on relationships and love. More recently his unique acrobatic approach has led him to work with other companies such as Cirk La Putyka and Cirque Du Soleil.

"My wheel teacher, Amy Welbourn, told me to 'Stay in the Wheel.' That's where new possibilities are found."

Edgar Zendejas - Ezdanza

Mexican-born Edgar Zendejas danced for Les Ballets Jazz de Montréal, Hubbard Street Dance Chicago. Zendejas explores new areas of artistic collaboration as a Creation Director with The National School of Circus in Montréal, The National Institute of Circus Arts in Melbourne. As a choreographer and artistic advisor for Cirque du Soleil, Cirque Eloize, Franco Dragone, and Starlight Circus.

"I have always witnessed that in circus art everything is possible, this applies to a production but my advice is that it also applies to movement and dance, always trust and you will be surprised."

Emilie Fournier - Machine de Cirque

After being part of the 2000 Olympic Games in Sydney, Emilie pursued a career as an artist with Cirque du Soleil for almost a decade. Parallel to her work, she obtained her degree in Arts in Business at the University of Phoenix. Later, she created the acrobatic duo Chilly & Fly and continues performing around the globe. She works as the international touring manager for Machine de Cirque.

"Just have fun and enjoy the process!"

Héloïse Bourgeois - Cirque Entre Nous

Heloise began acrobatics at five with equestrian vaulting, trampoline and dance. The Montréal circus school, Les "7 Doigts" [The Seven Fingers] and her duo with William gave her the opportunity to travel around the world. Specializing in hand to hand and Chinese pole, Heloise received a gold medal at the *Cirque de Demain* festival, performed in front of the Queen of England and at the Olympic Games of Turin.

"Trust yourself."

Michaël Hottier - Co-Founder, Back Pocket

The son of and actor and a musician, Hottier started performing at a young age. After attending ESAC in Brussels where he met his hoop diving partners and other co-founders of Back Pocket. A floor acrobat, hoop diver and aerial straps artist, he worked for numerous companies before founding his own. Back Pocket for him is the the place to express and share the artistic medium that he is passionate about: acrobatic movement.

James Tanabe - Director of Studies, National Circus School of Montréal; Executive Producer, 51/49 Productions

Prior to becoming Director of Studies at ENC, Tanabe was both Cirque du Soleil's Senior Director of Business and Creative Strategy and their youngest-ever Artistic Director. An MIT and Wharton graduate, he has produced projects in Japan, Taiwan, Holland, Canada, France, Spain, Italy, India, Thailand, Korea, Russia, Belgium, Vietnam, Lithuania, Turkey, Cambodia, Uganda, and the USA.

"Working for free is never a problem as long as you know exactly why you are doing it. On the other hand, letting yourself be exploited is a cardinal sin no matter how much you are getting paid."

Afton Benson - MS, Organizational Behavior and Business Management

Afton Benson uses their 15 years of leadership experience to help passionate artistic individuals and nonprofits thrive through relationship driven development and financial best practices. They are an IRS-Certified Tax Preparer who leads annual third-party audit reviews for performing arts nonprofits whose budgets are less than one-million dollars 990 and 990-T tax filings.

Afton works with nonprofits and individual artists throughout North America, with clients ranging from CLIMB Theatre, Benjamin Domask-Ruh, Bindlestiff Family Cirkus, International Jugglers' Association (IJA), and Prepare + Prosper. Afton serves as Treasurer for the IJA and Producer of the MONDO Juggling and Unicycle Festival in St. Paul, MN.

Sophie Picard - Mentor

Over the past 20 years, Picard has built an exciting career in the events and live entertainment industry. She is a creative, experienced, and highly skilled producer. She never just takes on a job or a project, she invests herself 100% in everything she does.

354

Tristan Nielsen - Co-Founder, Cirque Barcode

Tristan Nielsen is an American circus artist that specializes in basing hand to hand, Russian bar and banquine. He has worked for many companies, including The 7 Fingers, Cirque Éloize, Cirque du Soleil, Cirque Le Roux and cie XY and is a co-founder of Cirque Barcode.

"Don't get hung up on the problems; you will always find solutions if you keep pushing towards your goal."

Lydia Bouchard - Founder, La Résistance with Merryn Kritzinger; Project Director, Cirque du Soleil

Lydia Bouchard is an artist with numerous creation tools that refuses an etiquette. She aspires to an ever growing creative playground, elastic time and true human encounter.

"Inspiration is an arrow that points in the direction you should take. That path often is the scariest and requires the most courage. Be brave."

Chris Lashua - Cirque Mechanics

Chris Lashua began his circus career as a BMX acrobat with Cirque du Soleil's *Fascination*. He was then commissioned to build a "German Wheel" act for Cirque du Soleil's production of *Quidam*, cementing his reputation as a visionary of circus gadgetry. His engineering chops and creative energy led him to 'run away' with his own circus company, Cirque Mechanics, now based in Las Vegas. Cirque Mechanics is currently finalizing casting for *Zephyr's* second North American tour.

"Nobody gets anything meaningful done alone.
Start building your community now."

Zander Howard-Scott - Founder, Creative Sovereignty

Zander Howard-Scott is a multi-disciplinary creative entrepreneur originally from Winnipeg, Canada. Now based in Montréal, Zander's work as a performer has brought him from Carnegie Hall in NYC as a classical cellist to participating in multiple World Expos, improvising with Cirque du Soleil, and as a featured soloist in Dubai. Zander thrives on adventure and uniting the seemingly contrasting elements of culture and creative disciplines into his performances and creations. With his company Creative Sovereignty he has directed the original creations *Dessa*, *Ardeo* and numerous other fundraising events.

"If you don't decide what you want in your life, it'll be decided for you. Stay the course and keep your vision strong in the unavoidable moments of doubt and uncertainty."

Di Robson - Arts Producer

Di delivers arts-based projects from performance to festivals. Key involvement with British experimental theatre; Producer/Director of major festivals including Millennium and London Olympiad; Lecturer City University London; Consultancy includes Jaipur Festivals and Coventry City of Culture '23; founding Producer of Barely Methodical Troupe. Currently International Producer with Strijbos & Van Rijswijk: https://www.strijbosvanrijswijk.com

"Remember time off is as important s time on!"

APPENDIX G: SAMPLE BUDGETS

Here are two sample budgets showing loose examples of how you could adapt a creation to fit your available resources. Use your creativity to think of how else you could make your budget work. On the following pages, you will find an extensive sample budget prepared by Sophie Picard, Barcode's general manager. Note that this is a mockup, filled with round numbers for ease of use. These figures do *not* represent industry standards.

Small Budget:

Space: Some rehearsals in open training spaces for part of the day, some rehearsals in private studio where you got a grant for 1 month

Rehearsal (artists): Unpaid rehearsals, asking friends to pull safety lines. Working on creating new material while on other shows or on breaks on tour.

Director: Comes for part of the day, or twice a week, or just at the end of the creation process to help bring the ideas together.

Production Phase

Light design: N/A or made the day before a presentation.

Sound: Royalty free music, or music you make yourself onstage. Recording of artists singing.

Set Design: Minimal. Mostly just the apparatuses.

Props & Costumes: Sourced second-hand. Maybe you know someone graduating from a design school that needs to build out their portfolio and would be interested in collaborating for cheap? One costume per artist.

Administration: Artists write the grants themselves, maybe hire someone to review the grant once written.

Big Budget

Creation Phase

Space: Private space in a rehearsal studio for 6 months

Rehearsal: All artists paid for 6 months plus daily coaching with paid coach

Director: Paid director for the whole six months

Production Phase

Light design: 1 month in a theater with light designer at end of 6 months to build the light design with a light designer

Set Design: Set designer hired to make custom everything: big set, everything custom-made to pack efficiently into road cases

Sound: Custom-made music

Props & Costumes: Custom-made props and costumes. Prop designer paid to source props (maybe still second hand), but adapt/ decorate them for the show. Costume designer makes made-to-measure costumes from scratch. Multiple costumes.

Administration: Paid producer writing grants, talking to agents, setting up funding and a tour. Also dealing with promotion.

#	Item	Detail			Qty		Number		Rate	Count	Total
26	**Creator Royalties**								- $		
27	Set	Royalties			1		10		10.00 $		1,000.00 $
28	Light Design	Royalties			1		10		10.00 $		1,000.00 $
29	Musical rights	Royalties					-		- $		- $
30	**TOTAL Royalties**						20 $				2,000.00 $
31									- $		- $
32	**Salaries, honorariums and per diem TECHNIQUE**								- $		- $
33	Artistic follow up - reserve	Production Assistant			1		150		150.00 $		15,000.00 $
34									- $		- $
35	Tour director	advance city			1		200		200.00 $		200.00 $
36		Setup & Tear Down Fee			1		225		225.00 $		225.00 $
37		show fee			1		225		225.00 $		22,500.00 $
38	Avance technique / City Technical director	show fee			1		200		200.00 $		200.00 $
39	Light plan				1		150		150.00 $		150.00 $
40	Technical Director/ Sound	Set up and Teardown			1		200		200.00 $	NMBRE	400.00 $
41	/fly in 7 shows + setup/teardown	Show fee			1		100		100.00 $	7	700.00 $
42	/fly in 7 shows + setup/teardown	Set up & tear down			1		150		150.00 $		150.00 $
43	TBC	Show fee			1		150		150.00 $	5	750.00 $
44	Light tech/fly in 7 shows + setup/ teardown	Setup			1		150		150.00 $		150.00 $
45	TBC	Show Fee					100		100.00 $	5	500.00 $
46	Opérateur Français en plus des 2 fournis				1		100		100.00 $	72	7,200.00 $
47	**TOTAL Salaries and Honorariums TECHNIQUE**						2,000 $		2,000.00 $		48,125.00 $
48									- $		

360

Sample Budget

#	Amortization/ Creation/ Show /3 Years	Visas/pers	Cost/Day/Ins	Cost/Day/Ins class 2	Private Worker's Co CNESST 1,091 Medical Emergency		WC private/d	Fee/show/DA
2								
3		50	18	18	7	0	5	5
4		usd/CDN	$ CAN/ usd	# people	Training days	# montage	per diem $	# weeks	# days
5		1.00 €	1.00 $	12	0.0	1	10.00 $ (10 euros)	1.0	3	150.00 $
6	Revised on (day, month, year)	1.00 $	1.00 $						1	# days 50
7		1.00 $	1.00 $							# show 100

#	Expenses		# days/ week	# set up	# show	# weeks/training	$	%	Total $CAN	Euro	# show
8	Expenses						$	%	Total $CAN	Euro	
9	Salaries, honorariums & per diems ARTISTS										
10	Artiste 1	Pre prod and rehearsal				0.0	100		- $	- $	- $
11		Show fee			1		100		100 $	100.00 $	10,000.00 $
12	Artiste 2	Pre prod and rehearsal				0.0	100		- $	- $	- $
13		Show fee			1		100		100 $	100.00 $	10,000.00 $
14	Artiste 3	Pre prod and rehearsal				0.0	100		- $	- $	- $
15		Show fee			1		100		100 $	100.00 $	10,000.00 $
16	Artiste 4	Pre prod and rehearsal				0.0	100		- $	- $	- $
17		Show fee			1		100		100 $	100.00 $	10,000.00 $
18	Artiste 5	Pre prod and rehearsal					100		- $	- $	- $
19		Show fee			1		100		100 $	100.00 $	10,000.00 $
20	Artiste 6	Pre prod and rehearsal				0.0	100		- $	- $	- $
21		Show fee			1		100		100 $	100.00 $	10,000.00 $
22	Artiste 7	Pre prod and rehearsal				0.0	100		- $	- $	- $
23		Show fee			1		100		100 $	100.00 $	10,000.00 $
24	TOTAL salary and honorariums ARTISTS								700 $	700.00 $	70,000.00 $
25									- $	- $	

#	Item						
57	Other					$	
58	Maintenance (set, tools, etc.)		1	10	10 $	10.00 $	1,000.00 $
59	Accessoires and consumables (tape, chalk, etc.)		1	40	40 $	40.00 $	4,000.00 $
60	Costumes (cleaning, touchups, etc.)		1	50	50 $	50.00 $	- $
61	Sound		1	0	- $	- $	- $
62	Lights	Buy	1	0	- $	- $	- $
63	Physiotherapy / accident reserve		1	50	50 $	50.00 $	5,000.00 $
64	Catering and show costs (meals)		1	50	20 $	20.00 $	5,000.00 $
65	Communications (cell, mail, etc.)		3	10	10 $	10.00 $	500.00 $
66	VISA and work permits		7		50 $	350.00 $	350.00 $
67	TOTAL current expenses				230 $	230.00 $	15,850.00 $
68	SUB-TOTAL EXPENSES				3,100 $	3,100.00 $	148,525.00 $
69						- $	
70	Contingency (usually 10%)		3,100	5%	155 $	155.00 $	7,426.25 $
71	Admin charges (usually 15%)		3,255	15%	488 $	488.26 $	23,392.69 $
72	TOTAL EXPENSES $				3,743 $	3,743.25 $	179,343.94 $
73	Cost per show $ CAD				- $	$	1,793.44 $
74	Cost per show EURO		0.71				1,267.96 $

ABOUT THE AUTHOR

Eric Bates grew up in Fayston, Vermont and now lives in Montréal, Quebec. Since graduating from the National Circus School of Montréal he has worked professionally as a contemporary circus performer specializing in cigar box juggling and Russian bar, and is the co-founder of Cirque Barcode. Besides making three original creations with Cirque Barcode, he has participated in numerous other creations with companies such as Cirque du Soleil, The 7 Fingers, Cirque Eloize, and more.

OTHER BOOKS BY MODERN VAUDEVILLE PRESS

Juggling: Or How to Become a Juggler (annotated edition)

Rupert Ingalese, annotated by Thom Wall
ISBN – 978-1733971201
99 pages
MSRP: $15 USD

The fully annotated edition of Rupert Ingalese's 1921 "how to juggle" manual. This book covers basic juggling technique, tricks with hats and canes, practice methodology, and more. Ingalese's manuscript provides an interesting look at the state of juggling pedagogy in Britain's music hall era. Annotations by juggler and circus researcher Thom Wall bring insight and context to Ingalese's descriptions and instructions.

Pottery in Motion

Sam Veale
ISBN – 978-1733971232
71 pages
MSRP: $15 USD

British juggler Sam Veale's *Pottery in Motion* is the first of its kind - a straightforward book that provides aspiring plate spinners both the specifics of the props (such as plates, sticks, and rack) and comprehensive instruction on the skill of plate spinning itself. This small but detail-packed guide appeals to individuals looking to learn plate spinning and provides the knowledge to take it to a performance-ready level, just add practice.

Juggling: From Antiquity to the Middle Ages

Thom Wall
ISBN – 978-0578410845
129 pages
MSRP: $25 USD

As with dance, so with juggling—the moment that the performer finishes the routine, their act ceases to exist beyond the memory of the audience. There is no permanent record of what transpired, so studying the ancient roots of juggling is fraught with difficulty. Using the records that do exist, juggling appears to have emerged around the world in cultures independent of one another in the ancient past. Paintings in Egypt from 2000 BCE show jugglers engaged in performance. Stories from the island nation of Tonga place juggling's creation with their goddess of the underworld—a figure who has guarded a cave since time immemorial. Juggling games and rituals are pervasive in isolated Inuit cultures in northern Canada and Greenland. Though the earliest representation of juggling is 4,000 years old, the practice is surely much older—in the same way that humans were doubtlessly singing and dancing long before the first bone flute was created.

This book is an attempt to catalogue this tangible history of juggling in human culture. It is the story of juggling, represented in art and writing from around the world, across time. Although much has been written about modern jugglers–specific performers, their props, and their routines–little has been said about those who first developed the craft. As juggling enters a golden age in the internet era, *Juggling: From Antiquity to the Middle Ages* offers a look into the past—to the origins of our art form.

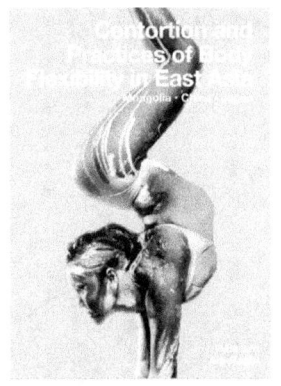

Contortion and Practices of Body Flexibility in East Asia - Mongolia, China, Japan

Mariam Ala-Rashi
MSRP: $25 USD
Coming June 2023!

This compendium includes three studies that examine contortion and practices of body flexibility in East Asia: China, Mongolia and Japan. It explores the performance art forms of Chinese contortion, Mongolian contortion and Japan's Kakubei Jishi lion dance of the Niigata prefecture.

These studies investigate the history and genesis of these art forms, illuminating how they developed in various political and social climates. This work further examines artists' training processes, their training environment, the development of aesthetics, symbolism in costuming and body movements, religious themes, mythology and natural phenomena, and costume designs.

This compendium includes data from a wide range of literature, material evidence, oral history, contemporary media reports, and considers recent work in anthropology, archaeology, and political history. A great fit for any interested reader, scholar, contortionist and contortion practitioner who's looking for a substantial treatise about contortionism and practices of body flexibility.

Juggling: What It Is and How to Do It

Thom Wall, et. al.
ISBN – 978-1-7339712-5-6
224 pages
MSRP: $25 USD

Juggling: What It Is and How to Do It teaches learners of all ages how to juggle – one of the world's oldest artforms. With a kind demeanor, humor, and enthusiasm, this authoritative manual explains the process of juggling through four different modalities, bolstered by the latest physical education research.

Juggling is an accessible primer that a middle-schooler can hit the ground running with, or that families can enjoy together. The result of six years of work by 2021 International Jugglers' Association *Excellence in Education* award winner and former Cirque du Soleil juggler Thom Wall and featuring guest chapters by some of today's juggling masters, *Juggling* provides great content for even the most serious adult learner.

Book plus Juggling Kit!
Includes juggling balls by Alchemy Juggling

MSRP: $60 USD

This exclusive kit makes the perfect gift for any aspiring juggler. Includes one copy of *Juggling: What It Is and How to Do It* and three professional-grade beanbags.

Beanbag specs: 90g ea., approx. 2.75" diameter. Machine washable / dryable. Made in USA.

Body Talk: Basic Mime

Mario Diamond
ISBN – 978-1733971218
73 pages
MSRP: $15 USD

Body Talk: Basic Mime covers the fundamental skills of mime in an easily accessible workbook format. Diamond brings over 40 years of teaching and performance experience to *Body Talk*, which includes rich photography illustrating various mime techniques.

"[*Body Talk: Basic Mime*] should be required reading for any theater participant looking to incorporate elements of mime into their routines." - *Midwest Book Review*

French Edition:
Corps Expressif: Base du Mime

Mario Diamond
ISBN – 978-1958604984
68 pages
MSRP: $15 USD

Mario a écrit un tour de force sur l'art du mime. Ce livre est éloquent et concis... riche en outils pour les élèves comme pour les professeurs, facile à comprendre et rempli d'exercices pratiques. Ce livre est brodé de segments historiques et anecdotiques qui en font un manuscrit amusant, plein d'observations charmantes et bouffonnes qui font de Mario un artiste phénoménal, prodigue de la caractéristique définitive du mime, la personnalité.

Circus Games (v1.1)

Compiled by Lucy Little & the American Youth Circus Organization (AYCO)
ISBN – 9781733971225
124 pages
MSRP: $15 USD

With over 100 games organized for optimal use in cooperative movement based settings, this is a must have for every circus school, teaching artist, and arts education program! Games are organized by age, number of participants, energy level, and social/emotional learning outcome, and also includes special notes for working with a variety of populations that may require adaptation or modifications to each game. Find more info about the project here: https://www.americancircuseducators.org/gamesproject/

The ABC Tour

Jon Udry
ISBN - 978-0578410852
MSRP: $25 USD

Ever felt like a challenge? For juggler and comedian, Jon Udry, the ABC Tour — 26 letters, 26 shows — seems the perfect way to shake things up.

What started as a silly idea he believed would take two to three months to complete, ended up being a mammoth three year project that included some of the toughest, most brutal and most enjoyable performances of his life.

From attempting to juggle while wearing roller skates and the unexpected discoveries of performing at a Naturist's Resort, to the challenges that came with working in rainforest conditions covered in ants or in snowy conditions at -10°C, Jon tells the full story from A to Z.

Circus Training Journal

Thom Wall & Rebecca Starr,
Consultant editor: Sarah Baker
ISBN – 978-1-7339712-9-4
9×6" paperback
380 pages
MSRP: $20 USD

What's measured is managed! The *Circus Training Journal* is the result of a year of collaboration between Thom Wall and Rebecca Starr, head aerial coach at Circadium: School of Contemporary Circus. This undated journal, spanning three months of daily training, tracks workouts, nutrition, goal-setting, and more. Heavyweight groundwood paper optimized for ballpoint and pencil.

Opulence & Ostentation

Steve Ward, PhD
ISBN: 978-1-958604-02-1
MSRP: $25 USD

Since the foundation of the 'modern' circus in the eighteenth century, the circus has been presented in defined spaces. Initially, performances were given in the open air and, over a period of time, these spaces first became enclosed and then later roofed. Temporary wooden structures often became semi-permanent until, in the nineteenth century, many permanent stone-built buildings were erected solely for the purpose of presenting circus. This phenomenon spread from the UK across Europe and beyond, creating a style of circus architecture that has never been repeated. The purpose of this book is to examine what caused these buildings to be constructed and their design and architecture. Examples of key structures will be explored in detail, some of them still surviving today and still being used for circus performances. The book will also look at the developments of contemporary circus architecture and raise questions as to the future of the circus building.

Artistes of Colour

Steve Ward, PhD
ISBN – 978-1-7339712-7-0
317 pages
MSRP: $25 USD

In a society that places an increasing value in ethnic diversity and cultural identity, the contribution that performers from a variety of ethnic backgrounds made to the development of the circus in the nineteenth century is often dismissed and largely forgotten. Using contemporary records and images, *Artistes of Colour* explores the wealth and depth of talented black and other performers of colour, and the contribution they made to the success of the nineteenth century circus. Ward draws iconic figures from the margins of history and gives them the recognition they deserve, illustrating what the BBC calls "a field of study that has been overlooked far too long."

Long-listed for the American Society for Theatre Research 2022 Book Award.

Cleverer Than God

CLEVERER
THAN
GOD

ERIK ÅBERG

Erik Åberg
ISBN – 978-1958604113
MSRP: $25 USD

Cleverer Than God is a book that tells the story of Paul Cinquevalli, a juggler who rose from the Circus circuit of the 1880s, to attain celebrity status in the British Music Hall and American vaudeville stages until the outbreak of WWI. Through quotes by Cinquevalli himself, woven together with excerpts from journalists and writers of his era, the book tells his story as poignant fragments, capturing the essence of Cinquevalli's triumphs, defining moments, and heart-rending tragedies.

Coming Soon:

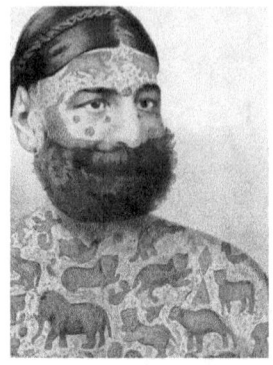

Captain George

| Amelia Osterud, Edited by Fritz Grobe
| **MSRP: $25 USD**
| Coming in 2024!

The life and times of the world's most celebrated illustrated man.

The Century's Juggler

| Reinhold Batburger, translated by
| Kathrin Wagner, edited by Thom Wall
| **MSRP: $25 USD**
| Coming in 2024!

He throws a ball in the air and makes millions. And millions of people watch – and did for more than fifty years.

His performance takes seven minutes, and that's his life. Reinhold Batberger tells a family story – the story of a world career, the story of the life and art of juggler Francis Brunn (1922-2004).

www.ingramcontent.com/pod-product-compliance
Lightning Source LLC
Chambersburg PA
CBHW061134120626
46546CB00005B/1779